Ready® | 3 Reading INSTRUCTION

Vice President of Product Development: Adam Berkin
Editorial Director: Katherine Rossetti
Executive Editor: William Kelleher
Project Manager: Audra Bailey
Editors: Melissa Brown, Anne Cullen, John Ham, Rob Hill, Susan James
Cover Design: Matt Pollock
Cover Illustrator: O'Lamar Gibson
Design/Production: William Gillis, Mark Nodland, Lisa Rawlinson, Jennifer Sorenson, Jeremy Spiegel

NOT FOR RESALE

ISBN 978-1-4957-0868-8

Acknowledgments

Mary Reina, "Teeny Tiny Tardigrades," Copyright © 2011 by Highlights for Children, Inc., Columbus, OH.

"Frozen Desserts" by Heidi Deal, *Appleseeds*, July 2014. All Cricket Media material is copyrighted by Carus Publishing Company, d/b/a Cricket Media, and/or various authors and illustrators. Any commercial use or distribution of material without permission is strictly prohibited.

Dale-Marie Bryan, "An Earful," Copyright © 2005 by Highlights for Children, Inc., Columbus, OH.

Vicky Alvear Shecter, "Cleopatra Finds Her Voice," Copyright © 2009 by Highlights for Children, Inc., Columbus, OH.

"Horses Helping Others" by Heidi Deal, *Appleseeds*, May 2011. All Cricket Media material is copyrighted by Carus Publishing Company, d/b/a Cricket Media, and/or various authors and illustrators. Any commercial use or distribution of material without permission is strictly prohibited.

"Oddball Allstars" by Jodi Wheeler-Toppen, *Ask*, October 2013. All Cricket Media material is copyrighted by Carus Publishing Company, d/b/a Cricket Media, and/or various authors and illustrators. Any commercial use or distribution of material without permission is strictly prohibited.

"Our Most Famous Immigrant" by Nancy Whiteslaw, *Cobblestone*, February 2006. All Cricket Media material Is copyrighted by Carus Publishing Company, d/b/a Cricket Media, and/or various authors and illustrators. Any commercial use or distribution of material without permission is strictly prohibited.

Jennifer Mattox, "Big Bugs," Copyright © 2009 by Highlights for Children, Inc., Columbus, OH.

George Cooper, "The Wind and the Leaves" from *Playtime Stories (Readers),* Published by First NY American Book Company (1921). Public domain.

"How the Animals Got Their Beautiful Coats" by Pat Betteley, *Faces*, February 2006. All Cricket Media material is copyrighted by Carus Publishing Company, d/b/a Cricket Media, and/or various authors and illustrators. Any commercial use or distribution of material without permission is strictly prohibited.

"Little Puppy," traditional Navajo poem, transcribed by Hilda Faunce Wetheril (1923). Public domain.

Edward Lear, "There Was an Old Man with a Beard" from *A Book of Nonsense* (1846). Public domain.

"Little By Little" by Anonymous, from *Required Poems for Reading and Memorizing,* Published by Third and Fourth Grades, Prescribed by State Courses of Study (1906). Public domain.

Lori Anastasia, "Basketball Ballet," Copyright © 2009 by Highlights for Children, Inc., Columbus, OH.

Mary Ann Hoberman, "Squirrel" from *A Little Book of Beasts*. Copyright © Mary Ann Hoberman. Copyright © 1973 by Mary Ann Hoberman. Used by permission of the Gina Maccoby Literary Agency.

"Eat This Spoon" by Elizabeth Preston, *Ask*, February 2017, by Carus Publishing Company.

Karin Gaspartich, "Patriotic Pizza," Copyright © 2007 by Highlights for Children, Inc., Columbus, OH.

"Writing on a Wasp's Nest" by Kacey Hartung, *Appleseeds*, November 2004. All Cricket Media material is copyrighted by Carus Publishing Company, d/b/a Cricket Media, and/or various authors and illustrators. Any commercial use or distribution of material without permission is strictly prohibited.

"Goodbye, Books?" by Jaime Joyce from *TIME for Kids*, November 20, 2009. Copyright © 2009 Time Inc. All rights reserved. Reprinted from *TIME for Kids* and published with permission of Time Inc. Reproduction in any manner in any language in whole or in part without written permission is prohibited.

Mary Pope Osborne, "Stormalong" from *American Tall Tales*. Copyright © 1991 by Mary Pope Osborne. Used by permission of Alfred A. Knopf, an imprint of Random House Children's Books, a division of Random House, Inc. Any third party use of this material, outside of this publication, is prohibited. Interested parties must apply directly to Random House, Inc., for permission.

"The Fox and the Goat" and "The Wolf and the Crane" from THE ÆSOP FOR CHILDREN with illustrations by Milo Winter, published by Rand McNally & Company (1919).

Alfred J. Church, Excerpts from "The Home of the Winds," "Of the Sirens and Other Wonders," and "The Cyclops" from *The Odyssey for Boys and Girls*. Copyright © 1906 by The Macmillan Company, New York. Public domain.

Common Core State Standards © 2010. National Governors Association Center for Best Practices and Council of Chief State School Officers. All rights reserved.

Table of Contents

UNIT 1 — Key Ideas and Details in Informational Text 8

Lesson

1 Ask and Answer Questions About Key Ideas 10

2 Finding Main Ideas and Key Details 24

3 Reading About Time and Sequence 38

4 Describing Cause and Effect 52

Interim Assessment 66

UNIT 2 — Key Ideas and Details in Literature 76

Lesson

5 Asking and Answering Questions About Stories 78

6 Describing Characters 92

7 Recounting Stories 106

8 Determining the Central Message 120

Interim Assessment 134

UNIT 3 **Craft and Structure in Informational Text** **144**

Lesson

9 Unfamiliar Words 146

10 Text Features 160

11 Author's Point of View 174

Interim Assessment 188

UNIT 4 **Craft and Structure in Literature** **198**

Lesson

12 Words in Context 200

13 What Are Stories Made Of? 214

14 What Are Plays Made Of? 228

15 What Are Poems Made Of? 242

16 Point of View 256

Interim Assessment 270

Table of Contents continued

UNIT 5 **Integration of Knowledge and Ideas in Informational Text** **280**

Lesson

17 Connecting Words and Pictures in Informational Text 282

18 Describing Connections Between Sentences and Paragraphs 296

19 Describing Comparisons 310

20 Comparing and Contrasting Two Texts 324

Interim Assessment 340

UNIT 6 **Integration of Knowledge and Ideas in Literature** **350**

Lesson

21 Connecting Words and Pictures 352

22 Comparing and Contrasting Stories 366

Interim Assessment 382

Glossary of Words to Know 392

Glossary of Terms 464

Language Handbook

Conventions of Standard English

Lesson

1 Nouns 398
2 Pronouns 400
3 Verbs 402
4 Adjectives 404
5 Adverbs 406
6 Plural Nouns 408
7 Abstract Nouns 410
8 Simple Verb Tenses 412
9 Regular Verbs 414
10 Irregular Verbs 416
11 Subject-Verb Agreement 418
12 Pronoun-Antecedent Agreement 420
13 Comparative and Superlative Adjectives and Adverbs . . . 422
14 Coordinating Conjunctions 424
15 Simple and Compound Sentences 426
16 Subordinating Conjunctions and Complex Sentences . . . 428
17 Capitalization in Titles 430
18 Punctuating Addresses 432
19 Punctuating Dialogue 434
20 Possessive Nouns 436
21 Possessive Pronouns 438
22 Adding Suffixes 440
23 Using Reference Works 442

Knowledge of Language

Lesson

24 Choosing Words and Phrases for Effect 444
25 Spoken and Written English 446

Vocabulary Acquisition and Use

Lesson

26 Using Context Clues 448
27 Prefixes and Suffixes 450
28 Root Words 452
29 Using a Dictionary or Glossary 454
30 Literal and Nonliteral Meanings 456
31 Real-Life Connections 458
32 Shades of Meaning 460
33 Words for Time and Space 462

UNIT 1

Key Ideas and Details in Informational Text

Do you think it would be fun to be a reporter? You'd get to write interesting news stories. How would you get the facts for these stories? You would ask questions and look for the answers. You would want to find out what happened, where it happened, and who it happened to. Next, you'd figure out when it happened. And finally, you'd figure out why it happened. In this way, a reporter is like a good reader.

In this unit, you'll learn to ask good questions and look for the answers. You'll read about events in history and see how one event leads to another. You'll read about kinds of weather, and learn how one event can cause another. These skills will help you become a better reader. Who knows, you may become a good reporter, too!

✔ Self Check

Before starting this unit, check off the skills you know below. As you complete each lesson, see how many more skills you can check off!

I can:	Before this unit	After this unit
ask and answer questions about what I read.	☐	☐
find the main idea and important details of a passage.	☐	☐
look for words that show time order.	☐	☐
find connections between ideas in a passage.	☐	☐
look for why things happened in a passage.	☐	☐

page 12

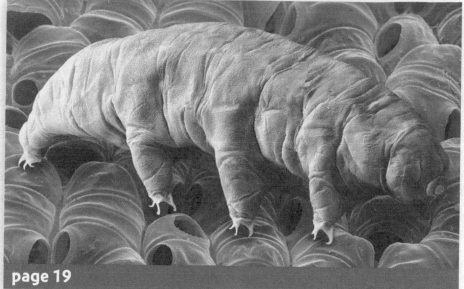
page 19

page 28

page 32

page 47

page 47

page 61

Lesson 1
Ask and Answer Questions About Key Ideas

Learning Target

Asking and answering questions about what you read will help you understand the text.

▶ **Read** We ask questions to get information or to understand something. Often questions begin with words such as *who, what, when, where, why,* and *how*. As you read, ask yourself questions about the text. Then look for **key details** in the text to answer your questions. Asking and answering questions will help you understand the **topic** of the text.

Look at this picture. What questions do you have about what you see?

Prairie Dog Homes

▶ **Think** What are some questions you could ask about the picture? Read the questions in the first column. Then use key details from the picture to answer these questions.

Question	Answer	Key Details
1 What are most of the animals in the picture called?		The title of the picture is "Prairie Dog Homes."
2 Where do these animals live?		
3 Why do these animals live underground?		

▶ **Talk** Take turns with your partner asking and answering questions about the picture.

◉ **Academic Talk**
Use this phrase and word to talk about the text.
- **key details**   • **topic**

▶ Read

BEAVER LODGES

by Bryan Davis

1   Do you know the saying "busy as a beaver"? People say this because beavers are always working. These crafty creatures spend a lot of time building their homes.

2   Beaver homes are called lodges. Lodges are found along streams, rivers, ponds, and lakes. Beavers build these homes from branches and rocks. They use mud to hold them together.

3   When they can, beavers build their homes into the banks along the water. Other times, they need to make a safe spot, first. To do this, they build a dam from logs, branches, and mud. They get the logs by gnawing at trees until they fall down. A dam is like a wall that blocks water from flowing. It then forms a pond. Once the dam is built, beavers can get to the business of building their lodge.

4   Beaver lodges are shaped like a dome. They are usually about 10 feet high and 20 feet across. Most lodges have at least one underwater opening. To get inside, the beavers must swim underwater. These "secret" openings keep out unwanted predators.

5   Inside the beaver lodge are different "rooms." There is an eating room and a nesting room. The floor of the lodge is built up out of the water. It is also made from rocks, branches, and mud. It is covered with plants and other soft materials.

6   A family of beavers lives in a lodge. Two parents and two sets of their offspring often live together.

Close Reader Habits

Think of two questions to ask about beaver lodges. Then **underline** words and phrases that help you answer your questions.

Explore | How can asking and answering questions as you read help you learn more about beavers and their homes?

▶ **Think**

You can ask questions that begin with *what, where, why,* and *how.*

1 Complete the chart by asking questions about the passage. Then answer your questions with key details from the text.

Question	Answer	Key Details
What do beavers use to build their lodges?		

▶ **Talk**

2 What does a beaver lodge look like? Using key details from the text, discuss the answer to the question.

▶ ✏ **Write**

3 **Short Response** Why are the beaver lodge openings underwater? Use key details from the text in your response. Use the space provided on page 16 to write your answer.

HINT Reread the passage to find key details.

Genre: Science Article

Termite Mounds
by Madeline Clark

1   Termites are insects that live together in nests. Some termites are called mound builders. They build their nests from mounds of clay. Some of these mounds are more like towers. They stand almost 35 feet tall!

2   Mound builders are found in Africa and Australia. They are also in parts of South America. Other animals in these areas use termite mounds, too. Some wait until the termites move away. Others ignore the termites and use the mound anyway.

3   Termite mounds are usually the highest place around. Cheetahs often use the mound as a lookout point. They climb to the top of the mound. There, they keep an eye out for their next meal.

4   Sometimes the termites move on to a new nest. That's good news for many of the other animals. These animals know how to put an empty termite mound to good use.

5   Some animals make the empty nest their new home. Mongooses are small animals in Africa. They make a hole in the mound to get inside. The termite mound keeps them safe from other animals. Snakes also use an empty termite mound as a home.

6   Termite mounds also come in handy for large animals. Elephants and rhinos use them as scratching posts. Bug bites and dry mud can make any creature itchy. These large animals stand near a mound and rub against them. Sometimes they even stand over a mound to scratch their bellies!

Close Reader Habits

How do other animals use termite mounds?
Underline some of the different ways.

> Think

1 This question has two parts. Answer Part A. Then answer Part B.

Part A
Why do cheetahs climb up termite mounds?

    A   They can see farther to find animals to hunt.

    B   They can sleep safely on top of termite mounds.

    C   They use termite mounds as scratching posts.

    D   They can call to each other more easily.

> Good questions often begin with the words *why, when, where,* and *how.*

Part B
Which sentence from the passage **best** supports the answer you chose for Part A above?

    A   "Other animals in these areas use termite mounds, too."

    B   "There, they keep an eye out for their next meal."

    C   "Some animals make the empty nest their new home."

    D   "Others ignore the termites and use the mound anyway."

2 Which question can be answered by reading paragraph 5?

    A   How tall is a termite mound?

    B   Why do mongooses move into termite mounds?

    C   What large animals use termite mounds?

    D   What animals are mound builders?

> Talk

3 How do large animals use termite mounds? Refer to specific details from the article as you talk with your partner.

> Write

4 **Short Response** Why are termite mounds important to so many animals? Include details from the passage in your response. Use the space provided on page 17 to write your answer.

> **HINT** What did you underline when you read the article?

▶ 📝 **Write** **Use the space below to write your answer to the question on page 13.**

BEAVER LODGES

3 **Short Response** Why are the beaver lodge openings underwater? Use key details from the text in your response.

> **HINT** Reread the passage to find key details.

_____

_____

_____

_____

_____

_____

_____

_____

> Don't forget to check your writing.

Write **Use the space below to write your answer to the question on page 15.**

Termite Mounds

4 **Short Response** Why are termite mounds important to so many animals? Include details from the passage in your response.

> **HINT** What did you underline when you read the article?

_____

_____

_____

_____

_____

_____

_____

_____

Check Your Writing

☐ Did you read the prompt carefully?

☐ Did you put the prompt in your own words?

☐ Did you use the best evidence from the text to support your ideas?

☐ Are your ideas clearly organized?

☐ Did you write in clear and complete sentences?

☐ Did you check your spelling and punctuation?

▶ **Read**

Genre: Science Article

Teeny Tiny Tardigrades

by Mary Reina, *Highlights*

WORDS TO KNOW

As you read, look inside, around, and beyond these words to figure out what they mean.

- **radiation**
- **survive**
- **thrive**
- **function**

1   What would you say if someone asked you to name Earth's toughest survivor? Camels can go a week without drinking. A cockroach can survive more radiation than a person. But there is a teeny tiny creature that can go without food or water for years. It is so small that it can be seen only under a microscope. Its real name is tardigrade. Most people call it a water bear.

🠒 Surviving Everything

2   Water bears look like soft, squishy bugs. People call them bears because they walk the way bears do. Most water bears are smaller than the period at the end of this sentence. Don't let their size fool you. They are found in places that would kill most living things.

3   Some water bears survive in the boiling water found in hot springs. Others live miles below the ocean surface. They survive with tons of water pressing down on them.

4   Not all water bears live in extreme places. They can be found in parks, forests, and gardens. They thrive in damp, woody areas where mosses and other plant life grow. Many feed by sucking juices out of plants. Others eat creatures that are smaller than they are.

This photograph of a water bear was taken with a microscope. A *microscope* is a tool that lets you see tiny objects or creatures.

➡️ Drying Up

5   Water bears must have water to stay active. It helps them eat, move, and breathe. So what happens when the water around one of these tiny creatures dries up? First, it pulls in its eight legs. Then it curls its body into a barrel shape called a tun. It loses 99 percent of its water. Then every single life function of the water bear stops.

6   When conditions get better, the water bear stretches its little legs and starts moving and eating again.

7   Water bears can survive the extreme cold and radiation of outer space. Scientists sent some water bears into space as part of an unmanned mission. They came back fine!

8   Not so long ago, most scientists believed life did not exist beyond Earth. Now, many think it is possible. If water bears can survive a visit to outer space, who knows what other creatures might live there?

Thousands of water bears spent more than a week in space before they were returned to Earth.

▶ Think Use what you learned from reading the selection to respond to these questions.

1 Which **two** questions can be answered by reading paragraph 2?

    A How do water bears survive in extreme surroundings?

    B What do tardigrades look like?

    C What do water bears need to stay active?

    D How and what do water bears eat?

    E How large are water bears?

    F Why does a tardigrade need water?

2 Why are tardigrades called "water bears"?

    A They have sharp claws like bears.

    B They are named after a type of bear.

    C They walk like bears.

    D They look something like bears.

3 Read the sentence from paragraph 4.

    Not all water bears live in extreme places.

Based on how it is used in the passage, what does the word *extreme* mean? Use key details from the text in your response.

_____

_____

_____

_____

_____

_____

_____

4 Based on details in the passage, what **three** types of places is this sentence talking about?

> **They are found in places that would kill most living things.**
>
>   **A** damp woody areas
>
>   **B** the boiling water of hot springs
>
>   **C** the deepest parts of the ocean
>
>   **D** parks and gardens
>
>   **E** inside volcanoes
>
>   **F** outer space

5 This question has two parts. First, answer Part A. Then answer Part B.

Part A

Read these sentences from paragraph 5.

> **Water bears must have water to stay active. It helps them eat, move, and breathe.**

Which question can be answered after reading these sentences?

   A How long can a water bear survive without water?

   B What types of food do water bears eat?

   C Where do water bears get their water?

   D Why is water so important to water bears?

Part B

Which other sentence from the text also helps answer the question you chose in Part A?

   A "Then every single life function of the water bear stops."

   B "Some water bears survive in the boiling water found in hot springs."

   C "When conditions get better, the water bear stretches its little legs and starts moving and eating again."

   D "But there is a teeny tiny creature that can go without food or water for years."

Write

6 **Short Response** Why are tardigrades important to scientists who are studying outer space? Use details from the article in your response.

_____

_____

_____

_____

_____

_____

_____

_____

Learning Target

Explain how asking and answering questions can help you better understand any text.

Lesson 2
Finding Main Ideas and Key Details

Learning Target

Retelling the main idea and key details of a text will help you understand what you've read.

▶ **Read** The **main idea** is what a text is mostly about. Details are all the facts and ideas in a passage that **support** the main idea, or help explain it.

Sometimes you will want to retell a passage that you've read. First, make sure you know the main idea. Then figure out the **key details,** which are the most important facts in the passage.

Read the cartoon below. What is it mostly about?

★★ Life in the American Colonies ★★

People had to chop wood for fuel.

Taking farm goods to sell in town could take hours.

Everyone in the family had to work.

▶ **Think** Use key details from the cartoon to complete the chart below.

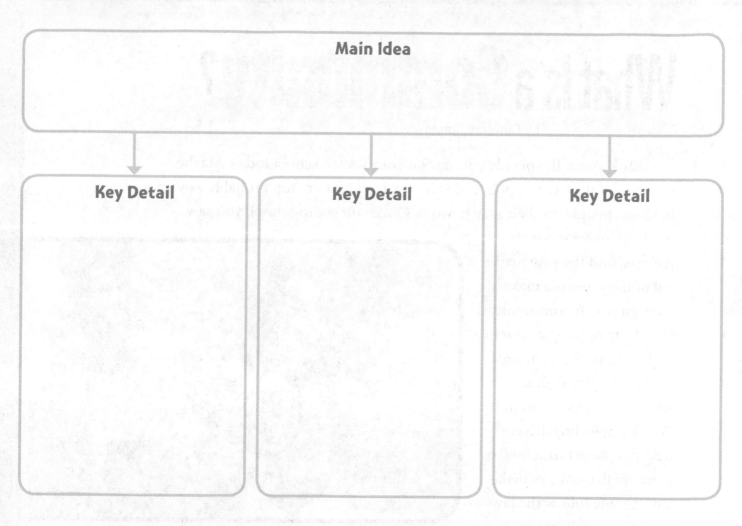

Main Idea

Key Detail

Key Detail

Key Detail

▶ **Talk** Discuss the key details you used to complete the chart. How does each detail support the main idea?

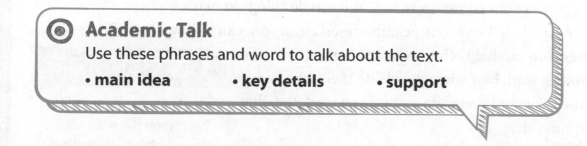

Academic Talk
Use these phrases and word to talk about the text.
- **main idea**
- **key details**
- **support**

What Is a Community?

by Clayton James

1   Think about the people you saw on your way to school today. Maybe you saw a bus driver, a police officer, or a mail carrier. You probably saw business people on their way to work. Once you got to school, you saw teachers, other students, parents, and the principal. All of these people make a community. A community is a group of people who live and work in the same area.

2   People play different parts to make a community. For example, bus drivers help people get to school or work. Police officers make sure people follow the laws and stay safe. Business people make or sell the things we buy. Parents and teachers make sure children have what they need to learn and be safe. Students learn so they can become good parents and workers.

3   You are a part of your community, too. You can do things to make a difference. You can help keep your neighborhood clean. You can follow rules and laws. You can help others who are in need.

4   Communities work best when people do their jobs and help each other. You and everyone around you work together to make a community.

Close Reader Habits

Circle the sentence that best states the main idea. As you reread, **underline** key details that tell more about the main idea.

Explore

What is the main idea of the text, and how do the key details support it?

▶ **Think**

As you reread the passage, ask yourself, "What is it mostly about?" Look for a sentence that answers this question.

1 Complete the chart with the main idea and key details of the text.

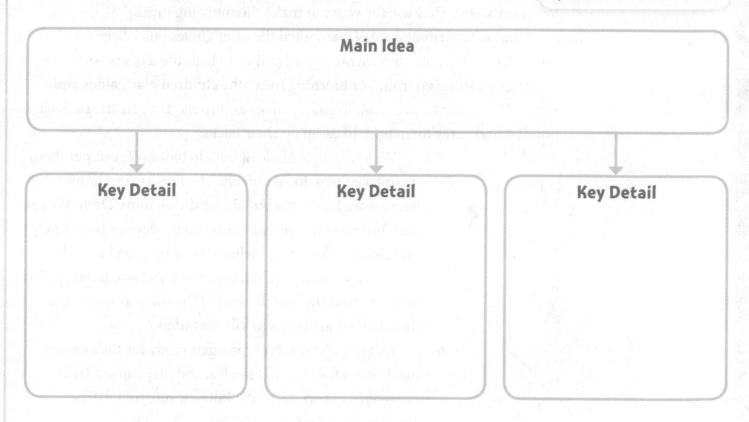

Main Idea

Key Detail   Key Detail   Key Detail

▶ **Talk**

2 One key detail is, "bus drivers help people get to school or work." How does this key detail support the main idea?

▶ **Write**

3 **Short Response** Choose another key detail you wrote in the chart. How does it support the main idea? Use the space provided on page 30 to write your answer.

HINT What does this detail say about the parts people play in a community?

▶ **Read**

Genre: **Personal Essay**

Life in My Village

by Maahe, a 19th-century Cheyenne Indian

1   My name is Maahe. I am a Cheyenne Indian. I live with my family on the plains. We work hard in my village, but we also have fun. Each morning before the sun rises, people in my village build a fire. Then women walk to the stream to collect water. They use the water to make the morning meal.

2   After our morning meal, a man called the crier circles our village on a horse. He makes announcements. We all gather to hear the day's news.

3   After cleaning up from our morning meal, the children play games and swim. The women leave camp to gather sticks and roots. They tie the sticks into bundles and carry them back to camp on their backs.

4   We live in tipis made of buffalo hides. We can put them up or take them down quickly. The tipis are our homes. Because we follow the buffalo herds, we move often. We can pack up our entire village in one hour! Dogs or horses help pull all our belongings, including our tipis, on big sleds.

5   When we hunt buffalo, both men and women help. The women chase the buffalo toward the men. The men use their bows and arrows to kill the buffalo.

6   As evening falls, everyone gets ready for the evening meal. We eat, dance, tell stories, and play music. Then everyone goes to sleep. We know tomorrow will be another busy day!

Close Reader Habits

What is the main idea of the passage? **Underline** the key details that helped you better understand the main idea.

> **Think**

1 This question has two parts. Answer Part A. Then answer Part B.

> A paragraph can have a main idea too. Pay attention to the key details in the paragraph. What idea do they all help explain?

Part A
What is the main idea of "Life in My Village"?

  A People in the village work hard but also have fun.

  B People in the village build a fire each morning.

  C The people live in tipis made of buffalo hides.

  D Women in the village make the morning meal.

Part B
Which sentence from the passage **best** supports your answer in Part A?

  A "After our morning meal, a man called the crier circles our village on a horse."

  B "After cleaning up from our morning meal, the children play games and swim."

  C "Because we follow the buffalo herds, we move often."

  D "When we hunt buffalo, both men and women help."

> **Talk**

2 What is the main idea of paragraph 5? What details in the paragraph support that idea?

> **Write**

3 **Short Response** Reread paragraph 4. Retell key details that show why the Cheyenne felt their tipis made good homes. Use the space provided on page 31 to write your answer.

> **HINT** Reread the text to find key details about the tipis.

Write **Use the space below to write your answer to the question on page 27.**

What Is a Community?

3 **Short Response** Choose another key detail you wrote in the chart. How does it support the main idea?

> **HINT** What does this detail say about the parts people play in a community?

> Don't forget to check your writing.

©Curriculum Associates, LLC   Copying is not permitted.

Write Use the space below to write your answer to the question on p. 29.

Life in My Village

3 **Short Response** Reread paragraph 4. Retell key details that show why the Cheyenne felt their tipis made good homes.

HINT Reread the text to find key details about the tipis.

Check Your Writing

- ☐ Did you read the prompt carefully?
- ☐ Did you put the prompt in your own words?
- ☐ Did you use the best evidence from the text to support your ideas?
- ☐ Are your ideas clearly organized?
- ☐ Did you write in clear and complete sentences?
- ☐ Did you check your spelling and punctuation?

▶ **Read**

Living in the Clouds

by Jeanette Cannon

1   Imagine living in a place so high that clouds are everywhere. And they're not just above you. They're all around you! This is what life is like in the Andes. The Andes are very high mountains in South America. The Inca people have lived in the Andes Mountains in Peru for over 500 years. But it is not easy to make a living on that rocky mountain land.

Mountain Farming

2   The mountainsides make farming difficult. Farmers need a flat area to plant. So they cut giant steps into the mountains. There they grow hundreds of kinds of potatoes. They also grow corn, wheat, and grains. Cotton, bananas, and sugarcane are common crops, too.

3   The Incas raise sheep, llamas, guinea pigs, and alpacas. Llamas were important to the Inca people 500 years ago and still are today. The animals are very surefooted. This means they do not easily trip or fall. The farmers use them to carry heavy loads through the mountains. People also drink the llama's milk.

Made in Peru

4   Beautiful handmade objects come from Peru. Many of them are made from the soft wool of llamas and alpacas. Spinners spin the wool into threads or yarn. The yarn is used for colorful sweaters and scarves. Weavers also form cloth from the threads. The cloth is used to make blankets, handbags, and hats.

Ancient Cities

5   Visitors come to Peru to see things they could not see anywhere else. One of the most famous places is Machu Picchu. The Incas carved this city on a mountaintop. People can walk there using the same trail the Incas used 500 years ago. The city and trail are kept very clean. Hikers and campers have to take their trash with them. Many people come every year. It is worth sore legs to see the ruins of this beautiful Inca city.

Peru's Garden of Eden

6   Peru is also home to beautiful Manu. Manu is one of the world's great rain forests. But too many of the trees there were being cut down. Some people are trying to stop more damage from happening. One reason is that rain forests are home to animals and plants that do not live anywhere else.

7   Life can be hard in the Andes. Still, the Inca people make the most of what the land offers. And more and more visitors are learning what life is like near the clouds.

▶ **Think** Use what you learned from reading the selection to respond to these questions.

1 What is the main idea of the entire passage?

    A The Incas raise sheep, llamas, and other animals.

    B The Incas make beautiful handmade crafts.

    C The Incas are working to protect the Manu rain forest.

    D The Incas live high in the Andes Mountains of Peru.

2 This question has two parts. First, answer Part A. Then answer Part B.

Part A
Which sentence **best** states the main idea of the section
"Mountain Farming"?

    A The Inca people have lived in the Andes Mountains for over 500 years.

    B Farming is hard work in the Andes.

    C A number of different crops are grown in the mountains.

    D Llamas are used to carry heavy loads through the mountains.

Part B
Which **two** sentences from the passage **best** support your answer
to Part A?

    A "The Andes are very high mountains in South America."

    B "The mountainsides make farming difficult."

    C "The Incas raise sheep, llamas, guinea pigs, and alpacas."

    D "Beautiful handmade objects come from Peru."

    E "So they cut giant steps into the mountains."

    F "There they grow hundreds of kinds of potatoes."

3 Which sentence states the main idea of paragraph 3?

    A "The Incas raise sheep, llamas, guinea pigs, and alpacas."

    B "Llamas were important to the Inca people 500 years ago and still are today."

    C "The farmers use them to carry heavy loads through the mountains."

    D "The animals [llamas] are very surefooted."

4 How do the key details in paragraph 4 support its main idea?

    A They describe different objects that are made.

    B They describe how sheep and alpaca wool is used.

    C They explain how wool is made into thread and yarn.

    D They describe what spinners and weavers do.

5 Read this sentence from paragraph 5 of the passage.

It is worth sore legs to see the ruins of this beautiful Inca city.

What does *ruins* mean in this context?

    A a place that has been destroyed

    B stones used to pave roads

    C what is left of old buildings

    D objects that were once used

6 The following question has two parts. First, answer Part A. Then answer Part B.

Part A
Reread paragraph 6.

> **Peru is also home to beautiful Manu. Manu is one of the world's great rain forests. But too many of the trees there were being cut down. Some people are trying to stop more damage from happening. One reason is that rain forests are home to animals and plants that do not live anywhere else.**

Which sentence **best** describes the main idea of the paragraph?

    A There are several great rain forests in the world.

    B Many animals and plants live in the rain forest.

    C The rain forest needs to be protected.

    D Tourists visit the rain forest.

Part B
Underline **two** key details in the paragraph that **best** support your answer for Part A.

Write

7 **Short Response** What is the main idea of the section "Made in Peru"? Use details from the passage to support your answer.

_____

_____

_____

_____

_____

_____

Learning Target

Explain how retelling key details can help you understand the main idea of a text.

Lesson 3
Reading About Time and Sequence

Learning Target

Using time and sequence words will help you understand how events in history are connected.

▶ **Read** Do you like a good story? Then you probably enjoy history. History is the story of events that happened in the past. **Historical** events are usually told in a **sequence,** which is the order in which they happened. The sequence can help you understand the **relationships,** or connections, between those events.

When you read, look for signal words that give clues about time order and sequence. *First, next,* and *finally* are signal words. So are phrases such as *later that year* and *in 1864.*

Read the cartoon below. What is happening? How are the events related?

First, the Vikings sailed to North America.

Next, they started a settlement.

After a few difficult years, the Vikings gave up and returned home.

▶ **Think** Read the cartoon again. Notice the signal words that are used. Now fill in the chart below by writing the events in the order in which they happened.

The Vikings Sail to North America		
First	**Next**	**After a Few Years**

▶ **Talk** Think about the second and third things that happen in the cartoon.

- What is the relationship between those two events?
- Was the third event what you expected?

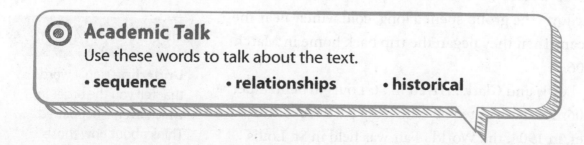

◉ **Academic Talk**
Use these words to talk about the text.
- **sequence**
- **relationships**
- **historical**

Adventures of the Growing Nation

by Teri Hillen

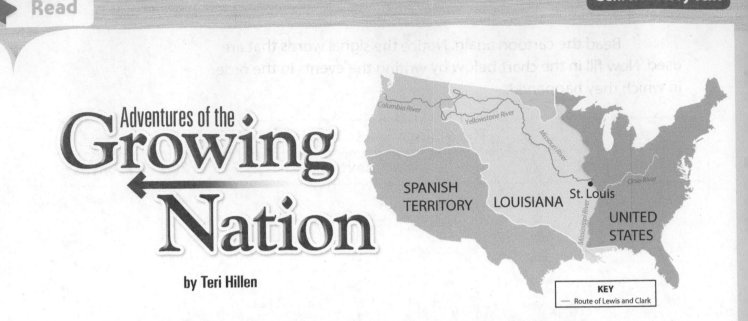

SPANISH TERRITORY

LOUISIANA

St. Louis

UNITED STATES

Columbia River

Yellowstone River

Missouri River

Ohio River

Mississippi River

KEY
—— Route of Lewis and Clark

1   Imagine that in one day, our country doubled in size. That's what happened to the United States in 1803. President Thomas Jefferson asked France to sell the United States a vast area of land. Overnight, America added more than 828,000 square miles of land west of the Mississippi River. This is known as the Louisiana Purchase.

2   Jefferson wanted to know the fastest way across the new land. At the time, there were no maps of the whole country. Jefferson asked Meriwether Lewis to explore the area. Lewis was an army captain whom Jefferson trusted. Lewis chose another soldier, William Clark, to help him lead the party.

3   To get ready, they first had a large boat built. The boat took the men down the Ohio River. Then they built a base camp near St. Louis, Missouri. They spent the winter of 1803 there. Finally, on May 14, 1804, Lewis and Clark began their famous trip into the new territory; 50 men went with them.

4   They traveled for over 18 months. Finally, the group made it to the Pacific Ocean. On November 7, 1805, Clark wrote, "Ocean in view! O! The joy." The group spent a long, cold winter near the ocean. Then they began the trip back home in March 1806.

5   Lewis and Clark arrived in St. Louis in September 1806. They were greeted with a big party. A century later, in 1904, the World's Fair was held in St. Louis. People honored Lewis and Clark's journey at the fair.

> ## Close Reader Habits
>
> **Underline** signal words that tell you the order in which events happened. Think about how those events are related.

Explore **What happened after the United States bought land from France?**

Think

1 Reread the text to find out the events of Lewis and Clark's journey. List those events in the graphic organizer.

Sometimes you need more than signal words to understand how events are related. Ask questions such as "Why did this happen?"

Lewis and Clark's Exploration	
First	President Jefferson asks Meriwether Lewis to explore the new land.
Winter 1803	
May 1804	
November 1805	
September 1806	

Talk

2 Reread paragraphs 2, 3, and 4. Talk with a partner about how the events in those paragraphs are related.

Write

3 **Short Response** What are the important events in the journey of Lewis and Clark? Include details from paragraphs 3, 4, and 5 in your answer. Use the space provided on page 44 to write your answer.

HINT Use details from your graphic organizer to organize your response.

WILLIAM BECKNELL
and the SANTA FE TRAIL

by Joy Adams

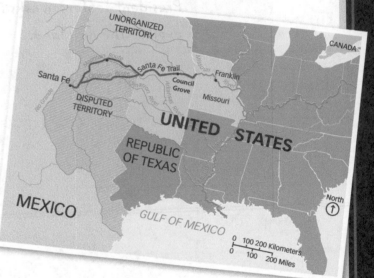

1   William Becknell was a trader and trapper. He was born in Virginia in the late 1700s. As a young man, Becknell moved to Missouri in 1810.

2   In Missouri, Becknell traded salt. His business wasn't very successful. So, in the summer of 1821, he planned a trip west. Traveling on horseback, Becknell and his group hoped to trade horses and mules and trap animals.

3   When the party started their trip, Spain owned New Mexico. The Spanish didn't allow traders from the United States to sell their goods there. As the party made its way, however, the Spanish lost control of New Mexico. Becknell heard this news and changed his plans. He headed straight to Santa Fe. There, they traded their goods for silver dollars.

4   About a year later, in May 1822, Becknell and his wagons left Missouri once again. This time Becknell followed a dangerous route. First, he followed the Arkansas River to what is today Dodge City, Kansas. Then he traveled southwest to the Cimarron River. The party ran out of water and almost died. But Becknell pushed them on to the river. Finally, they reached Santa Fe. They had blazed a new trail!

5   Becknell's route became known as the Santa Fe Trail. In 1825 it was marked as the main route to the Southwest. This route was important to the growth of the United States.

Close Reader Habits

What route did Becknell follow on his second trip to Santa Fe? **Number** the places where he stopped. The numbers should show the order in which he reached them.

Think

1 This question has two parts. Answer Part A. Then answer Part B.

> When two events are near each other in a sequence, think about how they might be related.

Part A
What important event happened soon after Becknell set off on his trip to the West?

A Becknell decided to trade horses instead of salt.

B Traders were told they couldn't go to Santa Fe.

C The Spanish lost their power in New Mexico.

D Becknell's group ran out of water and almost died.

Part B
Underline the sentence in this paragraph that supports your choice in Part A.

> **When the party started their trip, Spain owned New Mexico. The Spanish didn't allow traders from the United States to sell their goods there. As the party made its way, however, the Spanish lost control of New Mexico. Becknell heard this news and changed his plans. He headed straight to Santa Fe. There, they traded their goods for silver dollars.**

Talk

2 Discuss with a partner Becknell's second trip to Santa Fe. Use sequence words to describe the events of that journey.

Write

3 **Short Response** Describe Becknell's second trip to Santa Fe. Why was this an important historical event? Use the space provided on page 45 to write your answer.

> **HINT** Look at the last paragraph. What did Becknell's new trail help do?

Write Use the space below to write your answer to the question on page 41.

Adventures of the
Growing
Nation

3 **Short Response** What are the important events in the journey of Lewis and Clark? Include details from paragraphs 3, 4, and 5 in your answer.

> **HINT** Use details from your graphic organizer to organize your response.

> Don't forget to check your writing.

Write **Use the space below to write your answer to the question on page 43.**

WILLIAM BECKNELL
and the SANTA FE TRAIL

3 **Short Response** Describe Becknell's second trip to Santa Fe. Why was this an important historical event?

> **HINT** Look at the last paragraph. What did Becknell's new trail help do?

_____

_____

_____

_____

_____

_____

_____

_____

_____

_____

_____

Check Your Writing

- ☐ Did you read the prompt carefully?
- ☐ Did you put the prompt in your own words?
- ☐ Did you use the best evidence from the text to support your ideas?
- ☐ Are your ideas clearly organized?
- ☐ Did you write in clear and complete sentences?
- ☐ Did you check your spelling and punctuation?

▶ **Read**

SACAGAWEA'S JOURNEY INTO HISTORY
by Jeanette Cannon

WORDS TO KNOW

As you read, look inside, around, and beyond these words to figure out what they mean.

- **expedition**
- **fellow**
- **gap**

1   You may have seen this gold-colored dollar coin. It shows the face of a young Native American woman carrying a baby on her back. She is one of the only women on a U.S. legal coin. So who was she?

2   Sacagawea was a Shoshone Indian born at the end of the 1700s in an area now called Idaho. Her early life was difficult. Sometime between 1799 and 1801, she was captured by a group of Hidatsa Indians and taken away from her people. She was only 12 years old. By age 16, she was married to a French fur trader named Toussaint Charbonneau, who lived with the Hidatsas. Her adventures were just beginning.

3   In 1803, President Thomas Jefferson decided to map out the newly expanded nation. He sent Meriwether Lewis and William Clark on an expedition to explore the land.

4   In May of 1804, the explorers began traveling on the Missouri River in canoes. One of their jobs was to take notes about what they saw. They drew pictures of plants and animals they saw. They made maps as they went along. They carried with them special tools to help them as they traveled. Everything was wrapped so water would not damage anything.

5   In November of 1804, Lewis met Charbonneau and hired him as a translator. Sacagawea joined her husband on the expedition. Their baby was born soon after the journey began.

6   Though Sacagawea was not a guide on the journey, she helped the travelers in many ways. One of Lewis and Clark's diary entries from May 14, 1805, tells how Sacagawea's calm bravery saved important objects and information from being lost forever.

7   One day, a terrible storm caused Sacagawea's canoe to tip over. All the men were trying to get the canoe upright. Sacagawea calmly went into the water. Her baby was strapped to her back. She saved the notebooks and tools that would have floated away.

8   Later that year, the explorers came to Shoshone territory. Sacagawea helped them find a route through the mountains. She also helped them buy horses from her fellow Shoshone.

9   A few months later, the group had their first look at the Pacific Ocean. Before beginning the return journey, the explorers built a camp to stay in over the winter.

Lewis and Clark's winter camp at Fort Clatsop is now a National Historic Park near Astoria, Oregon.

10   In May 1806, a few months after they had started their journey home, the travelers met a group of Nez Perce Indians. Sacagawea helped the two groups speak to each other. On the way back east, Sacagawea guided the group along trails she remembered from her childhood. One important trail was a gap in the mountains that led them to the Yellowstone River.

11   The journey ended for Sacagawea in August 1806. People who traveled with her wrote about her cheerfulness and helpfulness. They all said she showed great courage.

12   In 2000, two centuries after Sacagawea was born, a special U.S. dollar coin was created. It honors a brave young woman who helped explore a new nation.

The U.S. Postal Service issued this stamp in honor of Sacagawea in 1994.

Timeline of Some Events in the Life of Sacagawea

1788 Sacagawea is born.

1799–1801 Sacagawea is captured by Hidatsas.

Lewis and Clark Expedition

1804

November 1804 Sacagawea and her husband Charbonneau join the Lewis and Clark expedition.

May 1805 Sacagawea saves important information during a storm.

August 1805 Sacagawea helps Lewis and Clark trade for Shoshone horses.

1805

November 1805 The company reaches the Pacific Ocean.

December 1805 The explorers build Fort Clatsop and camp there for the winter.

1806

May 1806 The group meets up with several Nez Perce chiefs. Charbonneau and Sacagawea translate.

July 1806 Sacagawea and the group reach Yellowstone River.

1811

March 1811 Sacagawea and Charbonneau move to South Dakota.

▶ **Think** Use what you learned from reading the selection to respond to these questions.

1 Look again at the time line. Based on the sequence shown there, which **two** statements are true?

    A Lewis and Clark spoke with the Nez Perce chiefs at Fort Clatsop.

    B Sacagawea met Charbonneau during the expedition.

    C Lewis and Clark reached the Yellowstone River near the end of their journey.

    D Sacagawea helped prepare for the journey by buying horses.

    E The group faced a dangerous storm early in their journey.

    F Sacagawea was captured by the Hidatsa Indians after moving to South Dakota.

2 This question has two parts. First, answer Part A. Then answer Part B.

Part A

What event happened **first** after Sacagawea helped the explorers buy horses from the Shoshone?

    A The group stayed at Fort Clatsop for the winter.

    B The group met with Nez Perce Indians.

    C Sacagawea married Toussaint Charbonneau.

    D Sacagawea remembered a gap in the mountains.

Part B

Where did you find the specific information needed to answer Part A?

_____

_____

3 Look at the sequence words and phrases in the first column. They show the order of events. Write the letter of the event that belongs with each one.

Sequence	Event
_____ In 1803	**A** Sacagawea and Charbonneau join the expedition.
_____ In May of 1804	**B** Sacagawea remembers trails that lead to the Yellowstone River.
_____ In November of 1804	**C** The explorers build a camp to stay in over the winter.
_____ In May of 1805	**D** Sacagawea saves important information from being lost.
_____ Later that year	**E** The explorers begin their journey to the American West.
_____ A few months after they cross the mountains	**F** Jefferson asks Lewis and Clark to explore the new land.
_____ Before beginning the journey home	**G** Sacagawea helps find a route through the mountains.
_____ On their way back east	**H** The explorers reach the Pacific Ocean.

4 What important sequence information does paragraph 5 include?

    A It explains why the expedition was necessary.

    B It describes Sacagawea's husband as a brave man.

    C It tells when Sacagawea joined the expedition.

    D It shows that the baby was born in the winter.

5 Read this sentence from paragraph 8.

    Sacagawea helped them find a route through the mountains.

What is the meaning of *route* in this context?

    A wide tunnel to travel through

    B train tracks in the mountains

    C way of getting from place to place

    D paved road for wagons to use

Write

6 **Short Response** How does the sequence of events in the biography help show how Sacagawea becomes more and more valuable to the expedition? Use details from the passage to support your response.

_____

_____

_____

_____

_____

_____

_____

_____

Learning Target

You've learned that it is important to understand the relationship between events in historical writing. Explain how a clear sequence can help you understand the relationship between events.

Lesson 4
Describing Cause and Effect

Learning Target

Understanding cause-and-effect relationships will help you understand how and why events happen.

▶ **Read** A heavy storm hits, and a large tree falls. The storm is the **cause,** or the reason the tree falls. The fallen tree is the **effect,** or what happens as a result of the storm. The connection between these two events is an example of a cause-and-effect **relationship.** Understanding cause and effect can help you see how events and ideas are related.

Writers often use words such as *because, if/then, since, so, therefore,* and *as a result* to signal and explain a cause-and-effect relationship.

Read this cartoon. What cause-and-effect relationship do you see?

Henry got a balloon at the party.

Henry blew up the balloon.

The balloon popped because Henry blew it up too much.

▶ **Think** Look at the cartoon again. Fill in this cause-and-effect chart to tell what happened.

Cause (Why It Happened)		Effect (What Happened)
	→	

Write one or two sentences describing what happened. Use words such as *because, so,* or *as a result* to show cause and effect.

_____

_____

_____

▶ **Talk** Imagine there is a fourth box in the cartoon. What do you think the cat would do? Why? Describe that cause and effect. Use a signal word in your description.

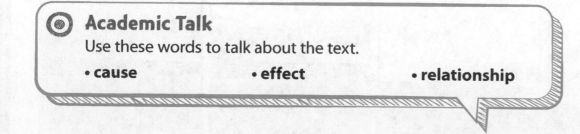

◉ **Academic Talk**
Use these words to talk about the text.
- **cause**   - **effect**   - **relationship**

Genre: **Science Article**

Cloudy

with a Chance of Cats and Dogs
by Nicole Sheffler

1   You may have heard the saying, "It's raining cats and dogs out there!" But what's really going on up in the sky? Read on to find out.

2   Rain comes from clouds. But where do the clouds come from? First, it's important to understand that all air contains water. This invisible water is called water vapor. When warm air rises, it cools down. Cool air can't hold as much water vapor as warm air. So the vapor grabs a ride on tiny pieces of dust in the air. The vapor forms water droplets around the bits of dust. A cloud is formed when billions of these water droplets come together.

3   Inside a cloud, the water droplets move around very quickly. When they move they may bump into each other. As a result, they may stick together. If they stick together, then they start to get bigger. When they get bigger, they get heavier. Sometimes they get too heavy for the cloud to hold them. Then they fall to the ground as rain. If it's cold outside, then they fall as snow.

4   Much of this rain and snow falls all the way back down to the ground. Then the whole process starts over again.

Close Reader Habits

Underline words and phrases that signal cause and effect. How do they help you understand how the ideas are connected?

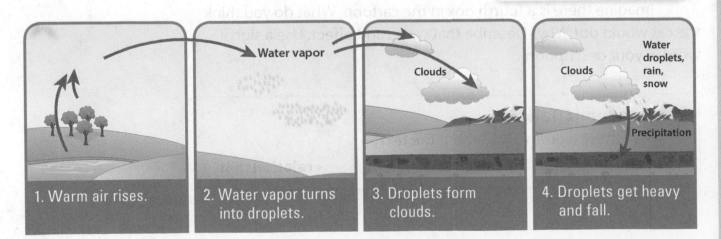

1. Warm air rises.

2. Water vapor turns into droplets.

3. Droplets form clouds.

4. Droplets get heavy and fall.

How do cause-and-effect relationships help explain how rain is formed?

Think

> When you read, pay attention to how and why things happen. This will help you spot causes and effects.

1 Finish this chart to show cause-and-effect relationships from the article about rain.

Cause	Effect
Warm air rises.	
	The water vapor attaches itself to dust to form droplets.
Billions of droplets come together.	
The droplets stick together and get heavier.	

Talk

2 Work with a partner to explain each cause-and-effect relationship from the chart. Use signal words to show how the ideas are connected.

Write

3 **Short Response** What happens inside a cloud that causes rain or snow to fall? Use signal words to explain the cause-and-effect relationship. Use the space provided on page 58 to write your answer.

> **HINT** Begin by making a list of the key details in paragraph 3 of the article.

from Frozen Deserts

by Heidi Deal, *AppleSeeds*

1   In spite of our image of deserts, some are freezing cold and covered with ice and snow. Cold deserts exist all over the world. They are found in Asia, Africa, South America, China, and even the United States.

2   The coldest place on Earth, Antarctica, is considered a desert. It gets very little snow or rain. When it snows, the snow never melts. Instead, it forms ice sheets that build up over time. This creates ice shelves and icebergs. It's too cold for plants. Only a few mosses and algae grow there. And people can't live there for long periods of time.

3   Another frozen desert, the Gobi, reaches from Mongolia to China. It is still expanding. The Gobi Desert is called a rain shadow desert. A large mountain range, the Himalayas, blocks the wet weather from reaching the area. Heavy winds whip through the Gobi plains. (That may explain why there's no sand there. Instead, the landscape is mostly bare rock with little plant life.) Temperatures are extreme. It isn't covered in ice like Antarctica is. But the Gobi can get as cold as 40° F below zero in the winter. In the summer, it can get as hot as 122° F.

4   Brrrr. It's the desert, but I'm freezing!

Close Reader Habits

Underline sentences that show the effects of extreme cold in Antarctica.

> ▶ **Think**

1 This question has two parts. Answer Part A. Then answer Part B.

Part A

In Antarctica, why do ice sheets build up over time?

    A because Antarctica gets very little snow or rain

    B because when it does snow, the snow doesn't melt

    C because there are few plants to stop the ice from forming

    D because there aren't enough people to break up the ice

Part B

What are **two** other effects of the extreme cold in Antarctica?

    A Ice shelves and icebergs form.

    B The plants become tougher and stronger.

    C It snows all the time.

    D Strong winds blow away any snow.

    E People can't stay there long.

    F There is no snow.

> Remember that one cause can have many effects, and one effect may have many causes.

> ▶ **Talk**

2 Reread paragraph 3 and discuss with a partner what the Gobi Desert looks like. What is one possible reason that there is no sand in the Gobi Desert?

> ▶ **Write**

3 **Short Response** Why is the Gobi Desert a desert? Explain at least two cause-and-effect relationships that might have caused this. Use the space provided on page 59 to write your answer.

> **HINT** What effect do the Himalayas have on the area where the Gobi Desert formed?

▶ 📓 **Write** **Use the space below to write your answer to the question on page 55.**

Cloudy
with a Chance of Cats and Dogs

3 **Short Response** What happens inside a cloud that causes rain or snow to fall? Use signal words to explain the cause-and-effect relationship.

> **HINT** Begin by making a list of the key details in paragraph 3 of the article.

_____

_____

_____

_____

_____

_____

_____

> Don't forget to check your writing.

Write **Use the space below to write your answer to the question on page 57.**

from
Frozen Deserts

3 **Short Response** Why is the Gobi Desert a desert? Explain at least two cause-and-effect relationships that might have caused this.

> **HINT** What effect do the Himalayas have on the area where the Gobi Desert formed?

_____

_____

_____

_____

_____

_____

_____

Check Your Writing

☐ Did you read the prompt carefully?

☐ Did you put the prompt in your own words?

☐ Did you use the best evidence from the text to support your ideas?

☐ Are your ideas clearly organized?

☐ Did you write in clear and complete sentences?

☐ Did you check your spelling and punctuation?

> Read

How Hail Happens

by Val Dumitrescu

WORDS TO KNOW
As you read, look inside, around, and beyond this word to figure out what it means.

• conditions

1   A soft rain is falling on the roof. You smile. Suddenly, the sound gets louder. It sounds like golf balls are bouncing off the roof. You race to the window. Outside, round balls of ice cover the ground. It is hailing! How did rain turn into hard hail in a matter of seconds?

Inside a Storm Cloud

2   It actually takes longer than a few seconds for hail to form. It all starts with a storm cloud. Storm clouds are made of water droplets. Large storm clouds are both very wide and very tall. At the top, air is much colder than it is lower down. Raindrops start to form at the bottom of the cloud, where it is warmer.

Journey of a Raindrop

3   As wind moves the storm cloud, it also moves some of the raindrops inside of it. Some of the raindrops move toward the top of the cloud. If the raindrops meet the very cold air there, then they turn to ice. These new "ice drops" get heavier. As a result, they fall to the ground as hailstones.

1

Wind blows raindrops up into a colder level of the cloud.

2

Raindrops freeze and become hailstones.

Clear and Cloudy Hail

4   Some hail is very clear. Other hail looks like pieces of white chalk. When the hailstone is clear, it is because there is little air in it. That happens when the raindrops freeze slowly. Then the air bubbles in the water have time to escape. Milky looking hailstones have many small air bubbles. That happens when the air at the top of the cloud is super cold. That cold air turns the raindrops into ice right away. The air bubbles are trapped inside.

Hailstones of Every Shape and Size

5   Sometimes, strong winds move up through a cloud. The wind can pick up the falling hailstones and push them back up. At the top, the hailstones meet the cold air again. There they get a new coat of ice. In a strong thunderstorm, that can happen several times. When you look carefully at a hailstone, you may see some rings. Each ring is one layer of ice. If you count the rings, then you will know how many times the hailstone has made the trip to the top of the cloud. This up-and-down movement causes hailstones to have very unusual shapes. It also makes the hailstones bigger. Some hailstones can be the size of a pebble. Other hailstones can be larger than a baseball!

6   Next time you see hail on your lawn, pick some up and look at it closely. It may have quite a story to tell!

3 Hailstones become larger and heavier.

4 Hail falls to the ground.

▶ **Think** Use what you learned from reading the selection to respond to these questions.

1 This question has two parts. First, answer Part A. Then answer Part B.

Part A
How do raindrops become hailstones?

    A Warm clouds form hailstones.

    B Raindrops in the cold air become ice.

    C The wind makes hailstones.

    D The soft rain makes hailstones.

Part B
Which sentence from the text **best** explains what causes raindrops to turn into hail?

    A "If the raindrops meet the very cold air there, then they turn to ice."

    B "As wind moves the storm cloud, it also moves some of the raindrops inside of it."

    C "Raindrops start to form at the bottom of the cloud, where it is warmer."

    D "At the top, air is much colder than it is lower down."

2 Match each cause to an effect. Write the letter from the second column on the correct line in the first column.

Cause	Effect
_____ Wind moves the storm clouds.	**A** The raindrops turn to ice.
_____ Air bubbles are trapped inside the freezing water.	**B** They fall to the ground as hailstones.
_____ Hailstones move up and down in the cloud.	**C** Raindrops inside the cloud begin to move.
_____ Raindrops meet cold air.	**D** The hailstones are milky white.
_____ The ice drops become heavier.	**E** Layers of ice are added.

3 Read this sentence from the article.

> **Storm clouds are made of water droplets.**

Notice the word with the ending -*let*. That ending means "a small type of something." According to the sentence, what are storm clouds made of?

    A   smaller clouds

    B   warm drops of water

    C   tiny drops of water

    D   heavy drops of water

4 What are **three** effects of hailstones moving up and down in the cloud?

    A   The hailstones break apart.

    B   The hailstones add layers of ice.

    C   The hailstones get stuck in a storm cloud and never fall.

    D   The hailstones warm up and turn back into raindrops.

    E   The hailstones grow larger.

    F   The hailstones may take on unusual shapes.

    G   The hailstones fill with air bubbles.

5 What causes rings to form in a hailstone?

    A   the hail's up-and-down movement in the clouds

    B   escaping air bubbles

    C   the warm air at the bottom of the cloud

    D   the cold air at the top of the cloud

6 Why are some hailstones clear?

    A   Air bubbles get caught inside the hailstones.

    B   There is almost no air inside the hailstones.

    C   The temperature inside the cloud is very cold.

    D   There are strong winds inside the cloud.

Write   Hailstones can be as small as pebbles or as large as baseballs. Some also have very unusual shapes. How does that happen? Reread the text. Draw a box around the section that tells why hailstones can be different shapes and sizes.

7 **Plan Your Response**   Reread paragraph 5. Underline details that explain how hailstones get their shape and size. You can use that information in your explanation.

8 **Write an Extended Response**   Explain what causes hailstones to get as big as baseballs and develop odd shapes. Use **two** details from the passage to help you show cause and effect.

_____

_____

_____

_____

_____

_____

_____

_____

_____

_____

Learning Target

You've seen that knowing about cause and effect can help you understand connections between ideas. Explain why looking for causes and effects is especially important when you are reading science texts.

▶ Read

Read the history article. Then answer the questions that follow.

Race to the Rescue

by Lisa Torrey

1   In the winter of 1925, a deadly disease broke out in Nome, Alaska. The disease was a serious threat to the children who lived there. Only one kind of medicine could stop the disease from spreading. However, the medicine was in Anchorage, Alaska. Anchorage was nearly 1,000 miles away from Nome.

2   People were in a hurry to get the medicine from Anchorage to Nome. There was an old mail route called the Iditarod Trail. It linked the two towns. But the trip along the route would be very hard. The route was covered with snow and ice. The howling winds were bitter cold. Rough mountains covered part of the route.

3   Their only hope was to use sled dogs. Sled dogs could endure the long, cold journey. They could get the medicine quickly to Nome.

The Journey Begins

4   More than 20 mushers, or drivers, put together teams of sled dogs. Each team played a key part in the relay to race the medicine to Nome. The first team soon left Anchorage on the first leg of the trip.

Statue of Balto in New York City

5   Reporters wrote articles about the heroic race to deliver the medicine to Nome. People all around the world read these reports in newspapers. They followed each leg of the journey. They became caught up in the drama that was taking place in Alaska. They cheered for the dog sled teams.

A dog sled team running in the Iditarod race.

Balto Leads the Way

6   Amazingly, the team on the final stretch of the journey arrived in Nome only six days later. The musher drove his dog sled team into Nome on February 2, 1925. The team brought the medicine that would keep the children in Nome safe.

7   A husky named Balto was at the lead. Soon people all over the world saw pictures of Balto. People everywhere recognized his black furry face and sparkling eyes. In 1926, a group of people built a statue in honor of Balto. They placed the statue in Central Park in New York City. Balto died in 1933.

8   Over forty years later, people in Alaska wanted to honor the heroic race that brought the medicine to Nome. They also wanted the race to celebrate Alaska and the important role of sled dogs.

9   The Alaskans held a sled dog race in 1967. It was a much shorter distance compared to the 1925 route. The first official Iditarod race was held in 1973. The trail covers nearly 1,200 miles. The race has been held every year since. Mushers and their teams of sled dogs come from all over to compete. It is called "The Last Great Race on Earth."

► **Think**

1 Which sentence from the passage **best** states the main idea of the article?

  A "The first team soon left Anchorage on the first leg of the trip."

  B "The team brought the medicine that would keep the children in Nome safe."

  C "A husky named Balto was at the lead."

  D "They also wanted the race to celebrate Alaska and the important role of sled dogs."

2 Paragraph 2 says the trip from Anchorage to Nome was "very hard." Explain why the trip was hard. Use details from paragraph 2 to support your answer.

_____

_____

_____

_____

_____

_____

_____

3 Which sentence from the article **best** explains why it was important to get medicine to Nome quickly?

  A "The disease was a serious threat to the children who lived there."

  B "People were in a hurry to get the medicine from Anchorage to Nome."

  C "Each team played a key part in the relay to race the medicine to Nome."

  D "Reporters wrote articles about the heroic race to deliver the medicine to Nome."

4 Look at the sequence words in the first column. They show the order of events in the article. Write the letter of the event that belongs with each one.

Sequence	Event
____ In the winter of 1925	**A** Balto's team brought medicine to Nome.
____ Six days later	
____ One year after the dog sled team arrived in Nome	**B** A statue of Balto was built.
	C The first Iditarod race was run.
____ Four decades after the race to Nome	**D** A terrible sickness broke out in Alaska.
____ In 1973	**E** The Alaskans organized a sled dog race.

5 Reread paragraph 5.

> **Reporters wrote articles about the dog sled teams and the heroic race to deliver the medicine to Nome. People all around the world read these reports in newspapers. They followed each leg of the journey. They became caught up in the drama that was taking place in Alaska. They cheered for the dog sled teams.**

How do the key details in paragraph 5 support its main idea?

    A They explain how far the dog sled teams traveled.

    B They explain how the dog sled teams became famous.

    C They describe the route the dog sled teams took to Nome.

    D They describe the problems the dog sled teams faced.

6 Read this sentence from paragraph 8.

> **Over forty years later, people in Alaska wanted to honor the heroic race that brought the medicine to Nome.**

What does *heroic* mean in this context?

    A very old

    B difficult to win

    C very interesting

    D done with courage

▶ **Read**

Read the science article. Then answer the questions that follow.

The Strange Power of Volcanoes

by Magnus Krako

1   In 1963, a ship's captain sailing near Iceland saw smoke rising from the sea. He thought it was a ship on fire, but what he found was much stranger. Lava, or liquid rock, was shooting up to the water's surface from below. Ash, tiny bits of rock crushed to a powder, also shot up to the surface. This eruption went on for more than three years. When it was over, all that lava had formed a new island called Surtsey.

Photo taken 16 days after the Surtsey eruption in 1963.

2   Surtsey was born from a volcano. Volcanoes are found all over the world. They can be underwater or on land. They can also be found in deserts or jungles. Volcanoes can create new islands. They can also destroy things when red-hot lava pours out of them.

3   Volcanoes are mostly the same on the inside. A long skinny tube called a pipe forms the center of a volcano. The pipe starts at a pool of hot, liquid rock called a magma chamber. The pipe goes all the way up to the crater. The crater is the opening at the top of the volcano. This is where the volcano's vent is found. The vent is a crack in Earth's surface. It lets smoke, ash, and lava out of the volcano.

4   To understand how a volcano erupts, or explodes, think about a bottle of soda. When you shake soda in a closed

bottle, bubbles form. The bubbles create a special kind of gas. As more bubbles form, more gas forms. Inside the bottle, the gas and bubbles press harder and harder against the sides of the bottle. This pressure builds and builds. Finally, when the lid is taken off, the soda sprays out.

5   This is how a volcano works. Hot, liquid rock makes different gases. The pressure from these gases builds up. When the pressure gets too great, the gases push up the pipe and through the vent. The gas pushes other things out with it. Sometimes hot, liquid lava sprays out of the vent. Sometimes tiny bits of rock blast in a huge ash cloud. Not all volcanic eruptions are the same. Some are quick and loud. Others move more slowly with lava that flows like thick honey.

6   The ash from volcanic eruptions can change Earth's weather. In April 1815, Mount Tambora in the Pacific Ocean erupted. It was one of the biggest volcanic eruptions of all time. It sent a huge ash cloud into the sky. For more than a year, the weather everywhere on Earth was different. Summers were cold and cloudy. Snow fell and lakes froze, even in June! All this because a volcano erupted!

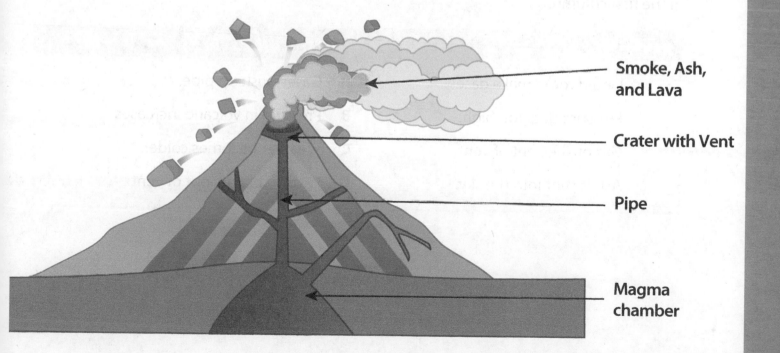

Smoke, Ash, and Lava

Crater with Vent

Pipe

Magma chamber

7 Choose **two** questions that can be answered by reading paragraph 2.

    A   Where are volcanoes found?

    B   How can volcanoes affect the world?

    C   How do volcanoes erupt?

    D   When was Surtsey formed?

    E   What is lava made from?

    F   How do volcanoes form in deserts?

8 Read these sentences from paragraph 1.

> **Lava, or liquid rock, was shooting up to the water's surface from below.
> Ash, tiny bits of rock crushed to a powder, also shot up to the surface.**

What is the meaning of *surface* in this context?

    A   to come into sight

    B   to break through

    C   the middle part of something

    D   the top part of something

9 Match each cause to an effect. Write the letter from the second column on the correct line in the first column.

Cause	Effect
_____ Liquid rocks make gases.	**A** Gases push up pipe.
_____ Pressure gets too high.	**B** Pressure in volcano increases.
_____ Gas pushes out of vent.	**C** Weather becomes colder.
_____ Ash is sent into the sky.	**D** Lava is sprayed out of vent.

10 This question has two parts. First, answer Part A. Then answer Part B.

Part A

What is the main idea of paragraph 6?

    A Volcanoes send ash into the sky.

    B Volcanoes can be very powerful.

    C Volcanoes can have an effect on the weather.

    D Volcanoes have erupted throughout history.

Part B

Underline **three** sentences in paragraph 6 below that **best** support its main idea.

> **The ash from volcanic eruptions can change Earth's weather. In April 1815, Mount Tambora in the Pacific Ocean erupted. It was one of the biggest volcanic eruptions of all time. It sent a huge ash cloud into the sky. For more than a year, the weather everywhere on Earth was different. Summers were cold and cloudy. Snow fell and lakes froze, even in June! All this because a volcano erupted!**

11 Which question is answered in paragraph 3?

    A How does the magma chamber get filled?

    B How does liquid rock get out of a volcano?

    C How are smoke, ash, and lava different?

    D Why do volcanoes erupt in different ways?

12 What is the main idea of the entire passage?

    A Volcanoes are all the same inside.

    B Volcanoes are found all over the world.

    C Volcanic eruptions are the reason islands form.

    D Volcanic eruptions are a powerful force of nature.

✎ **Write**

13 **Extended Response** How and why does a volcano erupt? How can volcanic eruptions affect Earth? Use details from the article in your answer.

In your answer, be sure to
- explain how and why a volcano erupts
- describe how volcanic eruptions can affect Earth
- use details from the article in your answer

Check your writing for correct spelling, grammar, capitalization, and punctuation.

_____

_____

_____

_____

_____

_____

_____

_____

_____

_____

_____

_____

_____

_____

Key Ideas and Details in Literature

You probably have heard the story "Jack and the Beanstalk." What is the first thing you remember about it? Most likely it's Jack and the giant. These are two of the characters. What do you remember about Jack's adventures? Is it how Jack climbs up the beanstalk? Or is it the part about Jack escaping from the giant? These are some of the important events in the story. Do you remember enough of the story to tell it in your own words? Perhaps you remember that it ends "happily ever after!" What do you like best about "Jack and the Beanstalk"? Have you read other stories that remind you of this story?

In this unit, you will learn to ask and answer questions about stories like "Jack and the Beanstalk." You will think about what characters say and do, and why. You'll pay attention to story events and see how one event leads to another. And you'll put all this together to figure out the message, or lesson, of the story. So get ready for a journey into storyland!

✓ Self Check

Before starting this unit, check off the skills you know below. As you complete each lesson, see how many more skills you can check off!

I can:	Before this unit	After this unit
ask and answer different kinds of questions about a story.	☐	☐
tell how and why characters make one event lead to another in stories.	☐	☐
tell the most important parts of a story using my own words, and in the order they happen.	☐	☐
describe the lesson that the characters learn in a story.	☐	☐

page 80

page 87

page 96

page 100

page 110

page 114

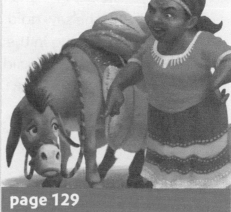

page 129

Lesson 5
Asking and Answering Questions About Stories

Learning Target

Ask questions about what you read, and use details from the text to support your answers.

▶ **Read** Stories are made up of characters, settings, and events. A **character** is person or animal. A **setting** is where and when a story takes place. An **event** is something that happens in a story.

When reading, you can ask questions about characters, settings, and events. You can also answer questions about those same things. When you answer a question about a story, support your answer with details from the text. This will show that you understand the story.

Erika was doing her homework. Her pencil rolled off the desk and under the bed. She was peering under the bed, looking for it, when she spotted an old wooden box she had never seen before. *How did that get there?* she asked herself. When Erika opened it, she saw gold coins glittering in the dim light. "Wow!" she said, "I think it's a treasure chest."

▶ **Think** You've learned about why it's important to ask and answer questions as you read. Now, look at the chart. Finish the chart to show how the questions can be answered with details from the story.

Question	Story Details	Answer
What does Erika find under the bed?		
Why does Erika think she has found a treasure chest?		

▶ **Talk** Which question had an answer in the text? Which one did you have to think more about? Explain how you figured out each answer in the chart.

⊚ **Academic Talk**
Use these words to talk about the text.
- **character**   • **setting**   • **event**

▶ **Read**

Grandma's Secret

by Kat Williams

1   Annie dreamed of being a famous singer one day. She and her grandmother both liked watching competition shows on TV that transformed ordinary people into singing stars.

2   One night Grandma brought down a small, dust-covered box from the attic. "I'd like to show you some old photographs," she said. "I think you might find them interesting."

3   One photo showed four girls singing on a stage, gathered around a microphone. They were wearing matching dresses, and their hair was elaborately styled. "Who are those people?" Annie asked.

4   "Look at the girl on the right," Grandma said. Annie leaned closer, peering at the photograph.

5   "Oh my gosh, Grandma, that's you! What are you doing??"

6   "I'm singing on a TV show with my group, The Wildflowers," Grandma said. "It was about 40 years ago. We recorded a song, and it played on the radio. It was so popular that we were asked to perform it on TV."

7   "Why didn't you tell me this before?" asked Annie.

8   Grandma smiled. "Oh, I guess I just haven't thought about it for a long time."

9   Now it was Annie's turn to smile. "So, Grandma, what else have you done that you haven't told me about?"

Close Reader Habits

What questions do you have about Grandma and her secret? **Underline** sentences that tell important details about Grandma's secret.

Explore

How can details from the story help you answer questions about Grandma and her secret?

▶ **Think**

Good readers ask what's happening in a story and whom it's happening to. They also ask where and why events happen.

1 Finish the chart by using details from the text to find answers. Add a question of your own in the second row.

Question	Story Details	Answer
Who are the girls in the picture?		

▶ **Talk**

2 What is one thing Annie and her grandmother have in common? How do you know?

✎ **Write**

3 **Short Response** Describe the secret that Grandma had been keeping. Why didn't Annie know about it? Use the space provided on page 84 to write your answer.

HINT What does Grandma say when Annie asks why her grandmother hadn't shared her secret before?

The TERROR of Green Street

by Julian Green

1   Frankie Ortiz had a secret. Each day after school, he would climb into a pine tree and wait for his friends to leave. Then he would climb down and ride his bike home as fast as he could. As he reached Green Street, Frankie would cross the street. On the other side, a white dog tied in a yard would bark fiercely. Its barking echoed around the neighborhood.

2   Today's trip home was a little different. Frankie's friend Mike lived next door to the dog. Today Mike was in his driveway when Frankie rode by. "Frankie, come here!" he called.

3   When Frankie didn't stop, Mike got on his own bike and caught up to him. "What do you want?" Frankie asked angrily, hoping Mike would leave him alone.

4   But Mike didn't leave. He said, "How come you always go home by yourself?"

5   Frankie stopped his bike to catch his breath. "That dog," he said quietly.

6   Mike started to laugh until Frankie glared at him. "Are you scared of that mutt? Snowball's noisy, but she's harmless. You just have to get to know her."

7   Frankie frowned, but he followed Mike back down the street. The closer they got to Snowball, the louder she barked, and the slower Frankie pedaled. His heart was pounding hard enough to break down a door. He wanted to cry, he wanted to run away, but he knew Mike would laugh again.

8   Frankie watched as Mike knelt on the ground and scratched the dog's chin. "Hiya, Snowball, you loudmouth fur ball," Mike said. Snowball sniffed around Frankie's legs and then wandered away.

9   Frankie let out a long sigh and said, "I still don't like that dog. But let's ride home together tomorrow." Mike just smiled.

Close Reader Habits

Why does Frankie hide from his friends and ride home alone? **Underline** details that answer the question.

▶ **Think**

1 This question has two parts. Answer Part A. Then answer Part B.

Part A

Why does Frankie cross Green Street on his way home?

- **A** He doesn't want his friends to see him.
- **B** He wants to avoid his friend Mike's house.
- **C** He is afraid of the dog on the other side.
- **D** He likes to be left alone.

> Think about what characters say. They may be providing important details.

Part B

Which **two** details from the story **best** support the answer to Part A?

- **A** "... he would climb into a pine tree and wait for his friends to leave."
- **B** "On the other side, a white dog tied in a yard would bark fiercely."
- **C** "Frankie's friend Mike lived next door to the dog."
- **D** "'Are you scared of that mutt?'"
- **E** "'Snowball's noisy, but she's harmless.'"
- **F** "'Hiya, Snowball, you loudmouth fur ball.'"
- **G** "Snowball sniffed around Frankie's legs and then wandered away."

▶ **Talk**

2 Why doesn't Frankie run away when the dog keeps barking? What detail from the text helps you answer the question?

▶ **Write**

3 **Short Response** What are two good things that come from what happens to Frankie? Use details from the story in your answer. Use the space provided on page 85 to write your answer.

> **HINT** What does Frankie ask Mike to do the next day?

Write **Use the space below to write your answer to the question on page 81.**

Grandma's Secret

HINT What does Grandma say when Annie asks why her grandmother hadn't shared her secret before?

3 **Short Response** Describe the secret that Grandma had been keeping. Why didn't Annie know about it?

_____

_____

_____

_____

_____

_____

_____

_____

_____

Don't forget to check your writing.

Write Use the space below to write your answer to the question on page 83.

The TERROR of Green Street

3 **Short Response** What are two good things that come from what happens to Frankie? Use details from the story in your answer.

> **HINT** What does Frankie ask Mike to do the next day?

_____

_____

_____

_____

_____

_____

_____

_____

Check Your Writing

☐ Did you read the prompt carefully?

☐ Did you put the prompt in your own words?

☐ Did you use the best evidence from the text to support your ideas?

☐ Are your ideas clearly organized?

☐ Did you write in clear and complete sentences?

☐ Did you check your spelling and punctuation?

▶ **Read**

Genre: Realistic Fiction

AN EARFUL

by Dale-Marie Bryan, *Highlights*

> **WORDS TO KNOW**
> As you read, look inside, around, and beyond these words to figure out what they mean.
>
> • **chores**
> • **stall**
> • **corral**

1   "Your homework is to collect sounds," Mrs. Olson said. She handed out sheets of paper shaped like giant ears. Then she held up a shiny blue kazoo. "Everyone who gets an 'earful' will get one of these." The class laughed.

2   Later, Jacob glared out the school bus window. Not fair, he thought. How could he collect enough sounds on his family's farm? There were plenty of noises in town. If only he lived where tires squeal.

3   Jacob scrambled off the bus when it screeched to a stop at his mailbox. But he wasn't in the mood to wave as it drove away.

4   When he threw open the gate, it groaned like a ghost. That was how he felt about his homework.

5   On the porch, Jacob knelt beside the kittens curled on the rug. They sounded like tiny motors when they purred.

6   "I'm home!" Jacob called. He thumped his book bag down on a kitchen chair.

7   The rocker in the nursery stopped creaking.

8   "How was school?" his mother asked, walking in with his baby brother on her shoulder. She was patting his little back.

9   "I've got homework," Jacob grumbled.

10   The baby burped, and Jacob laughed. "That's what I think about it, too!"

11   "Have a snack before you do your chores," his mother said. She took the animal crackers down from the cupboard.

12   Jacob rattled the carton. Not many left. He crunched two tigers, three lions, and a seal, then gulped down some milk. Grrr, roar, ork! If only animal crackers were real. He would have plenty of noises to list!

13   Goldie, Jacob's collie, woofed as Jacob walked toward the barn. Her puppies were yipping in a straw-filled stall. Jacob plinked dog-food pellets into their pan, and the pups snuffled and crunched.

14   In the chicken house, Jacob shooed two cackling hens from their nests. He slipped their warm eggs into his jacket. Wouldn't it be funny if he forgot about the eggs and they hatched? He'd have a peeping pocket!

15   In the corral, a black cow napped in the sun. Jacob woke her when he poured corn into her pan. "Moo, thank you!" she seemed to say.

16   Tap, clatter, clink. Dad drove the tractor into the yard. The lid on the tractor's smokestack rattled when it chuffed and chugged to a stop.

17   "How was school?" Dad asked, stepping down from the cab.

18   Jacob shrugged. "OK, I guess," he said. "I have some homework."

19   Jacob put the eggs in the kitchen, then climbed to his tree house. He could see Dad's beehives by the hay field. Six hives usually meant plenty of humming. But today he couldn't hear it over the scolding of the blue jays and the chattering of the sparrows. How could a person think?

20   "QUIET!" Jacob shouted.

21   Suddenly, he sat up straight. Cows mooed and puppies yipped. Chickens cackled in their yard. When Goldie began barking below, Jacob grinned. There were plenty of noises on the farm. "I hear you!" he called. He hurried down from the tree. He had an earful of homework to do.

▶ **Think** Use what you learned from reading the selection to respond to these questions.

1 Based on details from paragraph 1, how would you describe Mrs. Olson?

    A Rules are very important to her.

    B She likes learning to be fun.

    C She only uses books to teach.

    D She enjoys music.

2 This question has two parts. First, answer Part A. Then answer Part B.

Part A
Why is Jacob so upset about his homework assignment?

    A He has other plans after school.

    B He was already in a bad mood.

    C He thinks there will not be enough noises on a farm.

    D He hates homework of any kind.

Part B
Underline a sentence from paragraphs 2–4 of the story that **best** supports your answer from Part A.

    Later, Jacob glared out the school bus window. Not fair, he thought. How could he collect enough sounds on his family's farm? There were plenty of noises in town. If only he lived where tires squeal.

    Jacob scrambled off the bus when it screeched to a stop at his mailbox. But he wasn't in the mood to wave as it drove away.

    When he threw open the gate, it groaned like a ghost. That was how he felt about his homework.

3 Which detail explains why Jacob wished the animal crackers were real?

    A "She took the animal crackers down from the cupboard."

    B "Jacob rattled the carton. Not many left."

    C "He crunched two tigers, three lions, and a seal …"

    D "He would have plenty of noises to list!"

4 This question has two parts. First, answer Part A. Then answer Part B.

Part A

Why does Jacob need a lesson on collecting sounds?

    A He needs to learn to follow directions.

    B He doesn't hear the sounds around him.

    C He can't tell one sound from the other.

    D He doesn't listen to his teacher or parents.

Part B

Reread paragraphs 13–16. Put at least **four** sounds that Jacob could have collected into each column.

Animal Sounds	Machine Sounds

5 Read this sentence from paragraph 16.

> **The lid on the tractor's smokestack rattled when it chuffed and chugged to a stop.**

Read the sentence for context clues. The word *smokestack* is made from two smaller words. What does the whole word mean?

   A a chimney used for letting out smoke

   B a stack of metal on a train or tractor

   C a column of smoke in the sky

   D lids piled on top of each other

6 Which noise finally made Jacob aware that the farm had plenty of sounds?

   A the humming bees in the hives

   B the noisy blue jays and sparrows

   C the cackling chickens in their yard

   D the yipping puppies in the stall

7 How does Jacob feel about his homework at the end of the story?

   A He still is upset about it.

   B He wants help to do it.

   C He is eager to start it.

   D He decides to do it later.

Write

8 **Short Response** The writer provides a number of details to show that Jacob was missing the sounds around him. Use some of those details to demonstrate that Jacob just wasn't listening.

_____

_____

_____

_____

_____

_____

_____

Learning Target

Now that you understand how to use details from the text to support your answers to questions, tell how this can show how well you understand a story.

Lesson 6
Describing Characters

Learning Target

Understanding what characters are like, and why they act the way they do, can help you see how they drive what happens in a story.

▶ **Read** **Characters** are the people or animals in a story. When you read a story, think about what the characters say and do and why they act in certain ways.

Just like real people, characters have feelings. They have **traits,** or special qualities, such as courage, pride, or honesty. They also have **motivations,** or reasons for doing what they do. A character's actions **contribute,** or add, to the sequence of events in a story. The **sequence of events** is everything that happens, in the order it happens. Each action changes the story and what happens next.

Read this cartoon and look for clues about what the giant is like.

Hi! Let me help you over the mountain.

I'll be here when you want to go home.

▶ **Think** Look at the cartoon and then complete the chart below. Write one or two words that describe the giant's traits, motivations, feelings, and actions.

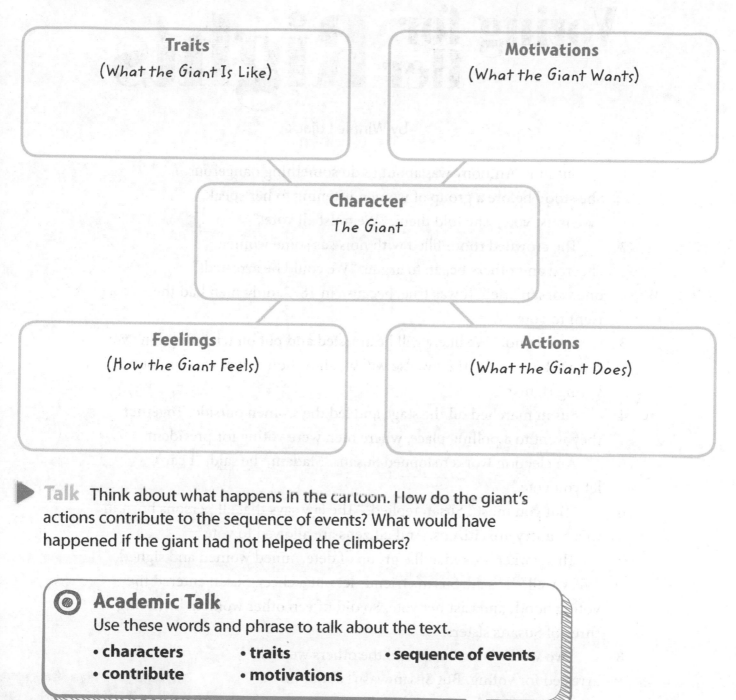

Traits
(What the Giant Is Like)

Motivations
(What the Giant Wants)

Character
The Giant

Feelings
(How the Giant Feels)

Actions
(What the Giant Does)

▶ **Talk** Think about what happens in the cartoon. How do the giant's actions contribute to the sequence of events? What would have happened if the giant had not helped the climbers?

◉ **Academic Talk**
Use these words and phrase to talk about the text.
- characters
- contribute
- traits
- motivations
- sequence of events

▶ **Read**

Genre: **Historical Fiction**

Voting for Her Rights

by Winnie Lujack

1   Susan B. Anthony was about to do something dangerous. She stood before a group of women listening to her speak. "We must vote," she told them. "We must all vote!"

2   The crowded room filled with noise as some women cheered and others began to argue. "We could be arrested!" one woman cried. It was true, because in 1872, only men had the right to vote.

3   Susan said, "We likely will be arrested and put on trial. But don't you see, we have to do it! How else will we show how much we want our voting rights?"

4   Susan marched off the stage and led the women outside. Together they went to a polling place, where men were voting for president.

5   An election worker stopped Susan. "Madam," he said, "I can't let you vote."

6   "But you must," Susan replied. "The law says that all persons born in this country are citizens. And citizens are allowed to vote."

7   The worker looked at the group of determined women and sighed. "Very well," he said. Susan's friends let out a cheer. Susan entered the voting booth and cast her vote. So did fifteen other women, including three of Susan's sisters.

8   Two weeks later, Susan and the others were all arrested for voting. But Susan wasn't about to give up her fight for women's rights.

Close Reader Habits

Underline sentences that tell why Susan thought fighting for rights was important.

Explore

How do Susan's traits, motivations, and feelings lead her to vote even though she knows she will be arrested?

Think

Sometimes you have to infer, or figure out, traits and feelings from what a character says or does.

1 Complete the chart to tell what you know about Susan from the story.

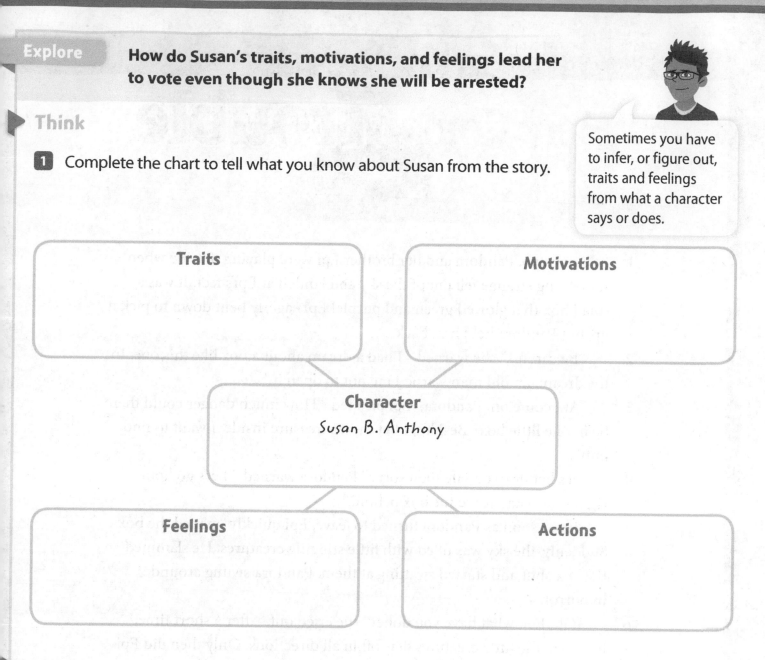

Traits

Motivations

Character
Susan B. Anthony

Feelings

Actions

Talk

2 Using the details from the chart, discuss the way Susan's actions contribute to the sequence of events. If Susan had not led the other women, how would the story be different?

Write

3 **Short Response** Explain why Susan B. Anthony casts a vote even though she expects to be arrested. Use details from the text in your answer. Use the space provided on page 98 to write your answer.

HINT Remember to look at what Susan says as well as what she does.

Here Comes Trouble

from a Greek myth

1   Long ago, Pandora and her brother Epi were playing outside when something strange fell out of the sky and landed at Epi's feet. It was a small box that glowed green and purple! Epi eagerly bent down to pick it up, but Pandora held him back.

2   "Be careful," she warned. "I had a dream about a box like this one. In the dream, an old man warned me not to open it."

3   "Aw, come on, Pandora," Epi pleaded. "How much danger could there be in one little box? Besides, I bet there's treasure inside. I want to find out!"

4   "It's better to be safe than sorry," Pandora warned. "Let's go home right now—and leave the box behind."

5   But as soon as Pandora turned to leave, Epi quickly opened the box. Suddenly, the sky was filled with little stinging creatures. He slammed the box shut and started swatting at them. Pandora swung around in horror.

6   "Oh, Epi, what have you done?" she cried out. After a short time, however, the little creatures flew off in all directions. Only then did Epi and Pandora hear a little voice coming from the closed box.

7   "Don't be afraid," the voice whispered. "I'm here to help you."

8   Pandora thought carefully for a moment. Then she slowly opened the box. A tiny green and purple fairy flew out.

9   "I am Hope," the fairy said. "You let all the troubles of the world out of this box, but I was put in the box to comfort the world. I will be with you always."

10   Epi felt sad that he hadn't listened to his sister. "Don't worry, Epi," she said kindly. "At least we have Hope."

Close Reader Habits

What can you learn about Pandora from details in the story? **Underline** words that show her traits. **Circle** words that describe her feelings.

▶ **Think**

1 At the beginning of the story, why does Epi want to open the box?

    A   He is curious to find out if the box is filled with treasure.

    B   He believes that the warning in Pandora's dream is only for her.

    C   He doesn't care if something bad happens when he opens the box.

    D   He knows that a green and purple fairy lives in the box.

> What each character says and does can show how they are similar and different.

2 Epi and Pandora each open the box. How do their actions change the story? Put an X by the **two** items that tell about the changes.

    ___ " 'Let's go home right now—' "

    ___ " 'You let all the troubles of the world out of this box . . .' "

    ___ " '. . . an old man warned me not to open it.' "

    ___ " 'I bet there's treasure inside.' "

    ___ "[Hope said,] 'I will be with you always.' "

    ___ ". . . something strange fell out of the sky . . ."

▶ **Talk**

3 Talk about what Epi did and how his actions affected the events in the story.

▶ **Write**

4 **Short Response** Contrast the characters in the story. Tell what Pandora and Epi do and say that show how they are different. Use the space provided on page 99 to write your answer.

> **HINT** How does each character act when the box first appears?

✏️ **Write** **Use the space below to write your answer to the question on page 95.**

Voting for Her Rights

3 **Short Response** Explain why Susan B. Anthony casts a vote even though she expects to be arrested. Use details from the text in your answer.

HINT Remember to look at what Susan says as well as what she does.

_____

_____

_____

_____

_____

_____

_____

_____

_____

_____

Don't forget to check your writing.

Write **Use the space below to write your answer to the question on page 97.**

Here Comes Trouble

4 **Short Response** Contrast the characters in the story. Tell what Pandora and Epi do and say that show how they are different.

> **HINT** How does each character act when the box first appears?

_____

_____

_____

_____

_____

_____

_____

_____

Check Your Writing

- ☐ Did you read the prompt carefully?
- ☐ Did you put the prompt in your own words?
- ☐ Did you use the best evidence from the text to support your ideas?
- ☐ Are your ideas clearly organized?
- ☐ Did you write in clear and complete sentences?
- ☐ Did you check your spelling and punctuation?

▶ **Read**

Genre: Historical Fiction

Cleopatra Finds Her Voice

by Vicki Alvear Shecter, *Highlights*

1   Eleven-year-old Princess Cleopatra sailed the Nile River on the royal barge. Her father, the king of Egypt, played his flute.

2   They were sailing from their palace in Alexandria to cities along the Nile. The king would often lead important ceremonies.

3   Cleopatra watched for slithering crocodiles and yawning hippos. Sometimes she would catch a glimpse of a Sacred Ibis bird tiptoeing along the marshy banks.

4   As the royal barge sailed, people crowded the banks, hoping to see the princess and her father. They sang and chanted and threw flowers. But it bothered Cleopatra that she could not understand what they said.

5   Her father explained that the people of Egypt spoke Egyptian, while Cleopatra's family spoke Greek.

6   But her father was the ruler of Egypt! Why didn't he and his family speak the native language?

7   They could thank their ancestors for that, the king said. The royal family traced its history back 250 years to the time of the Greek conqueror Alexander the Great. Alexander had conquered Egypt. When he died, his Greek general, Ptolemy, took over. Ever since, all of the rulers of Egypt had spoken Greek.

8   Once back at home, Cleopatra insisted on learning the Egyptian language. She believed that a ruler should know her people. And that meant knowing their words.

9   Cleopatra studied hard and soon learned to speak Egyptian. But she didn't stop there. She also learned Hebrew, Aramaic, Persian, Latin, and some African dialects. She loved learning and excelled in math and science, too.

10   Later, when she ruled as queen, one of her first acts was to visit the city of Memphis for an important religious ceremony. This time, she spoke to the people in Egyptian. The people loved her for learning their language. She showed them respect and honor in many other ways, too.

11   Cleopatra is remembered as a brilliant queen. She was the only Egyptian ruler in hundreds of years to learn the language of her people.

Think Use what you learned from reading the selection to respond to these questions.

1 This question has two parts. First, answer Part A. Then answer Part B.

Part A
What does Cleopatra find out about herself after she learns to speak Egyptian?

    A Speaking Egyptian helps her understand her religion better.

    B She no longer thinks her father is a good king.

    C Her family's old language no longer sounds right.

    D She realizes she has a love for learning.

Part B
Choose **two** details from the story that support the answer to Part A.

    A "She also learned Hebrew, Aramaic, Persian, Latin, and some African dialects."

    B "They sang and chanted and threw flowers."

    C "But it bothered Cleopatra that she could not understand what they said."

    D "Ever since, all of the rulers of Egypt had spoken Greek."

    E "She loved learning and excelled in math and science, too."

2 Why doesn't Cleopatra's father speak Egyptian?

    A Rulers of Egypt had spoken Greek for 250 years.

    B Alexander the Great had banned the teaching of Egyptian.

    C The king is more interested in playing the flute than learning a new language.

    D Cleopatra's father and the Greek general Ptolemy had agreed not to speak Egyptian.

3 Which sentence **best** explains why Cleopatra wants to learn to speak Egyptian?

    A She hopes it will help her with her studies of math and science.

    B She sees the love the people show for her father and for her.

    C Her father explains the history of her family's language.

    D She believes that as a ruler of Egypt, she should know Egyptian.

4 This question has two parts. First, answer Part A. Then answer Part B.

Part A

Which words **best** describe Cleopatra?

    A frightened and weak

    B spoiled and happy

    C thoughtful and caring

    D silly and careless

Part B

Which sentence from the story supports the answer to Part A?

    A "As the royal barge sailed, people crowded the banks, hoping to see the princess and her father."

    B "She believed that a ruler should know her people."

    C "She loved learning and excelled in math and science, too."

    D "Cleopatra is remembered as a brilliant queen."

5 Read these sentences from paragraph 6 of the story.

> **But her father was the ruler of Egypt! Why didn't he and his family speak the native language?**

What does *native* mean in this context?

    A foreign

    B difficult

    C local

    D ancient

6 Complete the chart. Base your answers on details from the story.

Character

Cleopatra

↓   ↓

Traits   **Actions**

Write

7 **Short Response** The author shows that Cleopatra was a curious person. Explain how we can tell that Cleopatra was curious. Use **two** details from the story to support your response.

_____

_____

_____

_____

_____

_____

Learning Target

Now that you've practiced describing characters, write about how characters' actions drive what happens in a story.

_____

_____

_____

_____

Lesson 7
Recounting Stories

Learning Target

Retell or recount stories from around the world by telling key events in the order in which they happened.

▶ **Read** When you **recount** a story, you are retelling the story in your own words. Be sure that you include the key details and **events** that happened in the beginning, middle, and end. Tell the events in the **sequence,** or order, in which they happened.

Read this story. Think about what happens at the beginning, middle, and end. Then reread the story. What are the most important details?

A Bundle of Sticks

Long ago, a mother had three children who were always arguing. "Your arguing sounds worse than the clucking of all the hens in the world," their mother told them. She wanted them to stop!

One day she got an idea. She gathered the children around her. Then she took a stick and broke it. "See how easy it is to break one stick?" she asked. Then she tied three sticks together. She asked each child to try to break the sticks. None of the children could break the bundle.

The mother told the children, "We're just like the sticks. When we don't stay together, our family is weak. When we stay together, nothing can break us apart."

The children understood! From that day forward, they didn't argue (as much).

▶ **Think** The chart below will help you to organize the most important details of a story. Think about what happened in the beginning, middle, and end of the story. Then add those details to the chart.

Beginning	Middle	End
	→	→

▶ **Talk** Using the key details in your chart, retell the story to your partner.

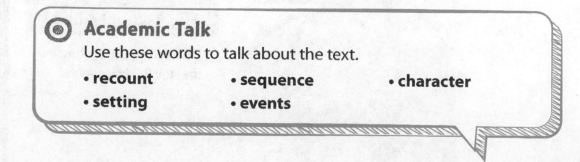

Academic Talk
Use these words to talk about the text.
- **recount**
- **sequence**
- **character**
- **setting**
- **events**

Genre: Folktale

Brother and Sister

a folktale from Korea

1   Long ago, a brother and sister grew rice to sell. Through the long summer, they worked together to care for the rice paddies. In the fall, they harvested all the rice and put the rice into bags. Each got the same number of bags.

2   After one harvest, the brother announced he was soon to be married. The sister knew her brother would need money to buy a new house for his bride. She didn't feel the rice was divided fairly, so that night, she took an extra bag of rice to her brother's house in secret.

3   The brother, too, felt the rice was not divided fairly. His sister had a large family. She would need more rice. So that night, the brother took an extra bag to his sister's house in secret.

4   The next day, the brother and sister counted their rice bags. Strange! Both had the same number as before. So that night, when the moon was full, they made another attempt. In the moonlight, the brother and sister each saw the other carrying a bag of rice! They laughed. The mystery was solved.

Close Reader Habits

Underline the sentences that tell the key events.

Explore How do you choose which details to include when you recount a story?

> To decide whether a detail is important, think about whether the story makes sense without it.

Think

1 Recount the folktale "Brother and Sister" by adding key details to the chart below.

Beginning	A brother and sister grow and sell rice. They each get the same number of bags of rice.
Middle	Sister Brother
End	

Talk

2 Using the details from your chart, take turns retelling the story with your partner.

Write

3 **Short Response** Which details from the chart do you think are most important? List them and tell why you chose them. Use the space provided on page 112 to write your answer.

> **HINT** What details would you need to help a friend understand what happens in the story?

Read

HOW THE BAT GOT WINGS

◀◀◀ A CHEROKEE NATION TALE ▶▶▶

1   A long time ago, the bat was a tiny mammal. It had no wings. One day, the mammals and birds decided to play a game. The birds played on one team, and the mammals played on the other team.

2   The bat wanted to play with the mammals, but the mammals laughed at her size. "You are too small," they said.

3   So the bat asked to play with the birds. The birds said, "You don't have wings, but we can make you some out of a drum." The birds stretched the skin of a drum into wings.

4   The birds put the wings on the bat and said, "Flap your wings." The bat jumped off a tree and flapped her wings, but she didn't fly in a straight line like the birds. Instead, she flew every which way in a crazy, zigzag pattern.

5   The birds let the bat play on their team. Just as she had done before, the bat flew in a crazy, zigzag pattern. The mammals on the other team could not catch the bat. The bat scored the winning points for the birds.

6   When the game was over, the mammals said, "Who is that superstar on your team?"

7   The birds said, "It is the bat. We gave her wings."

8   The mammals did not know what to say. After all, they had refused to let the tiny bat play on their team. The mammals had learned their lesson. From that day on, they let any animal of any size play on their team.

Close Reader Habits

Which details would you include to recount the story? **Underline** the most important ones.

▶ **Think**

1 Number the items to show the order of some events in the story.

_____ The bat flies in a crazy, zigzag pattern.

_____ The birds make wings for the bat.

_____ The mammals do not let the bat play on their team.

> When you get ready to recount a story, choose the most important details.

2 Why do the birds win the game?

   A The mammals cannot follow the bat's movements.

   B The mammals are surprised to see the bat on the team.

   C The mammals refuse to play against a bat.

   D The birds fly in a crazy, zigzag pattern.

▶ **Talk**

3 Using key details from the text, talk to your partner about how the bat's way of flying helps the birds win.

▶ **Write**

4 **Short Response** In your own words, recount what happens when the bat plays the game with the birds. Be sure to include the most important details from the story. Use the space provided on page 113 to write your answer.

> **HINT** Review the game in paragraphs 5 to 8.

Write Use the space below to write your answer to the question on page 109.

Brother and Sister

HINT What details would you need to help a friend understand what happens in the story?

3 **Short Response** Which details from the chart do you think are most important? List them and tell why you chose them.

_____

_____

_____

_____

_____

_____

_____

_____

Don't forget to check your writing.

Write Use the space below to write your answer to the question on page 111.

HOW THE BAT GOT WINGS

4 **Short Response** In your own words, recount what happens when the bat plays the game with the birds. Be sure to include the most important details from the story.

> **HINT** Review the game in paragraphs 5 to 8.

_____

_____

_____

_____

_____

_____

_____

_____

Check Your Writing

☐ Did you read the prompt carefully?

☐ Did you put the prompt in your own words?

☐ Did you use the best evidence from the text to support your ideas?

☐ Are your ideas clearly organized?

☐ Did you write in clear and complete sentences?

☐ Did you check your spelling and punctuation?

▶ **Read**

True or False

a folktale from Myanmar (Burma)

WORDS TO KNOW
As you read, look inside, around, and beyond these words to figure out what they mean.

- **fuss**
- **disbelief**

1   There once were three poor brothers who loved to tell tall tales. They traveled throughout the countryside telling wild stories. They always claimed that their tales were true, but no one ever believed them.

2   One day, the three brothers met a rich traveler. The man was dressed in fine clothes and wore shining jewels. The brothers wanted his things. "Let's ask him to play a game. Each of the four of us will tell a tale of a past adventure. The rule is that if anyone doubts the truth of another's story, he must become that person's servant. The man will never believe our stories. Getting him to doubt our stories will be like rolling off a log. He will have to become our servant."

3   The others liked this plan. They did not want a servant. But they wanted the man's fine things. The man agreed to the game.

4   The first brother told a story of how he had climbed a tree and could not get down. So he ran to a nearby cottage and borrowed a rope.

5   The second brother told of jumping into the stomach of a tiger who wanted to eat him. "I made such a fuss that the tiger spit me out," he said.

6   The third told of helping the village fishermen. He said he turned into a fish and jumped into the river. There, he turned back into a man and killed the big fish that were eating all the little fish.

7   The rich man listened to the three tales without saying one word of disbelief. Then he told his story. He said he was searching for three servants who had run away from him.

8   "You three must be the ones I am looking for," he said.

9   The brothers looked at him with alarm. If they doubted him, they must become his servants. That was their rule. But if they said his story was true, they would have to become his servants too!

10   They said nothing.

11   Finally, the man said he would let them go if they promised never to tell tall tales again.

12   The brothers agreed, and they kept their promise.

▶ Think Use what you learned from reading the selection to respond to these questions.

1 Number the items to show the order of some events in the story.

_____ Each brother told his make-believe story.

_____ Three brothers talked a rich traveler into playing a game.

_____ The rich man made them promise not to tell tall tales.

_____ The rich man told them a story.

_____ The rich man did not question the brothers' stories.

_____ The brothers realized they were trapped.

2 This question has two parts. First, answer Part A. Then answer Part B.

Part A
Why did the three brothers want to play a game with the traveler?

A They wanted to see if he would believe their tall tales.

B They wanted to trick him so they could have what he owned.

C They disliked people who had more money than they did.

D They were once the rich traveler's servants.

Part B
Write a sentence from paragraph 2 that supports the answer you chose for Part A.

_____

_____

©Curriculum Associates, LLC   Copying is not permitted.

3 Which is the **best** recounting of the third brother's story?

   A He plays a trick on the fishermen. He pretends to be a big fish catching small ones.

   B He gets away from the fishermen by swimming in the river like a fish.

   C He helps the fishermen. He turns himself into a fish and then back into a person to kill a big fish.

   D He becomes a fish so that he can help the fishermen chase fish into their nets.

4 Which is the **best** description of the brothers' problem at the end of the folktale?

   A The brothers think the rich man's story is the best of all the stories they have heard.

   B The rich man believes that the brothers are the runaway servants he is looking for.

   C The brothers promise never to tell tall tales again as they know they should not be doing that.

   D No matter how the brothers answer the rich man, they will have to become his servants.

5 Which **two** details could you leave out when recounting this story?

    A The brothers tell their tales throughout the countryside.

    B The brothers ask a rich traveler to play a game.

    C A tiger spit one brother out after eating him.

    D The rich man said nothing about the brothers' stories.

    E The rich man told a story about missing servants.

    F The brothers agreed not to tell any more tall tales.

6 Reread these sentences from paragraph 2.

> **The man will never believe our stories. Getting him to doubt our stories will be like rolling off a log.**

What does the word *doubt* mean in this context?

    A dislike

    B understand

    C mistrust

    D enjoy

Write

7 **Short Response** Use your own words to recount the folktale. Be sure to write about the events in the sequence that they happen in the story.

_____

_____

_____

_____

_____

_____

_____

_____

Learning Target

Explain why recounting the events in a story will help you understand it.

Lesson 8
Determining the Central Message

Learning Target

Use the key details and events of a story to figure out the central message, or lesson, that the author wants to share with readers.

▶ **Read** Many stories have a **central message,** or lesson, the author wants to share. The story teaches the lesson through the characters, the events that happen, and what the characters learn.

As you read, looking for the **key details** will help you to find the central message and understand what you read.

Look at the cartoon. Think about a lesson the boy learns by the end.

Don't let go of me!

I can do it!

▶ **Think** The events in the cartoon tell about a problem the boy has and what he does. Complete the chart by adding the key details. Use those details to figure out the central message of the cartoon.

Key Detail	Key Detail	Key Detail

What Is the Central Message?

▶ **Talk** Using the key details in the chart, talk about the central message of the cartoon.

◎ **Academic Talk**
Use these phrases to talk about the text.
- **central message**   - **key details**

Lesson 8 Determining the Central Message   **121**

> **Read**

Genre: Fable

The Girl and the Apples
by Tala Rutchel

1   One fall afternoon, a girl went to a farm to pick apples. She was in a hurry, so she picked carelessly both ripe apples and unripe ones. When she finished, her wagon was filled with a small mountain of apples.

2   The girl asked the farmer, "Quick, tell me how long you think it will take me to get back home."

3   The farmer thought carefully. Then he said, "Be patient. If you go slowly, you will be back soon. If you go fast, you will not get back until night. It's your choice."

4   The girl thought, "How can that be? How can it take so long if I go fast?"

5   The girl wanted to get back home as soon as possible, so she rushed her horse and wagon onto the road. She made her horse walk very fast.

6   And suddenly . . . bump! Off fell some apples.

7   Every time she hit a bump, more apples rolled off her wagon. Then she had to stop and put them back on the wagon. Because of all the delays, it was night before she got home.

Close Reader Habits

Underline key details that help you figure out the central message.

Explore How can key details help you figure out what lesson the girl in the story learns?

▶ **Think**

> To find the central message, think about what each key character says and does.

1 Complete the chart by writing some key details about what the characters say and do. Then write the central message, or lesson.

Key Details (the Girl)	Key Details (the Farmer)

↓   ↓

What Is the Central Message?

▶ **Talk**

2 Think about the message of the story. Talk about what the girl learned.

▶ **Write**

> **HINT** What might the girl think about the farmer's advice by the end of the story?

3 **Short Response** What is another lesson the girl might learn from what happened? Use the space provided on page 126 to write your answer.

Read ▶

Sharing the Crops

a folktale from England

1   Once a farmer rented some land. "How much does it cost to use this land?" the farmer asked the landowner.

2   The owner wanted to get the better part of the deal. So he said, "I'll take the top half of the crop, and you can take the bottom half."

3   But the farmer was clever. He planted potatoes because they grow in the ground. At harvest time, he gave the owner the potato tops, which are not good for anything.

4   The owner knew he had been outsmarted. He said, "Next year, I want the bottom half of your crops."

5   So the next year the farmer planted oats, which grow at the top of long grasses. The bottom half is useless grassy straw. That's what the farmer gave to the owner.

6   This time the owner said, "Next year, I'll take the top and the bottom. You can have the middle."

7   So this time, the farmer planted corn. At the top of each corn stalk are tassels. At the bottom are woody stalks. In the middle is where the tasty sweet corn grows.

8   For a third time, the owner had been outsmarted. Now it was the farmer's turn to suggest a deal. "From now on," he said, "why don't you take half of whatever I grow? Whatever I get, you will get the same."

9   This was a fair deal at last. From that day on, the owner and the farmer shared the crops equally.

Close Reader Habits

Why does the landowner keep changing the deal he made with the farmer? **Underline** the key details about the first deal between the landowner and the farmer.

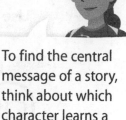

Think

1 This question has two parts. Answer Part A. Then answer Part B.

> To find the central message of a story, think about which character learns a lesson.

Part A

What is the central message of "Sharing the Crops"?

A   It is wrong to try to cheat others.

B   Never make a deal with a clever farmer.

C   The best part of a crop is usually at the top.

D   If a plan doesn't succeed, keep trying.

Part B

Which sentence from the story **best** supports the answer you chose for Part A above?

A   "Once a farmer rented some land."

B   "The owner wanted to get the better part of the deal."

C   "This was a fair deal at last."

D   "So this time, the farmer planted corn."

Talk

2 Using key details from the text, talk to your partner about how the farmer outsmarts the landowner.

Write

3 **Short Response** Explain which character in "Sharing the Crops" learns a lesson. Use one detail from the folktale to support your response. Use the space provided on page 127 to write your answer.

> **HINT** Reread to look for the character who learns a lesson.

▶ ✏️ **Write** Use the space below to write your answer to the question on page 123.

The Girl and the Apples

3 **Short Response** What is another lesson the girl might learn from what happened?

> **HINT** What might the girl think about the farmer's advice by the end of the story?

_____

_____

_____

_____

_____

_____

_____

_____

> Don't forget to check your writing.

Write Use the space below to write your answer to the question on page 125.

Sharing the Crops

3 **Short Response** Explain which character in "Sharing the Crops" learns a lesson. Use one detail from the folktale to support your response.

> **HINT** Reread to look for the character who learns a lesson.

_____

_____

_____

_____

_____

_____

_____

Check Your Writing

- ☐ Did you read the prompt carefully?
- ☐ Did you put the prompt in your own words?
- ☐ Did you use the best evidence from the text to support your ideas?
- ☐ Are your ideas clearly organized?
- ☐ Did you write in clear and complete sentences?
- ☐ Did you check your spelling and punctuation?

▶ Read

Genre: Folktale

WORDS TO KNOW
As you read, look inside, around, and beyond these words to figure out what they mean.

• **trotted/trotting**

• **stall**

ZEL,
the Gentle Donkey

A FOLKTALE FROM HAITI

1   Long ago, there was a gentle donkey named Zel. Everyone in town loved Zel because she was so pleasant and kind. But Zel's owner, Madame Charity, was angry and mean. She was so mean that she threw rocks at birds for singing too loud. She yelled at little boys when they laughed. But she was the meanest of all to poor Zel.

2   Every Saturday, Madame Charity sold sugar and rice at a market. Whoever arrived earliest sold the most. But Madame Charity always woke up late. Then she got angry and yelled at Zel, who had done nothing wrong.

3   In a huff, Madame Charity would then load heavy bags of rice and sugar onto Zel's back. Last, she climbed on top of it. "Hurry, Zel!" she yelled. "Get me to market as fast as you can!" Although Zel always trotted as fast as she could, it was never fast enough for Madame Charity.

4   One day, Zel's friend Touloulou the crab visited. "Did you have a good day at the market?" asked Touloulou.

5   "Madame Charity was mad at me all day. I work as hard as I can, but she is always mean to me."

6   "Madame Charity is always late. She won't blame herself, so she blames you," said Touloulou.

7   "Yes," said Zel. "And because everyone is afraid of her angry tongue, she never sells much at the market."

8   "I will help you," said Touloulou.

9   The next Saturday, Madame Charity woke up at 9 a.m. "Oh, no! I'm late again!" she yelled. As she tossed her heavy bags onto Zel's back, Touloulou the crab grabbed onto the hem of her long skirt. Madame Charity climbed on Zel's back. Touloulou held tightly to her skirt.

10   Zel started trotting. Madame Charity remembered how late she was. She opened her mouth to speak angrily, but Touloulou pinched her ankle.

11   "Ouch!" Madame Charity rubbed her ankle. She forgot how late she was. But soon she remembered. "Faster, Zel! Faster!" she yelled.

12   Again Touloulou pinched Madame Charity's ankle.

13   "Ouch!" shouted Madame Charity.

14   When they got to the market, Madame Charity saw that someone had taken the stall she liked to use. In a fit of rage, Madame Charity opened her mouth to yell. For the third time, Touloulou pinched her ankle. Madame Charity screamed.

15   "What's wrong?" people asked.

16   "Hurrying to get to market, I must have hurt my ankle. It's very painful. Ouch! Ouch! Ouch!"

17   The fish seller said, "Madame Charity, you should get up earlier. Then you will not have to rush. Next week, I will wake you at 6 a.m."

18   "Thank you," said Madame Charity. She was surprised at the man's kindness.

19   "Let me fix your ankle," said the fruit seller. In the past, the fruit seller had not talked to Madame Charity. Today he felt sorry for her.

20   When Madame Charity saw how kind everyone was, she smiled. For the first time, she sold all of her rice and sugar. At the end of the day, she saddled Zel gently and rode quietly home.

21   From that day on, Madame Charity tried not to raise her voice in anger. Sometimes she got angry, but she kept it to herself. And Zel the gentle donkey was happy at last.

▶ Think Use what you learned from reading the selection to respond to these questions.

1 Which detail in the first part of the story explains why Madame Charity is cruel to Zel?

    A Zel does not walk to the market as fast as she is able to.

    B Madame Charity is always angry and mean.

    C Madame Charity does not have enough sugar and rice to sell.

    D Everyone in town loves Zel because she is pleasant and kind.

2 Describe how Touloulou helps Zel.

_____

_____

_____

_____

3 This question has two parts. First, answer Part A. Then answer Part B.

Part A

What is the central message of this story?

    A Honesty is the best policy.

    B Kindness gets better results than anger.

    C Things are not always as they appear.

    D Beware of strangers.

Part B

Which sentence from the story is **most** important to the central message of the story?

    A "'Madame Charity, you should get up earlier.'"

    B "Then she got angry and yelled at Zel. . . ."

    C "From that day on, Madame Charity tried not to raise her voice in anger."

    D "Today he felt sorry for her."

4 What is the meaning of the word *market* as it is used in this sentence from the story?

> **Every Saturday, Madame Charity sold sugar and rice at a market.**

    A a store where food and spices are bought

    B a place where people buy and sell things

    C a street fair where people gather

    D a bank where money is exchanged

Write A central message of "Zel, the Gentle Donkey" is that being kind to others can cause good things to happen. Explain how the actions of the characters in the story show this central message.

5 **Plan Your Response** Make a list of things from the story that tell about the kindness of some of the characters.

_____

_____

_____

_____

6 **Write an Extended Response** Review the central message of "Zel, the Gentle Donkey." Explain how the characters in the story help deliver this message. Use details from the story to support your answer.

_____

_____

_____

_____

_____

_____

Learning Target

Explain why understanding the central message of a story will help you understand the text you read.

Read the folktale. Then answer the questions that follow.

The Lost Camel

a folktale from India

1   There were once some merchants from across the ocean who traveled from place to place selling their wares. Late one evening as they made their way up the river, they lost one of their camels. They discovered he was missing when they stopped to make camp that night.

2   Early the next morning when they set out to look for him, they met a man coming along the road. They stopped and asked him if he had seen a camel. The man told them he had not seen the camel, but he was sure he could tell them where the camel was to be found. The merchants were puzzled by this, and they began to question the man. Was the camel carrying a load? they asked.

3   "Yes," the man answered. "He was carrying bags of wheat on his left side and a large jar of honey on his right side. Furthermore, the camel is blind in one eye and he has a missing tooth. But like I said, I haven't seen him. I can only tell you where you can find him."

4   "But you have given a perfect description of our lost camel!" the surprised merchants exclaimed.

5   "You probably have hidden our camel and intend to steal him!"

6   "I haven't seen him and I'm not a thief!" the man retorted. "But I have lived in this land a long time and there are some things I know!"

7   "Then tell us, how do you know he was carrying wheat and honey?" the merchants asked suspiciously.

8   "I know he was carrying wheat on his left side because grains had fallen along the left side of the path. The bag was probably cut by some branches. Ants were gathering the grains on the left side of the trail. I know he was carrying jars of honey because, on the right side of the path, flies were swarming where the honey had dripped."

9   "Fine, but how do you know he is blind in one eye?" the merchants asked.

10   "Because I noticed he had been grazing only on the right side of the path," the man answered.

11   "And how do you know he has a tooth missing?"

12   "Because where he had chewed the grass he left a clump in the middle of the bite. That told me he had a tooth missing."

13   "If the directions you give us are correct," the merchants said, "then we will reward you for the good news you have given us."

14   And so they went off to look for the camel, and they found him near the place where the man said he had seen the signs. They were very pleased to find their lost camel, and they rewarded the man who had been so clever.

Think

1 This question has two parts. First, answer Part A. Then answer Part B.

Part A
Why do the merchants think the man they meet on the road is a thief?

A The man knows that a camel is missing from their camp.

B The man is carrying bags of wheat and a jar of honey.

C The man tells them where to find the camel.

D The man gives them a perfect description of the camel.

Part B
Choose the **two** sentences from the story that **best** support the answer to Part A.

A "The man told them he had not seen the camel, but he was sure he could tell them where the camel was to be found."

B "Was the camel carrying a load? they asked."

C "'He was carrying bags of wheat on his left side and a large jar of honey on his right side.'"

D "'Furthermore, the camel is blind in one eye and he has a missing tooth.'"

E "'You probably have hidden our camel and intend to steal him!'"

F "'But I have lived in this land a long time and there are some things I know!'"

2 Number the events from the story in the order in which they happen.

_____ The man explains how he knows about the camel without having seen it.

_____ The merchants search for their lost camel.

_____ The merchants find their lost camel and reward the man.

_____ The merchants meet a man who describes the camel perfectly.

_____ The man gives the merchants directions for where to find their camel.

3 This question has two parts. First, answer Part A. Then answer Part B.

Part A

How do the merchants learn the man is not a thief?

- **A** They find the camel where the man said it would be.
- **B** The man tells them he is not a thief, and they believe him.
- **C** The man tells them what the camel is carrying and what it looks like.
- **D** The man explains how he used clues to describe the camel.

Part B

Underline the sentence in paragraph 14 below that **best** supports the answer to Part A.

> **And so they went off to look for the camel, and they found him near the place where the man said he had seen the signs. They were very pleased to find their lost camel, and they rewarded the man who had been so clever.**

4 How does the man know the camel is blind in one eye?

- **A** The camel becomes lost in the dark night.
- **B** The camel grazes on only one side of the path.
- **C** The camel follows a path of ants back to camp.
- **D** The camel is found not too far from the camp.

5 What is the central message of this story? Use details from the story to support your answer.

_____

_____

_____

_____

_____

▶ **Read**

Genre: Realistic Fiction

Read the story. Then answer the questions that follow.

The Bicycle Parade

by Thomas Silva

1   It was a sunny summer day, but Gina was in the garage with the door closed. She wouldn't open the door because she didn't want Tony to see what she was working on. Tony lived down the street and was in her class at school. He always wanted to win, and so did Gina.

2   Gina was working on her entry for the back-to-school bicycle parade. The school gave out prizes for the best decorations. Last year, Tony had won first place, and Gina had come in second. This year, Gina knew she was going to win. She was turning her bike into a musical instrument.

3   Gina had found some plastic pipes that her dad kept in the garage. By taping the pipes together, she made her bike look like a giant horn. Next Gina tied bells and rattles to her bike. She also glued sleigh bells around the wheels.

4   It was hard work, and Gina was getting sweaty in the stuffy garage. Outside, she could hear her little brother and sister splashing in a wading pool. Their squeals of delight made Gina want to go play with them. But she had to beat Tony, so she kept working.

5   Finally, the musical bike was done. It was six o'clock. Tony would be eating supper. So Gina put on her helmet and took her bike out for a test ride. At first it was a great success. The rattles rattled, the bells rang, and the pipes whistled in the wind.

6   But when Gina tried to turn, the pipes got in her way. She tipped to the side, toppling the bike to the ground. The pipes, bells, and rattles all came clattering apart, clanking and clanging on the sidewalk.

7   Gina wasn't hurt, but she was furious. Rebuilding the musical bike would take hours! She picked up all the junk and tossed it into a box. As she carried the box up the driveway, she watched her brother pedaling his tricycle as fast as he could. Her sister chased him, giggling. Gina smiled, set the box down, and ran after them. She felt happier than she had all day.

8   The next morning, Gina decorated her bike with long blue and white streamers. She left the little bells on the wheels. When she got her bike to school, she saw Tony and his amazing parade entry.

9   Tony had turned his bicycle into a pirate ship. He had cut the sides of the ship from a huge cardboard box. A black pirate flag flew from a long pole.

10   As they rode in the parade, the wind blew the ship up and down. Tony had to pedal hard to keep his bike moving. He frowned and complained the whole way.

11   Gina rode next to Tony, her blue and white streamers tossing in the wind like ocean waves. Her wheels jingled merrily. Tony and his pirate ship won first prize, but somehow, it didn't bother Gina at all.

Think

6 This question has two parts. First, answer Part A. Then answer Part B.

Part A

Which word **best** describes how Gina feels about the contest at the beginning of the story?

A happy

B angry

C serious

D calm

Part B

Which sentence from the story **best** supports the answer to Part A?

A "Last year, Tony had won first place, and Gina had come in second."

B "Gina had found some plastic pipes that her dad kept in the garage."

C "By taping the pipes together, she made her bike look like a giant horn."

D "But she had to beat Tony, so she kept working."

7 How does Gina's test ride of her bike change the story?

A When her bike decorations fall apart, Gina decides to have simpler decorations.

B When her bike decorations fall apart, Gina decides not to enter the contest.

C Gina decides to decorate her bike as a musical instrument.

D Gina decides to decorate her bike as a pirate ship.

8 Read the sentence from the story.

Gina wasn't hurt, but she was furious. Rebuilding the musical bike would take hours!

What is the meaning of the word *furious*?

A very sad

B very angry

C very excited

D very foolish

9 Recount the **most** important events in the story using your own words. Be sure to retell the events in the order that they happen in the story.

_____

_____

_____

_____

_____

_____

_____

_____

10 This question has two parts. First, answer Part A. Then answer Part B.

Part A
What is a central message of the story?

    A It is more important to have fun than to win.

    B Always test your ideas before sharing them.

    C Asking for help is nothing to be ashamed of.

    D Working with others is better than keeping secrets.

Part B
Which sentence from the story **best** supports the answer to Part A?

    A "She wouldn't open the door because she didn't want Tony to see what she was working on."

    B "But when Gina tried to turn, the pipes got in her way."

    C "Rebuilding the musical bike would take hours!"

    D "She felt happier than she had all day."

Write

11 **Extended Response** At the end of the story, Gina loses the decorating contest to Tony, but she remains happy. What does this tell the reader about Gina? Describe what Gina is like and explain how her feelings and actions affect the events of the story. Be sure to include details from the story in your answer.

In your answer, be sure to
- describe what Gina is like
- explain how Gina's feelings and actions affect the events of the story
- use details from the passage in your answer

Check your writing for correct spelling, grammar, capitalization, and punctuation.

_____

_____

_____

_____

_____

_____

_____

_____

_____

_____

_____

_____

Craft and Structure in Informational Text

How is an author like a carpenter and an artist? Well, just like carpenters and artists, authors have special tools. They use these tools to help them do their jobs. Carpenters use hammers and nails to build things. Artists use paints and brushes to make paintings. And authors use words in special ways. For example, words in **bold print** or in a box in a passage stand out to help readers find information. Authors can also provide word clues to help readers figure out difficult words. And some words tell opinions to help readers know how the author feels about a topic. All of these word tools help readers search for and use information in a passage.

In this unit, you'll practice using word clues to figure out new words. You'll learn to use special parts of the text to look for information. And you'll see that understanding how writers view their topics can help you build your own views about what you read. So, be on the lookout for word tools!

✓ Self Check

Before starting this unit, check off the skills you know below. As you complete each lesson, see how many more skills you can check off!

I can:

	Before this unit	After this unit
look for word clues to help me find the meanings of new words.	☐	☐
use special parts of a passage, such as titles and headings, to find information.	☐	☐
use special parts of a passage, such as sidebars, key words, and hyperlinks, to find information.	☐	☐
discover how an author thinks or feels about what they have written.	☐	☐
decide how I think or feel about what I read.	☐	☐

page 148

page 155

page 162

page 169

page 178

page 183

Lesson 9
Unfamiliar Words

Learning Target

Context clues in the text can help you figure out the meaning of unfamiliar words.

▶ **Read** When you are reading about new **topics,** it is important that you read like a word detective by asking questions about words you don't understand. Word detectives look around an unknown word for clues that the author may have included to help them figure out the meaning and understand new topics. These clues are called **context clues.**

Read the paragraph below about cats in ancient Egypt. Circle any words you don't know.

Cats played an essential role in ancient Egypt. They were prized pets. But they were also useful. For example, cats killed dangerous snakes. They caught mice and rats to protect stores of grain. Some cats even helped gather food. Egyptian hunters trained them to bring back birds and fish from the marshes.

▶ **Think** Circle the word *essential* in the cat passage. Reread the passage and underline context clues in the text that helped you figure out the meaning of the word. Then complete the chart by adding the text evidence that you found in the passage. Ask yourself, does this meaning make sense?

Unknown Word: *Essential*	
Context Clues	**What the Word Means**

▶ **Talk** Take turns with your partner talking about the context clues you you used to figure out the meaning of the word *essential*.

◎ **Academic Talk**
Use this phrase and word to talk about the text.
- **context clues**   - **topic**

Read Me a Story

by Kara Williams

1   Dogs cannot read. But they can help children who may not like to read, or who find reading difficult. Reading therapy dogs and their owners visit schools and libraries. The child sits on the floor with the dog. Then he or she reads the dog a story. The dog helps its new friend relax. It offers the child support.

2   Only some dogs can be reading therapy dogs. First, dogs are tested to make sure they are calm and friendly. They have to be able to handle different situations. Then the dogs are trained to be good listeners. Some even learn how to turn the pages of a book with their noses or paws.

3   Studies show that reading therapy dogs can enhance reading skills. The children can practice reading to the dogs without being afraid of making mistakes. Shy readers gain confidence. They begin to feel better about their reading. As a result, they enjoy reading more. The more that children read, the more their reading skills improve.

Close Reader Habits

As you read, **circle** words you don't know. When you reread, **underline** clues that help you figure out what the words mean.

Explore How can you figure out the meaning of unfamiliar words in the passage about reading therapy dogs?

Think

Sometimes the clue to the meaning of a word is another word with the *opposite* meaning.

1 Complete the chart to help you figure out the meaning of the word *therapy*. Fill in context clues in the first column. Then write your definition.

Unknown Word: *Therapy*	
Context Clues	**What the Word Means**

Talk

2 Reread the third paragraph. Work with your partner to figure out the meaning of the word *enhance*. Look for clues in the text. How do therapy dogs enhance children's reading skills?

Write

3 **Short Response** Use details from the article to explain how therapy dogs help children gain confidence. Reread paragraph 3 and use context clues to make sure you understand what *confidence* means. Use the space provided on page 152 to write your answer.

HINT What are the children like before they begin working with the dogs?

The BUZZ on Sniffer Bees

by Heather Roberson

1   Did you know that bees have a great sense of smell? You've seen the antennae, or feelers, on their heads. Those feelers have more than three thousand tiny smell organs. The organs help the bees identify more than 170 different odors. This is how they find food, water, and pollen.

2   Many animals have a better sense of smell than humans do. That's why people train dogs to sniff out scents. Bees have an even stronger sense of smell than dogs. So, scientists are looking for ways that trained bees can help people.

3   Scientists can teach bees to follow specific smells. First, the bees are given a smell to learn. Then they are sent toward the same smell in another area. When they find where the smell is coming from, they are rewarded with sugar water. Scientists repeat this process over and over. Finally, the bees connect the smell with a treat. Bees can be trained in about ten minutes.

4   Sniffer bees have been trained to find harmful materials. They can also sniff out health problems. They can smell a disease in someone's breath. They can uncover some kinds of cancer. They can spot a lung disease called tuberculosis (too ber kyoo LOW sis). They can also smell dangerous chemicals. In addition, they can find plant diseases or pests such as bedbugs. Sniffer bees make few mistakes.

5   One day, these tiny helpers may work in airports, farms, hospitals, and war zones. They will alert people to possible danger.

Close Reader Habits

How can rereading a passage help you understand unfamiliar words? **Underline** context clues that help you understand them.

Think

1 Explain the meaning of *antennae* as it is used in this passage. Use clues from the passage in your response.

_____

_____

_____

> Remember that what you already know about a topic can help you figure out new words.

2 Read these sentences from the passage.

> **Scientists repeat this *process* over and over. Finally, the bees connect the smell with a treat.**

What is the meaning of *process* as it is used above?

A a series of actions taken for a certain purpose

B a reward for having done something correctly

C something that can happen only once

D a secret way of training animals

Talk

3 Find the word *alert* in the last paragraph. Talk to your partner about what it means. What kinds of danger could bees alert humans to in airports?

Write

4 **Short Response** Describe the different ways sniffer bees can help humans. In your description, use some of the science words you learned from the passage. Use the space provided on page 153 to write your answer.

> **HINT** Reread paragraph 4. Look for three things sniffer bees can detect.

📝 **Write** Use the space below to write your answer to the question on page 149.

Woof! Woof!

Read Me a Story

3 **Short Response** Use details from the article to explain how therapy dogs help children gain confidence. Reread paragraph 3 and use context clues to make sure you understand what *confidence* means.

> **HINT** What are the children like before they begin working with the dogs?

_____

_____

_____

_____

_____

_____

_____

> Don't forget to check your writing.

Write Use the space below to write your answer to the question on page 151.

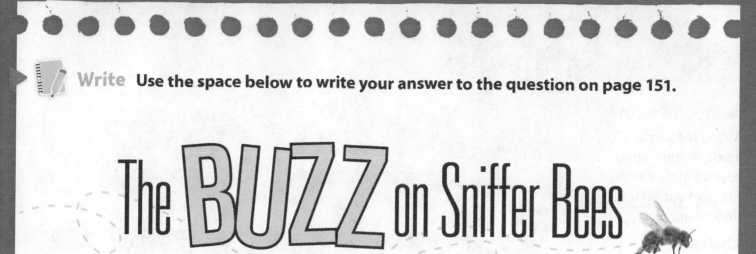

The BUZZ on Sniffer Bees

4 **Short Response** Describe the different ways sniffer bees can help humans. In your description, use some of the science words you learned from the passage.

HINT Reread paragraph 4. Look for three things sniffer bees can detect.

_____

_____

_____

_____

_____

Check Your Writing

☐ Did you read the prompt carefully?

☐ Did you put the prompt in your own words?

☐ Did you use the best evidence from the text to support your ideas?

☐ Are your ideas clearly organized?

☐ Did you write in clear and complete sentences?

☐ Did you check your spelling and punctuation?

> Read

from

Horses Helping Others

WORDS TO KNOW
As you read, look inside, around, and beyond these words to figure out what they mean.

- **halter**
- **interactive**

by Natasha Yim, *Appleseeds*

1   In 1993, when Erin Livingston was just 11, she had an idea. She wanted to use horses to help kids with special needs. Along with two friends, she researched different programs. With the support of the Mendocino County 4-H, Ridgewood T.R.A.I.L.[1] was born.

2   Freya, Kiss, Easy, Ginger, and Robin are horses with a very important job. They help kids with special needs. Some of these kids are in wheelchairs and walkers. Some can't talk. Some are very high energy and need to learn how to focus.

3   Erin uses games to help kids learn to communicate with horses. For example, a rope is attached to the halter of a horse. The student holds the other end and wiggles it to make the horse back up. Then the student wiggles it again to invite the horse back into his or her space.

[1] **T.R.A.I.L.:** Teaching Riding as an Access to Independence and Learning

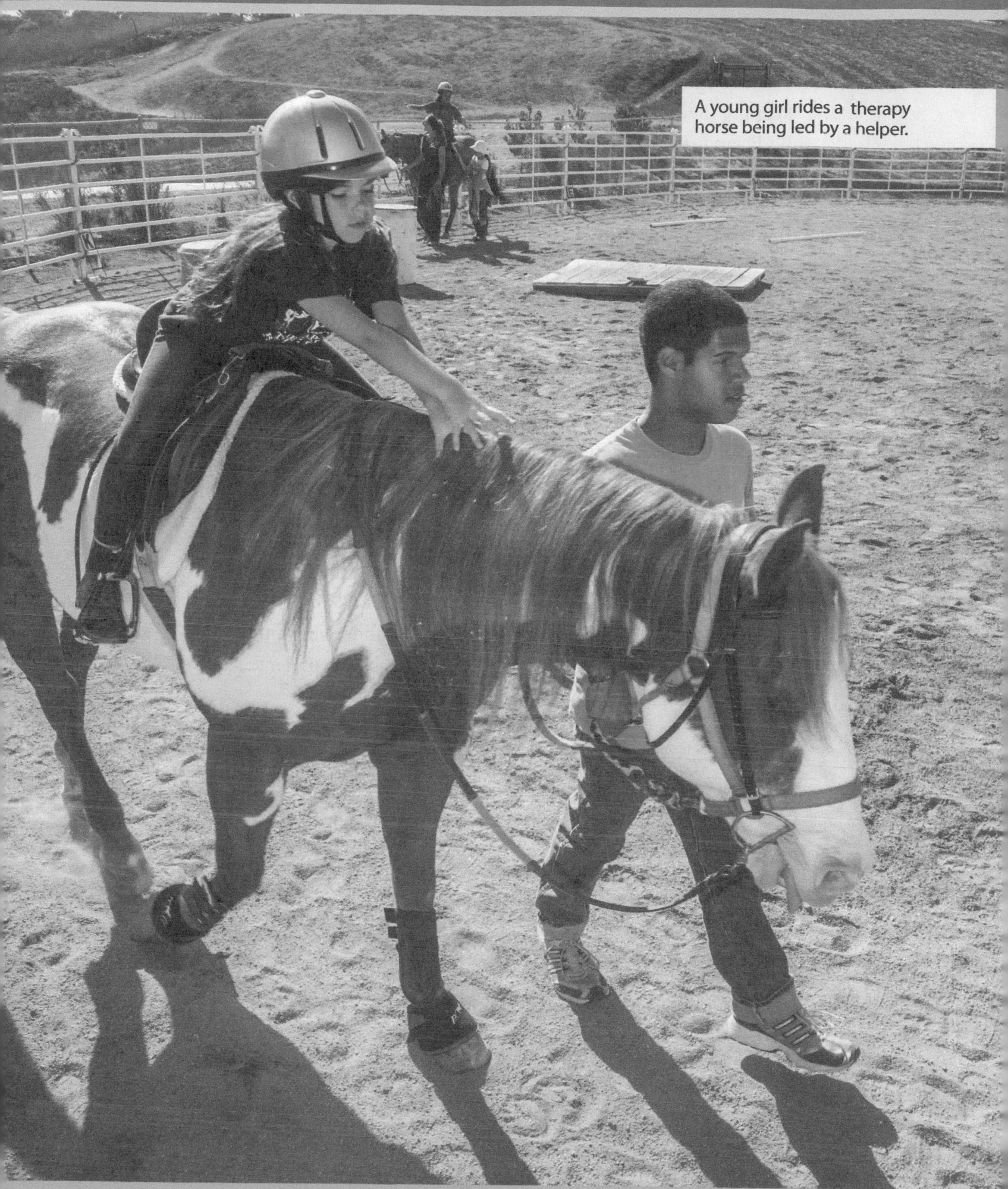

A young girl rides a therapy horse being led by a helper.

4   Through interactive games, the horses help the kids learn about trust, keeping themselves safe, and being sensitive to a horse's feelings and body language. If kids are loud and too full of energy, the horse may not want to come over to them.

5   "The kids learn to protect their space, and also to invite the horse into their space," says Erin Livingston, the founder of Ridgewood T.R.A.I.L.

6   For a child who can't walk, riding works her leg muscles. A horse's walking motion is very similar to our own hip movements. Children who have a hard time staying on task learn to pay attention. If they turn to the left when they want to go right, the horse may not do what they want it to do. For a kid who has a hard time talking, Erin has her use words to command the horse. One boy uttered his first sentence, "Walk on, Woody," while riding a horse! Another student is now a helper in the program. "She has so much confidence and pride in what she does," says her mother.

7   "We focus on the kids' abilities, not their disabilities," Erin says.

8   Good program horses are calm, patient, and understanding. They have to be used to people (there could be up to two or three helpers walking alongside a rider), loud noises, and sudden movements. It's exhausting work. But the next day, they're back at it, patient as ever—just another day at the office for these amazing horses!

Children get ready to ride therapy horses.

Think Use what you learned from reading the selection to respond to these questions.

1 This question has two parts. First, answer Part A. Then answer Part B.

Part A
Reread paragraphs 3 and 4. What is the meaning of *interactive* in paragraph 4?

    A acting apart from each other

    B acting like each other

    C acting in response to each other

    D acting politely with each other

Part B
Write one sentence from paragraph 3 or 4 that helped you understand what *interactive* means.

_____

_____

_____

_____

2 Read this sentence from the article.

> **Erin uses games to help kids learn to communicate with horses.**

Which words from paragraph 2 provide a clue to the meaning of *communicate?*

    A "can't talk"

    B "need to learn"

    C "with special needs"

    D "very high energy"

3 This question has two parts. First, answer Part A. Then answer Part B.

Part A
What is the meaning of the word *sensitive* in paragraph 4?

  A unfeeling

  B understanding

  C fearful

  D amazed

Part B
Underline the sentence in paragraph 4 that supports your answer in Part A.

> **Through interactive games, the horses help the kids learn about trust, keeping themselves safe, and being sensitive to a horse's feelings and body language. If kids are loud and too full of energy, the horse may not want to come over to them.**

4 Read these sentences from paragraph 6 of the passage.

> **For a kid who has a hard time talking, Erin has her use words to command the horse. One boy uttered his first sentence, "Walk on, Woody," while riding a horse!**

What does the word *uttered* mean as used in this passage?

  A spoke

  B wrote

  C understood

  D heard

5 In paragraph 7, Erin states, "We focus on the kids' abilities, not their disabilities." Explain what *disabilities* means. Tell what clue you used.

_____

_____

_____

Write

6 **Short Response** Using evidence from the text, describe how working with horses helps build confidence in children with special needs. Use some of the new words you learned in your response.

_____

_____

_____

_____

Learning Target

You've learned how to figure out the meaning of words you don't know. Describe some strategies that you could use to figure out the meaning of _migration_ in the following paragraph.

Every year, millions of monarch butterflies journey to California and Mexico to avoid the harsh winters in other parts of the country. This huge migration begins in fall, ahead of the cold weather. The journey can cover up to 3,000 miles.

Lesson 10
Text Features

Learning Target

By using special text features and search tools, you can find important information quickly and easily.

▶ Read   When you go into a store, you use signs and labels to help you find what you need. **Text features** are similar to those signs and labels. They are special parts of a text that help you locate the facts and details you're looking for.

Text features include **headings, key words** that are shown in bold print, and boxed information called **sidebars.** Digital texts that you read online have **search tools** such as **hyperlinks.** These text features let you access more information by clicking on the link.

Read this science article on the lungfish. How do the text features help you?

Long Live the Lungfish

If you had to be a fish, you might want to be a lungfish. Why? Because the lungfish can do some amazing things that most other fish cannot.

A Fish Out of Water

The lungfish can breathe air. If its lake or river dries up, the lungfish drags itself over land until it finds water in which to live.

A Fish Under Ground

If the lungfish can't find water to live in, it digs a hole in the ground and sleeps there until the water returns. This type of sleep is called **estivation.**

FUN FACTS
- Lungfish live in South America, Australia, and Africa.
- Lungfish can live for more than 80 years.
- Lungfish have been around since *before* the dinosaurs.

▶ **Think** Look again at the article on lungfish. Then look at the features listed in the box below. Write each feature where it belongs in the first column of the chart.

| sidebar | title | key word | heading |

Feature	What It Does
	tells what the whole passage is about
	shows what part of the passage is about
	calls attention to an important word that you should pay attention to
	gives more information related to the main article

▶ **Talk** The "Academic Talk" box below lists several text features. Which features would you use to preview an article to get a feeling for what it was about? What would each feature tell you?

◎ **Academic Talk**
Use these words and phrases to talk about the text.
- **text features**
- **sidebars**
- **search tools**
- **headings**
- **key words**
- **hyperlinks**

> **Read**

Brrr... Polar Bears in the Arctic

by Devonte Thomas

1   Polar bears live in the Arctic. The Arctic is one of the coldest places on Earth. How do polar bears survive in the ice and snow?

Built for the Arctic

2   Polar bears have thick, white fur. The outer layer of fur is made of oily, hollow **guard hairs.** These hairs keep the bears dry. The inner layer of fur next to their skin acts like a sweater. It traps in heat and keeps the bears warm. Under their fur, polar bears have a thick layer of fat. Also, polar bears have black skin and black noses. The color black **absorbs,** or takes in, more of the sun's heat.

Behavior

3   Polar bears have other ways to cope with the cold. They stay in a **den** all winter. Their body functions slow down. They do not eat or drink.

Close Reader Habits

Find and **circle** the text features in the passage. How do they help you as you read?

FAST FACTS

Baby, It's Cold Outside!

The Arctic is a cold, snowy region around the North Pole. In winter, the temperature can drop as low as −40°F.

Explore   How can text features help you learn how polar bears survive in the winter?

Think

> Before reading, look at the title, headings, and pictures. They give an idea of what the article is about.

1 Finish the chart. Write an example from the article in the second column. Tell how it is used in the article in the third column. Be as specific as you can.

Feature	Example from the Article	What It Does in This Article
Title	"Brrr ... Polar Bears in the Arctic"	shows that the article will be about polar bears and where they live
Heading		
Key Word		
Sidebar		

Talk

2 Imagine you're doing a report on polar bears. You need some facts about what they do to survive the cold. Where would you look in this article, and why?

Write

3 **Short Response** Explain how polar bears survive winter in the Arctic. Tell how you found the information in the article. Use the space provided on page 166 to write your answer.

> **HINT** Remember to use all the text features to help you locate information.

Genre: Science Article

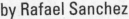

How Plants Live in a Desert

by Rafael Sanchez

1   A desert gets less than 10 inches of rain per year. It can get as hot as 100 degrees in the summer. Yet at night, it can be quite cold. It's not easy to live in a desert, but some plants do.

Plants That Store Water

2   Many cactuses have a waxy coating. The wax helps stop water from **evaporating,** or escaping through tiny holes in the plant. Cactuses are good at storing water. When it rains, a cactus stores water to live on during dry periods. For more information on cactus plants, research the topic.

Plants with Long Roots

3   A second type of desert plant grows very long roots. One example is the **mesquite** (meh SKEET) tree. The roots of the mesquite find water deep in the ground. Some mesquites have roots that are 80 feet long!

Plants with Hardy Seeds

4   A third type of plant grows only in the spring, following winter rains. It grows quickly. Soon it drops seeds. These seeds can live for a long time. If the following spring is wet, the seeds will grow. If not, the seeds may wait two or three springs to grow.

Deserts Around the Globe

There are many deserts around the world. The Sahara Desert is in Africa. The Gobi Desert is in Asia. The Great Basin and Mojave (moh HAHV ee) Deserts stretch across the American Southwest.

Close Reader Habits

Circle each of the main headings in the article. How are they similar?

▶ **Think**

1 Which text feature would help you find more facts about how seeds help plants survive in the desert?

    A   the picture of the mesquite tree

    B   the sidebar "Deserts Around the Globe"

    C   the key word **evaporating** in paragraph 2

    D   the heading "Plants with Hardy Seeds"

> Authors often use headings to organize the information in a piece of writing. You can use those headings to figure out key ideas.

2 Why do authors include key words in a text?

    A   to show which words are hard to say

    B   to use as headings within the article

    C   to help readers spot important words

    D   to call attention to the sidebar

▶ **Talk**

3 In what places around the world might you find some of the plants you read about? Which text feature gave you this information?

▶ **Write**

4 **Short Response** Plants have three main ways of surviving in the desert. Tell what they are, and how the author uses text features to call attention to them. Use the space provided on page 167 to write your answer.

> **HINT** Think about the three ways plants survive. Where do you see those ways listed in the article?

✏️ **Write** Use the space below to write your answer to the question on page 163.

Brrr... Polar Bears in the Arctic

HINT Remember to use all the text features to help you locate information.

3 **Short Response** Explain how polar bears survive winter in the Arctic. Tell how you found the information in the article.

_____

_____

_____

_____

_____

_____

Don't forget to check your writing.

✏️ **Write** Use the space below to write your answer to the question on page 165.

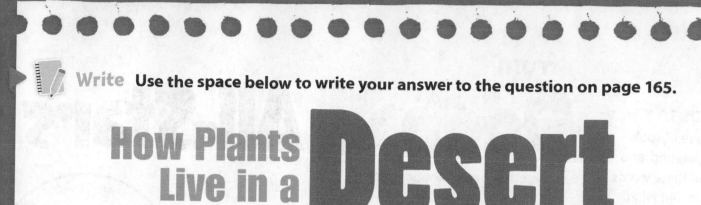
How Plants Live in a Desert

> **HINT** Think about the three ways plants survive. Where do you see those ways listed in the article?

4 **Short Response** Plants have three main ways of surviving in the desert. Tell what they are, and how the author uses text features to call attention to them.

_____

_____

_____

_____

_____

_____

_____

Check Your Writing

☐ Did you read the prompt carefully?

☐ Did you put the prompt in your own words?

☐ Did you use the best evidence from the text to support your ideas?

☐ Are your ideas clearly organized?

☐ Did you write in clear and complete sentences?

☐ Did you check your spelling and punctuation?

▶ Read

from
Oddball All-Stars

by Jodi Wheeler-Toppen, *Ask*

WORDS TO KNOW
As you read, look inside, around, and beyond these words to figure out what they mean.

- **current**
- **coast**
- **volunteering**

Turn Up the Heat

1   The Galápagos Islands are home to some unusual penguins. They swim. They waddle. They lay eggs. They do the same things other penguins do. But they do them on **tropical** islands, where the rocks can get hotter than 100°F (38°C). It's so hot that the penguins' eggs will cook if they are left out in the sun.

2   What are penguins doing in the tropics? Scientists think the first penguins got to the Galápagos by following a cool current. It flows up the coast of South America. Now small changes, called **adaptations,** let them live where it's too hot for other penguins.

©Curriculum Associates, LLC   Copying is not permitted.

Keeping Cool

3   When people are hot, sweat helps them cool off. But birds can't sweat. At the hottest time of day, Galápagos penguins hang out in the cool water. But eventually, they have to return to land. And when they do, their feathers trap heat like a heavy winter coat.

4   Unlike Antarctic penguins, Galápagos penguins have bare skin around their beaks, on their feet, and under their flippers. When they need to cool off, they strike a funny pose. They hunch over to keep the sun off their feet. Then they hold their wings out to let the wind blow across the bare places. The wind carries the heat away. They also open their mouths and pant, like dogs. Galápagos penguins protect their eggs by building nests under the shade of rocks, out of the sun.

Galápagos Penguin

Scientific Name: *Spheniscus mendiculus*
Home Base: Galápagos Islands, off the coast of Ecuador
Size: 21 inches (53 cm) tall, a little bigger than a newborn baby

Penguin Hide and Seek

As a boy growing up on the Galápagos Islands, Hernan Vargas had no idea how special the plants and animals around him were. In high school, he started volunteering with scientists who came from all around the world to study them. Now he is a scientist himself. Counting penguins is an important part of his job.

Scientists regularly count the penguins to see how they're doing. But how many are hiding? To answer this question, Vargas and his team caught a bunch of penguins and painted some of their feathers yellow, then released them. When they counted penguins that year, they kept a separate count of the ones with yellow feathers. They found about half of their painted penguins, so they knew that about half were hiding somewhere. If half the painted penguins were hiding, probably about half of all of the penguins were hiding, too. So now they know that when they count penguins, they are getting about half of the total number.

▶ **Think** Use what you learned from reading the selection to respond to these questions.

1 What key words are called out in this article?

    A   **Oddball All-Stars**

    B   **Scientific Name, Home Base, Size**

    C   **tropical, adaptations**

    D   **Penguin Hide and Seek**

2 Where in the article would you tell someone to look for facts about how scientists keep track of the Galápagos penguins?

    A   the trading card titled "Galápagos Penguin"

    B   "Turn Up the Heat"

    C   "Keeping Cool"

    D   "Penguin Hide and Seek"

3 Next to each fact about the Galápagos penguins, write the letter of the section name that shows where that fact was found. You will use some letters more than once.

    A   **Turn Up the Heat**

    B   **Keeping Cool**

    C   **"Galápagos Penguin" Trading Card**

    D   **"Penguin Hide and Seek" Sidebar**

_____ The penguins pant like dogs to cool off.

_____ The birds are about 21 inches tall.

_____ The penguin eggs will cook if left out in the sun.

_____ Penguins may have reached the Galápagos by following a cool current.

_____ Scientists paint some birds to help them count the penguins.

_____ Bare skin on parts of the penguins helps them cool off.

4 Look at the underlined antonyms in this sentence from the "Penguin Hide and Seek" sidebar. Antonyms are words that have the opposite meanings.

> **To answer this question, Vargas and his team <u>caught</u> a bunch of penguins and painted some of their feathers yellow, then <u>released</u> them.**

The word *caught* is the antonym of the word *released*. What does *released* mean?

  A trapped

  B hid behind

  C colored

  D let go of

📓 **Write**

The Galápagos penguins are different from Antarctic penguins. How have they had to change in order to survive in the tropics? Reread the article. Draw a line under each detail that shows how the Galápagos penguins deal with the heat. Then complete numbers 5 and 6.

5 **Plan Your Response** Make a 2-column chart. In the first column, list examples of how the penguins have changed in order to live in the tropics. In the second column, explain how each change helps them survive the heat.

6 **Write an Extended Response** Explain the similarities and differences between the Galápagos penguins and their Antarctic cousins. First, tell how the penguins are similar. Then explain why the Galápagos penguins have had to change. Finally, tell what those changes are and how they help the penguins to survive.

_____

_____

_____

_____

Learning Target

Now that you understand how text features and search tools can help you find information, explain how using them could help you complete a science report.

Lesson 11
Author's Point of View

Learning Target

Understanding the difference between an author's point of view and your own will help you understand different ways of looking at a topic.

▶ **Read** **Point of view** is the way we think or feel about something. For example, you might like a certain kind of music, but a friend of yours may think it's terrible. You both have different points of view about that kind of music.

Authors often give their points of view about **topics.** They do this by using opinion words such as *best, worst, beautiful, like, dislike, feel,* and *believe.* As you read, try to figure out the author's point of view by noticing these types of word clues.

Look at the cartoon below. How does the woman feel about the art?

Look at the cartoon again. Notice the words the woman uses as she writes about the art. What does that tell you about her point of view?

▶ **Think** Look back at the cartoon. Complete the chart by telling the woman's point of view about the art.

Author	Point of View	Details
Woman		

▶ **Talk** What do you think of the art in the cartoon? Give reasons for your point of view. Does your partner share your point of view?

◎ **Academic Talk**
Use this phrase and word to talk about the text.
- **point of view**
- **topics**

Make Way for *the Mallard Family*

by Jesse Green

1   *Make Way for Ducklings* is a children's book by Robert McCloskey. In it, a mother and her eight ducklings walk to a park in Boston, Massachusetts. Today, a delightful bronze sculpture of Mrs. Mallard and her ducklings stands in Boston's Public Garden. The statue is almost as popular as the book! It seems to bring the duck family to life.

2   Nancy Schön made this charming creation in 1987. It is a series of nine adorable statues. Mrs. Mallard and her ducklings proudly parade in a row. Children cuddle these lifelike statues all the time. All this petting means they never need to be polished.

3   A thief stole one of the ducklings in 2009. The cowardly criminal snapped the bird off at its webbed feet. This senseless attack angered many people. Boston's Mayor Menino said, "This act is not a prank, it is a crime."

4   Fortunately, the missing statue was found four blocks away. It was leaning against a tree. The people who found the stolen duckling returned it right away. Soon, the duckling was back in the parade where he belonged.

5   Nancy Schön loves to come to the park and watch children enjoy her sculpture. She feels lucky to have made something that "has given so much pleasure to so many."

Close Reader Habits

As you read, **circle** words that show how the author feels about the statue.

Explore

How can you figure out the author's point of view and compare it to your own?

Think

> To figure out the author's point of view, look at the words used to describe the topic.

1 What words help you decide how the author feels about the sculpture? Add two more examples to the first column of the chart. Then write what you think the author's point of view is about the sculpture.

Words Describing the Sculpture	Author's Point of View on the Sculpture
• "delightful bronze sculpture"	

Talk

2 Look again at the picture of the sculpture. What do you think of it? Explain your point of view.

Write

> **HINT** Think of opinion words that describe something you liked or something you disliked. Use them in your response.

3 **Short Response** Is your point of view different from or the same as the author's? Tell how it is the same or different. Use the space provided on page 180 to write your answer.

SNOW SCULPTURE CONTEST

by Kim Wu

1   The town of Butler held its first Winter Fest this week. The highlight of the outdoor event was the snow sculpture contest. Teams of snow carvers worked tirelessly to create amazing works of art. The crowds were delighted!

2   Snow sculpture is a very difficult kind of sculpture to make. Teams of snow carvers made fantastic sculptures from huge blocks of snow. Each team could use only common hand tools. Shovels and cheese graters were very popular. For a whole day, they cut away packed snow from the heavy blocks. By late afternoon, these snow artists had created amazing sculptures. Some were over nine feet tall!

3   My favorite snow sculpture won second prize. This sculpture of a giant dragon was incredible. It had detailed scales and a pair of giant wings. It also had a long tail. This fierce dragon even breathed fire made of snow!

4   The snow sculpture that won third prize was a good choice by the judges. It was a copy of the White House in Washington, D.C.

5   I was disappointed by the snow sculpture that captured first prize. It was a covered wagon. The team of carvers made the wagon wheels too small! They made other mistakes, too.

6   I really do believe that my favorite sculpture should have won the grand prize. But Butler's first Winter Fest was still a great success. I can't wait for the next one!

Close Reader Habits

What is the author's point of view about the dragon sculpture? **Circle** words and details in paragraph 3 that show how the author felt about the sculpture.

Think

1 This question has two parts. Answer Part A. Then answer Part B.

Part A
Which choice **best** describes the author's point of view about snow sculpture?

A Snow sculpture is interesting, but it's just for kids.

B Snow sculpture is an impressive type of art.

C Snow sculpture requires very little effort.

D Snow sculptures are not as good as regular sculptures.

Part B
Which sentence from the review **best** supports your answer in Part A?

A "The highlight of the outdoor event was the snow sculpture contest."

B "Snow sculpture is a very difficult kind of sculpture to make."

C "This sculpture of a giant dragon was incredible."

D "The snow sculpture that won third prize was a good choice by the judges."

> Authors sometimes use words that show strong feelings in order to convey their point of view.

Talk

2 Based on the review, do you think the author, Kim Wu, believes that Butler should have another Winter Fest? What details helped you know what Kim Wu's point of view would be?

Write

3 **Short Response** In the second paragraph, the author says, "Snow sculpture is a very difficult kind of sculpture to make." Explain whether or not you agree. Compare your point of view with Kim Wu's. Use the space provided on page 181 to write your answer.

> **HINT** Reread the details that tell about how a snow sculpture is made. Think about what it takes to complete those steps.

▶ 📓 **Write** Use the space below to write your answer to the question on page 177.

Make Way for *the Mallard Family*

3 **Short Response** Is your point of view different from or the same as the author's? Tell how it is the same or different.

> **HINT** Think of opinion words that describe something you liked or something you disliked. Use them in your response.

_____

_____

_____

_____

_____

_____

_____

_____

_____

> Don't forget to check your writing.

 **Write** Use the space below to write your answer to the question on page 179.

SNOW SCULPTURE CONTEST

3 **Short Response** In the second paragraph, the author says, "Snow sculpture is a very difficult kind of sculpture to make." Explain whether or not you agree. Compare your point of view with Kim Wu's.

> **HINT** Reread the details that tell about how a snow sculpture is made. Think about what it takes to complete those steps.

Check Your Writing

☐ Did you read the prompt carefully?

☐ Did you put the prompt in your own words?

☐ Did you use the best evidence from the text to support your ideas?

☐ Are your ideas clearly organized?

☐ Did you write in clear and complete sentences?

☐ Did you check your spelling and punctuation?

Read

Our Most Famous Immigrant

by Nancy Whitelaw, *Cobblestone*

1 America's most famous immigrant arrived here in 1885. She was packed in 214 boxes. She was about 10 years old then. America had been waiting nine years for her. She was the Statue of Liberty. Her story begins long ago in France.

2 It is April 1876. Frederic Auguste Bartholdi, a French sculptor, has a problem. He has been commissioned to complete a statue as a gift from France to America for America's 100th birthday.

3 "July fourth, July fourth," he mutters over and over. "It can't be done."

4 Plaster dust swirls through the air around the partly finished statue. Gobs of wet plaster fall in heaps on the floor below it. Workmen climb up and down the scaffolds, hauling pails of materials and tools.

5 The noise is deafening. Men are shouting directions. Saws are rasping at ragged edges. Mallets are clanging copper sheets into molds. Hammers are nailing wood strips together.

6 An idea comes to Bartholdi. "I'll finish the arm and torch. I'll send them in time for the 4th of July so the Americans can at least imagine the whole statue." This is no small present. The hand alone is 16 feet high.

7 When the arm and torch finally are completed, Bartholdi has them shipped to the Philadelphia World's Fair. The Americans are amazed and delighted. The sculptor feels some relief that his art is appreciated. But he still has a great deal of work to do to finish building the world's largest statue.

Frederic Auguste Bartholdi visited the United States and chose the place where the Statue of Liberty would stand.

In 1878, the head of the Statue of Liberty was displayed in Paris, France. A small copy of the complete statue was shown with it.

8   Finally, in 1884, she stands tall and proud. She looks over the rooftops of Paris, France. She stays there until January 1885, while the Americans build a pedestal for her. Then, Bartholdi orders his crew to dismantle the statue and pack her into boxes.

9   Two hundred fourteen boxes arrive at Bedloe's Island in New York Harbor on June 17, 1885. A reporter opens some of the boxes. "I found one case that had just the eyebrows and forehead," he writes. "Another contained the left ear and some pieces of hair. One box that was eight feet long held one of her curls." Workmen in America assemble the statue—all 216 feet of her—on an 89-foot-tall pedestal.

10   On October 28, 1886, crowds of cheering spectators gather at the shore to watch the unveiling. The 300 boats in the harbor clear a path to the statue for President Grover Cleveland and his party. Bartholdi, positioned high in the torch of the statue, pulls the cord to unveil the face of the statue called *Liberty Enlightening the World.* Thousands cheer, wave banners, blow whistles, sound sirens, beat drums, and ring bells.

▶ **Think** Use what you learned from reading the article to respond to the following questions.

1 This question has two parts. First, answer Part A. Then answer Part B.

Part A
With which statement would the author of this article **most likely** agree?

   A Building the Statue of Liberty was an amazing accomplishment.

   B The sculptor Frederic Auguste Bartholdi was not a patient man.

   C Americans did not appreciate the statue as much as they should have.

   D The Statue of Liberty cost too much money to make.

Part B
Write **two** sentences that support the answer you chose in Part A.

_____

_____

_____

_____

_____

_____

_____

_____

_____

2 Which of the following **best** describes the author's point of view about the Statue of Liberty?

    A   Late delivery of the statue was the result of poor planning.

    B   More statues like the Statue of Liberty should be built in this country.

    C   The story of how the statue was built is both interesting and amazing.

    D   The Statue of Liberty is the greatest statue in the world.

3 This question has two parts. First, answer Part A. Then answer Part B.

Part A
According to the author, how did most Americans feel about the statue while they waited for it to be completed?

    A   They weren't very interested in seeing it.

    B   They were excited and eager for it to arrive.

    C   They were worried that it wouldn't fit in the harbor.

    D   They didn't think the statue was worth the long wait.

Part B
Which key event mentioned in the article caused Americans to feel the way they did about the gift they'd be receiving?

    A   the nine-year delay as the statue was built

    B   the display of the arm and torch at the World's Fair

    C   the arrival of 214 boxes at Bedloe's Island in New York Harbor

    D   the completion of the statue in France

4 Read these sentences from paragraph 7.

> **The Americans are amazed and delighted. The sculptor feels some relief that his art is appreciated.**

What does the word *appreciated* mean in this context?

- **A** felt, touched
- **B** found, discovered
- **C** valued, enjoyed
- **D** covered, hid

5 Read these sentences from paragraph 10.

> **Bartholdi, positioned high in the torch of the statue, pulls the cord to unveil the face of the statue called *Liberty Enlightening the World*. Thousands cheer, wave banners, blow whistles, sound sirens, beat drums, and ring bells.**

Which word **best** describes the author's point of view on the 1886 unveiling of the Statue of Liberty?

- **A** disappointed
- **B** confused
- **C** upset
- **D** excited

Write

6 **Short Response** The author describes the Statue of Liberty as America's most famous immigrant. Do you agree with her point of view? Explain your point of view and support it with details from the article.

_____

_____

_____

_____

_____

_____

Learning Target

You have now compared several authors' points of view to your own. Explain how doing this can help you think about your own point of view more carefully.

_____

_____

_____

▶ Read

Read the science article. Then answer the questions that follow.

BIG Bugs

by Jennifer Mattox, *Highlights*

1   Imagine walking through the park on a sunny day. You look up to see a spider twice the size of your head. It looks so real that it seems to be creeping down its web toward you.

2   Before you scream and run away, look closer. That 50-pound spider is a wood sculpture. It was made by artist David Rogers and is one of 14 bugs he has on display in parks and gardens around the United States.

Ants the Size of a Bus!

3   David's collection is called **Big Bugs**. It includes three monster ants. Each one stretches 25 feet long. That's almost as long as a school bus! The collection also includes a praying mantis that weighs 1,200 pounds. How heavy is that? It would be like picking up six grown men at once. Some of David's other bugs are a grasshopper, an assassin bug, and a ladybug—all big enough to sit on.

4   Real bugs are tiny. So why did David build his so large?

5   David hopes his jumbo sculptures will help us to stop and notice bugs. We may not see them working. Sometimes we may not even want them around. But David points out that bugs are an important part of nature. They make the soil a better place for plants to grow, they pollinate flowers, they eat other insects, and they are food to many creatures.

Bugs Under Construction

6   Making such massive art is not easy. Some of the bugs took three months to construct.

7   David began by carving pieces of wood into just the right shape and size. He used a mix of black walnut, red cedar, and black locust woods to craft each bug. He also used young willow trees to show texture in his ladybug and ants.

8   He then connected the parts using metal rods. Finally, he gave them a coat of varnish for a smooth, shiny finish.

Sticks and Strings

9   As a child, David Rogers did not get the best grades. He was not even the best painter. But he loved to make things. Using only sticks and string, he would build tiny villages small enough for an insect.

10   One day when he was older, he saw a bent tree that reminded him of the backbone of an animal. He decided to form a giant beast by adding more branches. The result was a dinosaur named Goliath. Goliath was his first large sculpture.

11   David has also made sculptures by welding metal. By joining together old car parts, he made a housefly and a dragonfly. Does this sound like fun to you? Good news—David believes there's an artist in everyone.

12   Of course, you probably won't start out by making a 25-foot ant. It took David years to come up with his huge bugs. But as David says, "There's no right or wrong way to express yourself with art. Let your imagination run free."

▶ **Think**

1 Next to each fact about David Rogers and his Big Bug art, write the letter of the heading that shows where the fact can be found.

    A   **Ants the Size of a Bus!**

    B   **Bugs Under Construction**

    C   **Sticks and Strings**

_____ David built tiny villages when he was a child.

_____ All of David's bugs are big enough to sit on.

_____ Different kinds of wood are used in David's art.

_____ David named his first large sculpture "Goliath."

_____ David hopes his art will help people notice bugs more.

2 Read paragraphs 4 and 5 from the article.

    4   **Real bugs are tiny. So why did David build his so large?**

    5   **David hopes his jumbo sculptures will help us to stop and notice bugs. We may not see them working. Sometimes we may not even want them around. But David points out that bugs are an important part of nature. They make the soil a better place for plants to grow, they pollinate flowers, they eat other insects, and they are food to many creatures.**

What does the word *jumbo* mean in paragraph 5?

    A   beautiful

    B   large

    C   new

    D   tiny

3 With which statement would the author **most likely** agree?

    A Although David's sculptures are interesting, they are too large and heavy.

    B Although bugs are an interesting subject for sculptures, they are not an important part of nature.

    C Although David was not the best painter as a child, he became a talented artist as an adult.

    D Although David's sculptures are huge, they are not difficult to make.

4 Which text feature would **best** help you find facts about how David built his bug art?

    A the heading "Ants the Size of a Bus!"

    B the heading "Bugs Under Construction"

    C the keywords **Big Bugs** in paragraph 3

    D the picture of the ant sculpture

5 This question has two parts. First, answer Part A. Then answer Part B.

Part A
Reread paragraph 11. What does the word *welding* mean as it is used in paragraph 11?

    A connecting

    B making bigger

    C adding branches

    D imagining

Part B
Write **one** phrase from paragraph 11 that **best** supports the answer to Part A.

_____

_____

_____

▶ **Read**

Genre: Science Article

Read the science article. Then answer the questions that follow.

The Praying Mantid

by Sophie Burmeister

1   The praying mantid is an insect that looks like a thin green or brown stick. It gets its name from the way its two front legs can bend. It looks as if it were praying. Most people call this insect a "praying mantis." But its real name is the "praying mantid."

Helpful Eaters

2   Praying mantids are **carnivores**. They eat other small animals and insects. They eat moths, grasshoppers, and flies. Some even eat lizards and frogs!

3   The eating habits of mantids are helpful to people. Farmers like mantids because they eat insects that could hurt their crops. Gardeners also like mantids. Mantids eat pesky insects that eat fruit and flowers.

Mighty Hunters

4   Tiny but mighty, mantids are skillful hunters. They have an interesting way of hunting their meals. Mantids camouflage themselves. They change their body color to match plants and trees near by. This makes them seem like a part of their background.

5   They can sit patiently for a long period of time and look like a branch or leaf. When their prey gets close enough, they quickly catch and hold it with their front legs. These legs have sharp spines that prevent escape. Most mantids eat the head of the animal first.

The Amazing Mantid

6   The mantid has three main body parts. The **head** is shaped like a triangle. It sits on a long thin neck, called a **thorax**. The thorax is connected to a long body, called an **abdomen**. Mantids are the only insects in the world that can turn their heads 180 degrees. That's a full half turn.

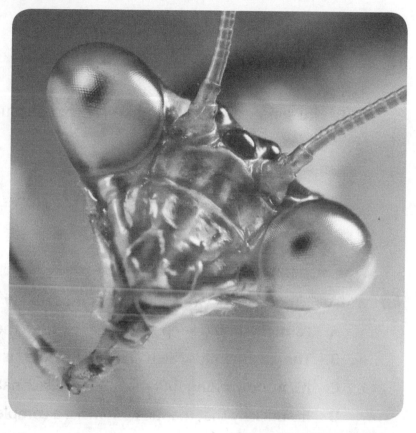

7   One of the most amazing features of mantids are their eyes. They have five of them! Two large eyes are on either side of their head. Three smaller eyes are set between the larger eyes. This gives the mantid excellent eyesight, which helps it catch its prey.

8   Mantids are super fast, graceful jumpers. They can make a complete leap in less than a second. Right before it leaps, the mantid wiggles its body back and forth. It can twist and turn its body in different directions. When it finally leaps, its body spins as it shoots through the air.

9   People have been fascinated with praying mantids for thousands of years. There are even rock paintings of mantids made by ancient people. The mantid is an awesome insect!

Fast Facts

- North America has only 20 kinds of mantids, while Africa has 880 species.

- Mantids live in warm or hot areas of the world.

- Most mantids are less than six inches long.

▶ **Think**

6 This question has two parts. First, answer Part A. Then answer Part B.

Part A
What does the word *prey* mean in paragraph 5?

    A an animal that is very similar in size to another animal

    B an animal that is caught and eaten by another animal

    C an animal that looks like it is praying

    D an animal with legs that look like spines

Part B
Write **two** sentences from paragraph 5 that **best** support the answer to Part A.

_____

_____

_____

_____

7 With which statement would the author **most likely** agree?

    A Farmers should keep mantids away from their crops.

    B The way mantids catch and eat their prey is cruel.

    C It's not surprising that mantids have fascinated people for a long time.

    D It's unlikely that mantids can make a complete leap in less than a second.

8 Mantids have three main body parts. Tell what they are. Then identify the text feature the author uses to call attention to those body parts.

_____

_____

_____

_____

9 This question has two parts. First, answer Part A. Then answer Part B.

Part A
Which text feature would help you find out why gardeners like mantids?

  A the heading "Helpful Eaters"

  B the picture of the mantid on a leaf stem

  C the key word **"carnivores"** in paragraph 2

  D the sidebar "Fast Facts"

Part B
Write a sentence from the article that supports the answer to Part A.

_____

_____

_____

_____

10 Read the sentences from the article.

> **They have an interesting way of hunting their meals. Mantids camouflage themselves. They change their body color to match plants and trees near by.**

Which phrase from these sentences provides the **best** clue to the meaning of *camouflage*?

  A "an interesting way"

  B "hunting their meals"

  C "change their body color"

  D "plants and trees near by"

✏️ Write

11 **Extended Response** What is the author's point of view about praying mantids? Find examples in the article to support your answer.

In your answer, be sure to
- explain the author's point of view about praying mantids
- give examples from the article that show the author's point of view about praying mantids
- use quote marks around words and sentences taken directly from the article

Check your writing for correct spelling, grammar, capitalization, and punctuation.

_____

_____

_____

_____

_____

_____

_____

_____

_____

_____

_____

_____

_____

_____

Craft and Structure in Literature

How do you make a castle? You start by building a floor. Next, you put up the walls. You build a few towers. Then you put the roof on top of the walls. Each part of the castle is built on the part before it. And all parts are necessary for the castle to be finished. Like building a castle, an author uses parts to create a story. The author begins with the first part, or chapter. Then he or she adds more chapters until the book is finished. Each chapter builds on the one before it and is important to the whole book.

In this unit, you will see how each chapter in a book builds on the chapter that came before and still adds something new. You'll also learn what poems and plays are made of and how they are built. Understanding how the parts work together will help you enjoy what you read!

✔ Self Check

Before starting this unit, check off the skills you know below. As you complete each lesson, see how many more skills you can check off!

I can:

	Before this unit	After this unit
choose the right meaning of a word based on how it is used in a text.	☐	☐
read chapters of a story to see how they build on each other.	☐	☐
read scenes of a play to see how they build on each other.	☐	☐
read stanzas of a poem to see how they build on each other.	☐	☐
tell the difference between my own point of view and those of the storyteller or the characters.	☐	☐

page 202

page 209

page 250

page 223

page 237

page 265

Lesson 12
Words in Context

Learning Target

By noticing when authors are using words and phrases in special ways, you can better understand and enjoy a story.

▶ **Read** Words and phrases may have more than one meaning. For example, a "clown" is someone who works for the circus. That's its **literal,** or usual, meaning. But, if you call your friend a clown, you don't *literally* mean that he or she is a circus clown. You just mean that your friend's behavior is silly. You're using the **nonliteral** meaning of "clown." *Nonliteral* means "not literal" or "not usual."

Authors often use nonliteral language to describe story characters, settings, and events more colorfully. If you come across a word or phrase with an unexpected meaning, use **context clues**—nearby words, phrases, and sentences—to figure out its meaning.

Read this passage. Notice the underlined phrases.

Arthur liked nothing better than to stay up reading, long after he was supposed to be asleep. He would pull his blanket over his head like a tent, turn on his book light, and <u>get lost</u> in his story. Tonight, though, his dad caught him. "Turn off that light, <u>night owl</u>," said his dad. "You've got school tomorrow."

▶ **Think** The chart below shows how to use context clues to find the meanings of nonliteral words and phrases. First, look at the literal meanings. Then read the context clues from the passage. Finally, write what you think the phrases mean in the passage.

Literal Meaning	Context Clues	Meaning in the Passage
night owl: a big-eyed bird that is usually awake at night	• stays up reading • should be asleep • awake later than he is supposed to be	
get lost: not know where you are or how to get where you want to go	• lost in his story	

▶ **Talk** Why is "night owl" a good way to describe Arthur in the passage?

◎ **Academic Talk**
Use these words and phrase to talk about the text.
• **literal**   • **nonliteral**   • **context clues**

▶ Read

Seaside Surprises

by Wendell Riley

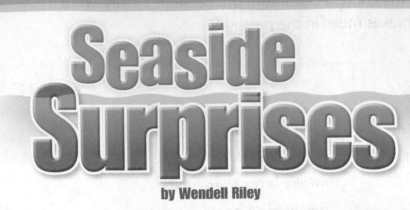

1   I didn't know what to expect when my family went hiking on the Oregon coast. I'd never seen the Pacific Ocean before. But I sure knew what I wanted to see—a whale!

2   After a picnic lunch, we hiked through a thick rainforest. We saw chipmunks, a lizard, and a hawk. The trail gently snaked its way up the steep mountainside to the top of a huge rocky cliff with a great view of the ocean. But I couldn't spot any whales. Then we heard something move through the woods right behind us! We turned, and there stood a huge elk with giant antlers. We all froze in place, barely breathing, until the animal slowly walked away. Then we finally relaxed. We all started laughing and jumping around in excitement.

3   Next, the trail wound down to a sandy beach. Waves hammered the shore. We saw seagulls, crabs, clams, and even some seals happily baking themselves out on the warm rocks—but no whales. It was fun, but then it was time to go.

4   Everyone else started walking back to our trail, but my eyes were locked on the ocean. And then it happened. Not just one whale but a whole pod of them broke the surface of the water. I was so stunned that I could barely shout, "Look!"

Close Reader Habits

Which words and phrases are unfamiliar, or used in unusual ways? **Underline** details that help you figure out their meanings.

Explore How can you figure out the meanings of words and phrases with nonliteral meanings?

Think

1. Look at the phrase *froze in place* in paragraph 2. Complete the chart to figure out the meaning.

> When you read a word or phrase whose literal, or usual, meaning doesn't make sense, look for context clues that help you figure out what the author really means.

Literal Meaning	Context Clues	Meaning in the Passage
froze in place: turned from water into ice	• barely breathing	

Talk

2. Look at the phrase *seals happily baking themselves* in paragraph 3. What is the literal meaning of *baking*? What does the word *baking* mean in this passage? Use context clues to help you decide.

Write

3. **Short Response** Look at the description of the waves in paragraph 3. Describe the literal meaning of *hammered*. Then explain how *hammered* is used in the text. Tell which context clues helped you figure out the meaning. Use the space provided on page 206 to write your answer.

> **HINT** Use what you know about *actual* hammers to picture how the waves must have looked, sounded, and felt.

▶ Read

The Wind and the Leaves

by George Cooper

1   "Come, little leaves," said the wind one day,
    "Come over the meadows with me and play.
    Put on your dresses of red and gold, —
    For summer is gone, and the days grow cold."

5   Soon as the leaves heard the wind's loud call,
    Down they came fluttering one and all.
    Over the brown fields they danced and flew,
    Singing the soft little songs they knew.

    Dancing and whirling, the little leaves went;
10 Winter had called them, and they were content;
    Soon fast asleep in their earthy beds,
    The snow laid a coverlet over their heads.

Close Reader Habits

What words in the last stanza have nonliteral meanings? **Underline** words in lines 9–12 that would normally be used to describe people. **Circle** clues that help you figure out what the words may mean here.

▶ **Think**

1 How does the poet use the word *dresses* in line 3 of the poem?

   A to describe leaves changing color in the fall

   B to describe girls getting dressed for a party

   C to describe the sky changing colors at sunset

   D to describe the movement of the wind

> This is a poem, so look for words used in unusual and creative ways.

2 Read these lines from the poem.

> **Soon fast asleep in their earthy beds,**
> **The snow laid a coverlet over their heads.**

The poet uses the word *coverlet* to show that

   A the snow looks like a blanket.

   B the leaves have fallen.

   C the snow looks like a dress.

   D the singing has stopped.

▶ **Talk**

3 How do the words the poet uses help you picture what is happening to the leaves?

✎ **Write**

4 **Short Response** Tell how the poet uses nonliteral word meanings to describe how the leaves look and sound when they fall. Use the space provided on page 207 to write your answer.

> **HINT** Look at lines 5–9 for words that tell how the leaves move.

Write Use the space below to write your answer to the question on page 203.

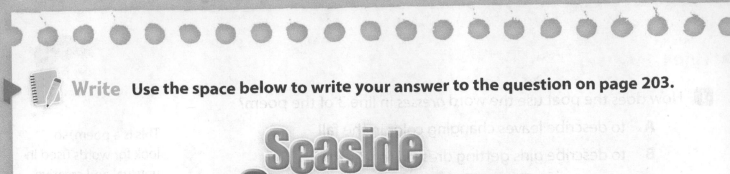

Seaside Surprises

3 **Short Response** Look at the description of the waves in paragraph 3. Describe the literal meaning of *hammered*. Then explain how *hammered* is used in the text. Tell which context clues helped you figure out the meaning.

> **HINT** Use what you know about *actual* hammers to picture how the waves must have looked, sounded, and felt.

Don't forget to check your writing.

Write Use the space below to write your answer to the question on page 205.

The Wind and the Leaves

4 **Short Response** Tell how the poet uses nonliteral word meanings to describe how the leaves look and sound when they fall.

> **HINT** Look at lines 5–9 for words that tell how the leaves move.

_____

_____

_____

_____

_____

_____

_____

Check Your Writing

☐ Did you read the prompt carefully?

☐ Did you put the prompt in your own words?

☐ Did you use the best evidence from the text to support your ideas?

☐ Are your ideas clearly organized?

☐ Did you write in clear and complete sentences?

☐ Did you check your spelling and punctuation?

▶ **Read**

Yosemite Morning

by Hilary Dumitrescu

WORDS TO KNOW
As you read, look inside, around, and beyond these words to figure out what they mean.

- **massive**
- **boulders**
- **exploration**
- **granite**

1   It is quiet in the park when my brother and I wake up. We pretend we are the only ones here, and not one of thousands of tourists. Fresh snow has fallen overnight and blankets the ground, the rocks, and the massive boulders with a silent quilt of white. I take a deep breath. The air smells green and icy. Suddenly, nearby, I hear a soft thump. I hear my brother gasp. When I turn around, he is standing there with his head covered in a thick crown of snow. He laughs and points up. The branches above him hold armfuls of snow. They are ready to have a snowball fight with us.

2   We walk further into the woods, our boots crunch, crunch, crunching in the snow. My brother walks ahead. At one point, his entire left leg sinks down into the snow. I run to help, and I, too, sink completely into the surprisingly deep snowbank. We are laughing, trying to free our legs from the snow's grip. I pull my foot out, finally, only to find that it's just my sock that has escaped. My boot is still buried. The forest echoes with our giggles, clear as bells.

3   We finally roll, exhausted, away from the deep snow. We continue our exploration. We wander deep into the woods. It feels like we are all alone. I wonder what it must have been like for the first people who lived here. What was it like before the cars, the tour buses, and the fancy hotels came along? Did they walk, quiet as rabbits, on the new-fallen snow? Did they stare up in awe at the great granite face of Half-Dome?

4   We come to a clearing. My brother holds up a hand, signaling me to stop. At the far edge of the clearing is a small creek, cutting an icy path through the snow. At the creek's edge, a deer is watching us. We freeze. The deer freezes. Slowly, never taking her eyes off of us, she dips her head quickly to the water. She takes a long drink. Her head suddenly shoots up, alerted to sounds only her deer ears can hear. In a flash, she is gone. In the woods, her white tail waves her goodbye.

5   We decide to head back to our cabin, as the cold air and snowy walk have left us famished. We talk about the breakfast we will have, pancakes with golden butter and syrup. Our parents, we know, will be waiting for us. They have been watching all along, sipping steamy cups of coffee on the porch of our cabin. Later, we will take them into the woods and show them the silence.

Think Use what you learned from reading the story to respond to the following questions.

1. Read the following sentence from paragraph 1.

> **Fresh snow has fallen overnight and blankets the ground, the rocks, and the massive boulders with a silent quilt of white.**

What do the words *quilt of white* mean in this sentence?

    A warm blanket

    B layer of snow

    C slippery ice

    D pebbles and dust

2. The following question has two parts. First, answer Part A. Then answer Part B.

Part A
Read this sentence from paragraph 1 about the author's brother.

> **When I turn around, he is standing there with his head covered in a thick crown of snow.**

What does this sentence really mean?

    A The brother has made a crown from the branches.

    B The brother has a pile of snow on his head.

    C The brother is turning in circles to look at the snow.

    D The brother is wearing a thick cap to keep off the snow.

Part B
Underline **two** details in these sentences from paragraph 1 that support the answer you chose in Part A.

> **Suddenly, nearby, I hear a soft thump. I hear my brother gasp. When I turn around, he is standing there with his head covered in a thick crown of snow. He laughs and points up. The branches above him hold armfuls of snow. They are ready to have a snowball fight with us.**

3 Read these sentences from paragraph 2:

> **I pull my foot out, finally, only to find that it's just my sock that has escaped. My boot is still buried.**

What has happened to the narrator?

    A   The narrator has buried her boot and sock in the snow.

    B   The narrator has lost her sock during the hike.

    C   The narrator's boot is still stuck in the snow.

    D   The narrator's boot and sock have been taken.

4 Read the following sentence from paragraph 4.

> **In a flash, she is gone.**

The author uses the words *in a flash* to show that the deer runs

    A   through a bright light.

    B   in a clumsy way.

    C   very quickly.

    D   when lightning struck.

5 When the deer runs away, the narrator says, "In the woods, her white tail waves her goodbye." Which is the **best** literal restatement of this idea?

    A   The deer turns and waves goodbye from the woods.

    B   The deer's tail begins twitching as she enters the woods.

    C   The deer uses her tail to wave goodbye to the children.

    D   The deer's tail is the last thing the narrator sees as the animal leaves.

6 What does the word *famished* mean in paragraph 5?

    A tired

    B hungry

    C unhappy

    D confused

7 Read these two sentences from the story. Both use words in nonliteral ways. Write what you think each sentence means.

The air smells green and icy.

_____

_____

_____

Later, we will take them into the woods and show them the silence.

_____

_____

_____

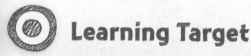 **Write**

8 **Short Response** The author described several things the children saw in Yosemite. Which description did you like the most? In your answer, include examples of how the author used both literal and nonliteral word meanings in the description.

_____

_____

_____

_____

_____

_____

Learning Target

You've practiced figuring out the literal and nonliteral meanings of words and phrases by using context. Explain how using the nonliteral meanings of words can help an author make the writing more interesting.

Lesson 13
What Are Stories Made Of?

Learning Target

Knowing how parts of a story are organized can help you better understand how events and ideas connect and build on each other.

▶ **Read** All stories have a beginning, a middle, and an end. To make longer stories easier to read, authors often divide them into parts or **sections.** The sections are called **chapters.** Every chapter adds new events and information to the story.

Read the table of contents and chapter summaries from the book *What They Found on Planet Z*.

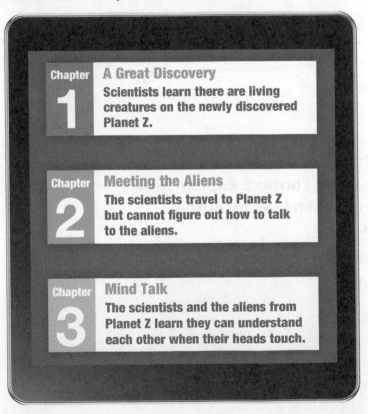

Chapter 1 **A Great Discovery**
Scientists learn there are living creatures on the newly discovered Planet Z.

Chapter 2 **Meeting the Aliens**
The scientists travel to Planet Z but cannot figure out how to talk to the aliens.

Chapter 3 **Mind Talk**
The scientists and the aliens from Planet Z learn they can understand each other when their heads touch.

Look again at the summaries. How do these chapters build on each other?

▶ **Think**   Reread the chapter titles and summaries. Then finish the chart below to see how the chapters build on each other.

Details from *What They Found on Planet Z*	
Chapter 1: A Great Discovery	• Scientists discover that there is life on Planet Z.
Chapter 2: Meeting the Aliens	
Chapter 3: Mind Talk	

▶ **Talk**   How does each chapter of *What They Found on Planet Z* add something new to the story?

🎯 **Academic Talk**
Use these words to talk about the text.
- **chapters**
- **sections**

Genre: Realistic Fiction

Keeping the LOST DOG LOST

by Siri Johnson

Please call 555-1432

CHAPTER 1:
Finding a Lost Dog

1   Three weeks ago I found a lost dog on my way home from school. Mom and I couldn't figure out whom he belonged to, so we called him "Mystery." There was no mystery, though, about what happened next. I fell in love with the dog and started hoping that he could stay with us forever.

2   Then one night, Mom sat down next to me and said, "Jillian, what if we can't find Mystery's owner? Do you think you're ready to become a pet owner?"

3   I said, "Yes, yes! Of course!" But then a darker thought crept into my brain: *What if we do find the owner?*

CHAPTER 2:
Mystery's Real Name

4   The next day, I was taking Mystery for a walk when I spotted, tacked to a telephone pole, a poster with a picture of a lost dog on it. I thought, *Oh no, it can't be!* But there was no question, it was Mystery—or I should say Barney, because it seemed that was his real name. "Are you Barney?" I asked, and he barked three times, wagging his tail happily.

5   Then we walked all over the neighborhood, and I tore down ten more posters from ten more poles. I knew that what I was doing was selfish and wrong, but I couldn't bear to lose . . . Barney.

Close Reader Habits

Underline phrases and sentences that tell important events. Then think about how each event builds on what came before it.

Explore How does the second chapter of "Keeping the Lost Dog Lost" build on the first one?

Think

> The beginning of a story usually introduces the main characters and a problem. The next chapters build on that problem.

1 Finish the chart with details from the story that help you understand Jillian's problem.

Details from "Keeping the Lost Dog Lost"	
Chapter 1: Finding a Lost Dog	
Chapter 2: Mystery's Real Name	

Talk

2 What happens in Chapter 2 that connects to Jillian's worry in Chapter 1?

Write

3 **Short Response** Explain the problem Jillian faces in Chapter 2. Use the space provided on page 220 to write your answer.

> **HINT** Why does Jillian tear down the posters even though she knows doing it is wrong?

Keeping the LOST DOG LOST Continued

CHAPTER 3:
Home at Last

6   After I took down all the posters I could find, though, my happiness vanished. I knew someone else loved Barney, and I even knew her name from the poster: Carol Greene

7   It was wrong to keep a lost dog lost, and I realized what I had to do. That night, my Mom said, "Mystery sure seems happy in his new home."

8   "His name is Barney, Mom," I said.

9   "Barney?" she said. "Are you changing his name?"

10   Then I told her the truth. Mom was upset with me at first, but she knew I'd only behaved that way because I loved Barney so much.

11   Mom called the phone number on the poster, and we headed over to Carol Greene's house. The minute we got out of the car, Mrs. Greene burst out of the house, crying "Barney!"

12   Mrs. Greene told us how it happened that Barney got lost. She had been out of town for a month and had put Barney in a kennel, but somehow he escaped. "He couldn't find me," Mrs. Greene said to me, "but I guess he found you."

13   Then Mrs. Greene surprised us. She told us she had to move out of state for a new job, and she wouldn't be able to take Barney with her. She announced, "Jillian, do you think Barney could live with you?" She was blinking back tears, but she was smiling.

14   "I think that would make everyone very happy," Mom said.

15   I grinned and then Barney barked and wagged his tail. Apparently, he agreed.

Close Reader Habits

How do the events in Chapter 3 build on the events in the first two chapters? **Number** several key events from this chapter in the order that they happen.

▶ **Think**

1 This question has two parts. Answer Part A. Then answer Part B.

Part A

How do the ideas in Chapter 3 build on the ideas from Chapter 2 in "Keeping the Lost Dog Lost"?

> Think about how events in a story build on each other. Ask questions like "What caused this?" or "Why did she act that way?"

A In Chapter 2, Jillian finds out that Barney has an owner. Chapter 3 shows why she decides to keep the dog anyway.

B In Chapter 2, Jillian realizes she has to return the dog. Chapter 3 builds on this by telling how she plans to find Barney's owner.

C In Chapter 2, Jillian is trying to find a way to keep Barney. In Chapter 3 she feels guilty about what she's done and looks for the owner.

D In Chapter 2, Jillian is trying to find a way to keep Barney. Chapter 3 shows how those actions lead to sadness.

Part B

Choose **one** detail from Chapter 2 and **one** detail from Chapter 3 that **best** support the answer to Part A.

A "I spotted, tacked to a telephone pole, a poster with a picture of a lost dog on it." (Chapter 2)

B "But there was no question, it was Mystery—or I should say Barney." (Chapter 2)

C "I knew that what I was doing was selfish and wrong, but I couldn't bear to lose … Barney." (Chapter 2)

D "… she knew I'd only behaved that way because I loved Barney so much." (Chapter 3)

E "It was wrong to keep a lost dog lost …" (Chapter 3)

F "She was blinking back tears, but she was smiling." (Chapter 3)

▶ **Talk**

2 Why did Jillian feel guilty after tearing down the posters?

▶ **Write**

3 **Short Response** Tell how Jillian's feelings change between Chapter 2 and Chapter 3. What causes the change? Use the space provided on page 221 to write your answer.

> **HINT** What did Jillian think about before she told her mother the truth?

▶ 📝 **Write** Use the space below to write your answer to the question on page 217.

Keeping the LOST DOG LOST

> **HINT** Why does Jillian tear down the posters even though she knows doing it is wrong?

3 **Short Response** Explain the problem Jillian faces in Chapter 2.

_____

_____

_____

_____

_____

_____

_____

_____

_____

_____

_____

> Don't forget to check your writing.

Write **Use the space below to write your answer to the question on page 219.**

Keeping the LOST DOG LOST Continued

3 **Short Response** Tell how Jillian's feelings change between Chapter 2 and Chapter 3. What causes the change?

> **HINT** What did Jillian think about before she told her mother the truth?

_____

_____

_____

_____

_____

_____

_____

_____

Check Your Writing

☐ Did you read the prompt carefully?

☐ Did you put the prompt in your own words?

☐ Did you use the best evidence from the text to support your ideas?

☐ Are your ideas clearly organized?

☐ Did you write in clear and complete sentences?

☐ Did you check your spelling and punctuation?

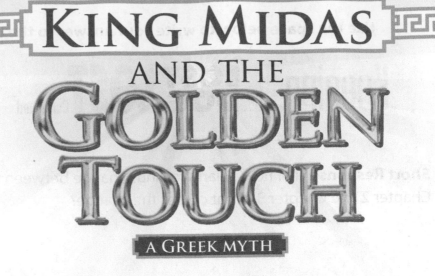

KING MIDAS
AND THE
GOLDEN TOUCH

A GREEK MYTH

WORDS TO KNOW

As you read, look inside, around, and beyond these words to figure out what they mean.

- **ancient**
- **immediately**
- **doubts**
- **wondrous**

CHAPTER 1: THE KING'S WISH

1   Long ago there was a king named Midas. You might think that a king would have to be wise and thoughtful, but unfortunately, Midas was a foolish king.

2   Although he was foolish, King Midas was not mean or unkind. He had a daughter whom he loved more than the moon and stars. And Midas himself was much loved by some of the gods who ruled over the ancient world. In fact, one of the gods told Midas that he would grant the king anything he wished for.

3   Midas thought this over. If he had thought a little longer, he might have made a wiser choice. But, besides being foolish, Midas was also a bit greedy. Surely, it was greed that caused Midas to ask for the power to turn everything he touched to gold.

CHAPTER 2: MIDAS'S GOLDEN TOUCH

4   Unfortunately for Midas, the god granted his wish. King Midas was overjoyed. He touched his chair, and it turned to gold. He touched the walls of the room, and they turned to gold. Then Midas went outside. Every plant, flower, and blade of grass he touched immediately became gold. He went to his orchard and pulled an apple from the tree. Midas's golden touch turned the fruit into a glittering ball of gold.

CHAPTER 3: TOO MUCH OF A GOOD THING

5   Midas returned to his palace. He called out for food and drink, for all this gold-making had made him hungry. His servants brought plates of food to

his table. But every bit of food that Midas touched turned to gold before he could taste it. Even the water in his glass turned to a flowing stream of gold as soon as it touched his lips. Midas was beginning to have some doubts about his wondrous new power. Just then, his beloved daughter came running into the room.

CHAPTER 4: WASHING THE GREED AWAY

6   "Father, father," the young girl cried. "Something terrible has happened in the garden. The soft green grass has turned hard and sharp. And the flowers, father, look at the flowers." She held out two blooms. Once living, they were now cold and hard and golden.

7   Midas reached out to comfort his crying child. As soon as his hand touched her, the girl became a statue of gold, a golden tear frozen on her golden cheek.

8   "What have I done?" cried Midas. He begged the god who had given him this gift to take it away.

9   The god took pity on Midas. He told the king to go to the nearby river to have his greed washed away. Once he did so, all that the foolish king had once made gold returned to what it had been. And his daughter came running to his arms.

Think Use what you learned from reading the myth to respond to the following questions.

1 What do you learn about King Midas in Chapter 1 of the story?

    A He was foolish and greedy, but kind.

    B He seldom thought about his daughter.

    C He had made enemies of the gods.

    D He had special powers.

2 How do the events of Chapter 2 build on those of Chapter 1?

    A Midas asks to be able to turn everything he touches into gold.

    B Midas realizes the power he asked for doesn't make him happy.

    C Midas looks for ways he can use his power to help others.

    D Midas shows his greed by turning everything into gold.

3 Read this sentence from Chapter 3.

> **Midas was beginning to have some doubts about his wondrous new power.**

What has caused Midas to begin questioning the power he was so happy about in Chapter 2?

    A He doesn't feel his power will make him rich enough.

    B He finds that his power means he can't eat or drink.

    C He worries that the power won't last.

    D The god who gave him the power is angry.

4 Look again at this sentence from Chapter 2.

Midas's golden touch turned the fruit into a glittering ball of gold.

What is the meaning of *glittering* in this context?

    A round

    B soft

    C shiny

    D rough

5 This question has two parts. First, answer Part A. Then answer Part B.

Part A

How does Chapter 4 build on what happens in Chapter 3?

    A Chapter 3 shows the king turning everything he can touch into gold, and Chapter 4 tells how his actions make his daughter angry with him.

    B Chapter 3 shows that Midas's power may not be all good, and Chapter 4 proves just how awful the power can be.

    C Chapter 3 describes how Midas realizes his power can be both good and bad, and Chapter 4 shows that he decides to use the power only for good reasons.

    D Chapter 3 describes Midas's foolish actions, and Chapter 4 shows that even what happens to his daughter doesn't change Midas.

Part B

Which **two** details from the story **best** support the answer to Part A?

    A "… all this gold-making had made him hungry." (Chapter 3)

    B "But every bit of food that Midas touched turned to gold before he could taste it." (Chapter 3)

    C "Midas was beginning to have some doubts about his wondrous new power." (Chapter 3)

    D " 'Something terrible has happened in the garden.' " (Chapter 4)

    E "He begged the god who had given him this gift to take it away." (Chapter 4)

    F "The god took pity on Midas." (Chapter 4)

6 Which sentence in Chapter 1 **best** helps you understand the king's sadness in Chapter 4?

    A "Although he was foolish, King Midas was not mean or unkind."

    B "He had a daughter whom he loved more than the moon and stars."

    C "And Midas himself was much loved by some of the gods …"

    D "If he had thought a little longer, he might have made a wiser choice."

▶ 📓✏️ **Write**

How do events in "King Midas and the Golden Touch" build on each other throughout the story? Think about what happens in each chapter. Then answer questions 7 and 8.

7 **Plan Your Response** What important events happen to King Midas in each chapter? Use a chart to organize your thoughts before you write.

8 **Write an Extended Response** How does King Midas change from the beginning to the end of the story? In your response, include the events from the story that lead to each change.

_____

_____

_____

_____

_____

_____

_____

_____

Learning Target

Why do authors organize stories into chapters? How does this help readers?

Lesson 14
What Are Plays Made Of?

Learning Target

Describing how each scene of a drama builds on the one before it will help you understand what you read.

▶ Read   A **drama,** or **play,** is a story that is performed by actors on a stage. Most plays are divided into parts, called **scenes.** The events and actions build from one scene to the next to tell the story.

The pictures below show four scenes from a play about Cinderella. How do the four scenes build on each other?

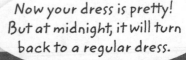

▶ **Think** Look again at the scenes from *Cinderella*. Complete the chart by describing each scene.

Scenes from *Cinderella*	
Scene 1	• Cinderella is dressed in rags and washing the floor.
Scene 2	
Scene 3	
Scene 4	

▶ **Talk** Using the information in your chart, take turns with your partner describing how each scene builds on the one before it.

◎ **Academic Talk**
Use these words to talk about the text.
• **scenes**   • **drama**   • **play**

Danger in Deep Space

by Annika Pedersen

Scene 1: *The deck of a spaceship. A young woman, Commander Lyla, is standing at the control panel, talking to the pilot. A robot-like figure enters and walks to her side.*

Lyla: (*to robot*) Well, Sam, I hope we don't have any trouble getting to Planet Juno. The people there are desperate for our help.

Sam: Yes. We must get the medicine to them as soon as possible.

(*Just then an alarm sounds, and a red light flashes over the control panel.*)

Lyla: (*looking at controls*) There's someone—or something—in the cargo bay! Come on, Sam. We need to make sure that medicine is safe.

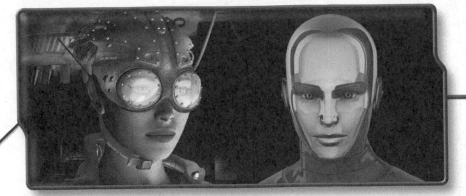

Scene 2: *Lyla and Sam slowly enter the cargo bay of the spaceship.*

Sam: (*to Lyla*) If there's trouble, let's hope our plan works. (*Just then a huge creature enters. It has an octopus-like head and six arms. It wears a white lab coat.*)

Creature: I am Dr. Blurg from the Planet Mord, and I will be taking your precious supplies. But first, I will put you to sleep.

(*Dr. Blurg sprays a green smoke toward Lyla, who falls to the floor. Then he pulls a handful of wires from Sam's back. Sam falls next to Lyla.*)

> **Close Reader Habits**
>
> **Underline** key events in Scene 1 and one in Scene 2.

Explore How does the second scene of *Danger in Deep Space* build on the first scene?

Think

The beginning of a play usually shows where the story takes place. It also introduces the main characters and a problem. The scenes that follow build on that problem.

1 Complete the chart with details from each scene of the play that help you understand the situation on the spaceship.

Details from *Danger in Deep Space*	
Scene 1	
Scene 2	

Talk

2 Think about the text. Talk to your partner about what problems Lyla and Sam will have to solve.

Write

3 **Short Response** How could the events in Scene 2 affect the mission that was described in Scene 1? Use the space provided on page 234 to write your answer.

HINT Why are supplies needed on Planet Juno?

Danger in Deep Space Continued

Scene 3: *Back on the deck of the spaceship. Dr. Blurg is at the spaceship's controls, all six arms working at once.*

Dr. Blurg: My plan is working perfectly! I'll dump Lyla and her helpless robot on some safe planet. Then I will return to my own planet with the medicine. I'll be a hero! (*Sam enters. Then Lyla appears, makes an impossible leap through the air, and lands next to Dr. Blurg.*)

Sam: I think there's been a change of plans, Dr. Blurg.

Dr. Blurg: But this is impossible! (*He looks to Lyla.*) My secret sleeping gas should have put you to sleep for at least 24 Earth hours! (*Dr. Blurg sprays Lyla again with the green gas. She fakes a yawn. Then she jumps ten feet in the air, lands, and shrugs.*)

Dr. Blurg: And you, robot. I cut your power supply! How . . . ?

Sam: Things are not what they seem, Dr. Blurg. (*Sam takes off his "head," which is more like a space helmet.*) You see, you've got things backwards. I'm the human. And Lyla, she's the most amazing "machine" in space.

Dr. Blurg: Why, she's hardly more than a girl! I'll take care of her. (*He goes after Lyla, who grabs Dr. Blurg and lifts him over her head with one hand. Dr. Blurg shouts.*) You tricked me!

Sam: The spies we have on your planet told us that you might try something like this. We were ready for you.

Dr. Blurg: But my poor planet! We won't survive without your special medicine.

Sam: If you're willing to make peace, we will get medicine to your people. Now let's take this ship to your Planet Mord.

(*Lyla sets Dr. Blurg down and gently brushes him off.*)

Close Reader Habits

How do the events in Scene 3 build on Scenes 1 and 2 to solve the problem? **Underline** events that help solve the problem. **Draw a box** around the sentence that describes the solution.

▶ **Think**

1 This question has two parts. Answer Part A. Then answer Part B.

Part A

How do the events in Scene 3 build on the events from Scene 2 in *Danger in Deep Space?*

To see how events in a play build on each other, look for the problem and then the solution.

A Scene 2 shows that Lyla and Sam are afraid of Dr. Blurg, but Scene 3 shows them finding the courage to fight back.

B Scene 2 shows that Lyla and Sam were not prepared for a problem, and Scene 3 shows the result of that mistake.

C Scene 2 describes the plan Lyla and Sam have ready, and Scene 3 shows them putting that plan into action.

D Scene 2 makes it seem that Dr. Blurg has overcome Lyla and Sam, but Scene 3 shows that they actually had tricked him.

Part B

Which **two** details from the play **best** support the answer to Part A?

A *"Lyla and Sam slowly enter the cargo bay of the spaceship."* (Scene 2)

B *"'If there's trouble, let's hope our plan works.'"* (Scene 2)

C *"Dr. Blurg sprays a green smoke toward Lyla, who falls to the floor."* (Scene 2)

D *"'Then I will return to my own planet with the medicine.'"* (Scene 3)

E *"'The spies we have on your planet told us that you might try something like this.'"* (Scene 3)

F *"'If you're willing to make peace, we will get medicine to your people.'"* (Scene 3)

▶ **Talk**

2 Talk to your partner about what surprised you in Scene 3. What details in earlier scenes caused you to feel that way?

▶ **Write**

3 **Short Response** How do Lyla and Sam trick Dr. Blurg? Show how details in Scene 2 lead to Dr. Blurg being fooled. Use the space provided on page 235 to write your answer.

HINT What does Dr. Blurg say in Scene 3 after Sam and Lyla enter the room?

📝 **Write** Use the space below to write your answer to the question on page 231.

Danger in Deep Space

3 **Short Response** How could the events in Scene 2 affect the mission that was described in Scene 1?

> **HINT** Why are supplies needed on Planet Juno?

_____

_____

_____

_____

_____

_____

> Don't forget to check your writing.

Write Use the space below to write your answer to the question on page 233.

Danger in DeepSpace Continued

3 **Short Response** How do Lyla and Sam trick Dr. Blurg? Show how details in Scene 2 lead to Dr. Blurg being fooled.

> **HINT** What does Dr. Blurg say in Scene 3 after Sam and Lyla enter the room?

_____

_____

_____

_____

_____

_____

_____

_____

_____

Check Your Writing

☐ Did you read the prompt carefully?

☐ Did you put the prompt in your own words?

☐ Did you use the best evidence from the text to support your ideas?

☐ Are your ideas clearly organized?

☐ Did you write in clear and complete sentences?

☐ Did you check your spelling and punctuation?

▶ Read

Genre: Drama

from HOW THE ANIMALS GOT THEIR
BEAUTIFUL COATS

a play based on a Zulu folktale, retold by Pat Betteley

WORDS TO KNOW

As you read, look inside, around, and beyond these words to figure out what they mean.

- **groomed**
- **glossy**
- **loped**
- **slunk**

Characters: Storyteller, Tortoise, Leopard, Zebra, and Hyena

ACT 1, SCENE 1

Storyteller: Sakubona, visitors. Welcome to our village. Sit down by the fire, and I will tell you a story. You all know that Zulus are very careful about their looks. Even the animals in this land are well groomed. But this was not always so. In the beginning, all animals in Africa were a dull brown color. Hyena was not only drab but also mean. He liked to play tricks on smaller animals. One day he knotted a piece of vine around one of Tortoise's feet and hung him from a high branch. Then Hyena ran away, laughing.

Tortoise: Help, someone! Please, help me!

Leopard: Calm down, little one. I'll help you.

Tortoise: Mr. Leopard, please hurry. I don't want to die!

Storyteller: Leopard quickly lowered Tortoise and untied him.

Tortoise: Thank you, friend Leopard. You could have made a meal of me, but instead you saved my life. Please let me do something for you in return.

Leopard: (*chuckling*) What can a little tortoise like you do for a big leopard like me?

Tortoise: I can make you beautiful.

Leopard: (*smiling*) Very well. I accept your offer.

ACT 1, SCENE 2

Storyteller: Tortoise mixed a silver-yellow color from the petals of flowers and painted Leopard's coat.

Zebra: My, my, that is the most handsome coat in the forest. Where did you get it?

Leopard: My friend, Mr. Tortoise, made it for me.

Zebra: I must find him. Maybe he'll make one for me as well.

Storyteller: Zebra hurried down the path until he came upon Tortoise.

Zebra: Oh, Mr. Tortoise, Mr. Leopard's coat is so handsome. Please paint my coat, too.

Storyteller: Tortoise painted black and white stripes all over Zebra's coat. He finished up by painting Zebra's dainty hoofs a glossy black.

Zebra: Thank you, Tortoise. These stripes will be perfect for hiding in the tall grass.

Act 1, Scene 3

Storyteller: Zebra went along down the path. Soon he met Hyena.

Hyena: (*sneering*) Hey, where'd you get that coat?

Zebra: From my friend, Mr. Tortoise. Do you like it?

Hyena: I'd never wear it, but it fits you, I suppose. Where's Tortoise?

Storyteller: Zebra pointed down the path, and Hyena loped off to find Tortoise.

Hyena: (*in a threatening voice*) I want a beautiful coat, too. Give me one or I'll hang you from the tree again.

Tortoise: (*looking him over carefully*) H-m-m-m. I think I see just what will be best for your size and shape.

Storyteller: So Tortoise mixed many colors together in one pot and smeared them all over Hyena's coat. When Hyena slunk away, it was a good thing he could not see himself, for he was all blotched, with a dirty white, gloomy gray, and dull brown coat. And he is still that way today —the messiest-looking animal in Africa—labeled clearly as a mean and unpleasant character!

Think Use what you learned from reading the play to respond to the following questions.

1 What does the storyteller say in Scene 1 that hints at what the play will be about?

    A that the animals were once all a dull brown color

    B that the leopard is kind to the tortoise

    C that the tortoise will make the leopard beautiful

    D that the hyena was both drab and mean

2 How do the events of Scene 2 build on the events of Scene 1?

    A The tortoise promises to make the leopard beautiful in Scene 1, and he keeps his promise in Scene 2.

    B The hyena plays a trick on the tortoise in Scene 1, and the tortoise makes plans to get even in Scene 2.

    C The leopard saves the tortoise in Scene 1, and the tortoise saves the zebra in Scene 2.

    D The tortoise makes the leopard beautiful in Scene 1, and the zebra becomes jealous of the leopard in Scene 2.

3 Look again at the sentence from the Storyteller in Scene 3.

> **. . . he was all blotched, with a dirty white, gloomy gray, and dull brown coat.**

What is the meaning of *blotched* in this context?

    A coated in mud

    B tangled in the weeds

    C covered with patches of color

    D wet and slimy

4 This question has two parts. First, answer Part A. Then answer Part B.

Part A

How do the events in Scene 3 build on the events from Scene 1 of *How the Animals Got Their Beautiful Coats?*

A Scene 1 describes the beauty of the animals in Africa, and Scene 3 shows how they got that way.

B Scene 1 shows how mean the hyena is to the tortoise, and Scene 3 shows how the tortoise makes sure the hyena's appearance matches his actions.

C Scene 1 describes the kindness of the leopard, and Scene 3 shows how the tortoise repays that kindness.

D Scene 1 shows how cruel the hyena is, and Scene 3 shows the hyena learning to be kinder to others.

Part B

Which **two** details from the play **best** support the answer to Part A?

A "'Even the animals in this land are well groomed.'" (Scene 1)

B "'In the beginning, all animals In Africa were a dull brown color.'" (Scene 1)

C "'One day he knotted a piece of vine around one of Tortoise's feet and hung him from a high branch.'" (Scene 1)

D "'I want a beautiful coat, too. Give me one or I'll hang you from the tree again.'" (Scene 3)

E "'When Hyena slunk away, it was a good thing he could not see himself. ...'" (Scene 3)

F "'And he is still that way today … labeled clearly as a mean and unpleasant character!'" (Scene 3)

Write

How do the events in the play build on each other to explain something in nature? Reread the play and underline important events. Then answer questions 5 and 6.

5 **Plan Your Response** How do the events in each scene build on the scene before to show why the hyena is ugly? Use a chart to organize your thoughts before you write.

6 **Write an Extended Response** How do the events of the play build on each other to show why the hyena is ugly and other animals are not? Use details from different scenes in your answer.

_____

_____

_____

_____

_____

_____

_____

_____

_____

_____

_____

_____

_____

_____

_____

_____

_____

 Learning Target

Explain how the events in each scene of the plays helped you
understand what you read. Use an example in your answer.

_____

_____

_____

_____

_____

Lesson 15
What Are Poems Made Of?

Learning Target When you understand the parts of a poem, you can see how each line and stanza builds on what came before it.

▶ **Read** Many poems tell stories. Like stories, they have a **speaker** who talks to the reader. They also have a beginning, a middle, and an end. Poems are made up of lines that are called **verses.** A group of verses is called a **stanza.** The stanzas in a poem work together to tell a story. Each stanza tells an important part of the poem's story, and the stanzas build on each other to present ideas and tell a story.

Read the poem below. Tell who the speaker is. Then think about the idea in each stanza. How does the second stanza build on the first stanza?

A Penguin's Life

1   I'm a bird with little wings,
    but they don't make me fly.
    The air above is not for me.
    The ocean is my sky.

2   In icy seas I swoop and soar,
    a swimmer fast and bold.
    You'd swim fast, if you were me—
    the water sure is cold!

▶ **Think** You've learned what verses and stanzas are and how stanzas make meaning in a poem. How do the stanzas in "A Penguin's Life" work together to present an idea about penguins? Complete the chart to show how the stanzas work together and what idea they develop.

Idea of Stanza 1	Penguins cannot fly.
Idea of Stanza 2	
Idea of Whole Poem	

▶ **Talk** Reread the last two lines of the poem. How do these lines change how the poem makes you feel?

⊙ **Academic Talk**
Use these words to talk about the text.
- **stanza**
- **verses**
- **speaker**

▶ **Read**

LITTLE PUPPY

FROM THE NAVAJO

1   Little puppy with the black spots,
    Come and herd the flock with me.
    We will climb the red rocks
    And from the top we'll see
    The tall cliffs, the straight cliffs,
    Where the eagles live.

2   We'll see the dark rocks,
    The smooth rocks,
    That hold the rain to give us
    Water, when we eat our bread and meat,
    When the sun is high.

Close Reader Habits

Circle things in each stanza the speaker in the poem tells about and sees.

Explore   How do the two stanzas of "Little Puppy" work together to build meaning?

▶ **Think**

As you read, summarize each stanza to help you understand the poem.

1 Finish the chart to figure out what this Navajo poem is saying about nature.

Idea of Stanza 1	The speaker and dog will climb the red rocks. They will see tall, straight cliffs where eagles live.
Idea of Stanza 2	
Idea of Whole Poem	

▶ **Talk**

2 What do the "dark rocks" make the speaker think about?

▶ **Write**

3 **Short Response** How are the ideas in the first stanza and the second stanza connected? How does that help you understand what the poem is about? Write your answer in the space provided on page 248.

HINT How do the rocks help the speaker and the dog?

Little by Little

Anonymous

1   "Little by little," an acorn said,
    As it slowly sank in its mossy bed,
    "I am improving every day,
    Hidden deep in the earth away."

2   Little by little, each day it grew;
    Little by little, it sipped the dew;
    Downward it sent out a thread-like root;
    Up in the air sprung a tiny shoot.

3   Day after day, and year after year,
    Little by little the leaves appear;
    And the slender branches spread far and wide,
    Till the mighty oak is the forest's pride.

Close Reader Habits

What is the poem about?
Underline what is
speaking in the first
stanza. **Circle** what
it becomes in the
last stanza.

▶ **Think**

1 What key idea is presented in the first stanza?

  A The acorn is improving every day.

  B The acorn knows it is very small.

  C The acorn knows it has to stay hidden.

  D The acorn believes it is slowly disappearing.

As you read, stop and summarize what is happening in each stanza. This will help you understand the story the poem is telling.

2 How does the second stanza build on the first one?

  A It shows that the acorn remains small.

  B It shows how the acorn is improving.

  C It describes the mossy bed where it disappeared.

  D It explains why the acorn needed to be hidden.

3 Describe how the acorn starts to change in the second stanza. Use examples from the poem in your answer.

_____

_____

_____

▶ **Talk**

4 Which words are repeated in every stanza? What do these words add to the meaning of the poem?

▶ **Write**

5 **Short Response** What story does this poem tell the reader? Use details from each stanza in your answer. Write your answer in the space provided on page 249.

HINT How long does it take the acorn to grow into an oak?

Write Use the space below to write your answer to the question on page 245.

LITTLE PUPPY

3 **Short Response** How are the ideas in the first stanza and the second stanza connected? How does that help you understand what the poem is about?

> **HINT** How do the rocks help the speaker and the dog?

_____

_____

_____

_____

_____

_____

_____

_____

_____

> Don't forget to check your writing.

Write **Use the space below to write your answer to the question on page 247.**

Little by Little

5 **Short Response** What story does this poem tell the reader? Use details from each stanza in your answer.

> **HINT** How long does it take the acorn to grow into an oak?

Check Your Writing

☐ Did you read the prompt carefully?

☐ Did you put the prompt in your own words?

☐ Did you use the best evidence from the text to support your ideas?

☐ Are your ideas clearly organized?

☐ Did you write in clear and complete sentences?

☐ Did you check your spelling and punctuation?

The Truth About the Dragon's Tooth

by John Hansen

WORDS TO KNOW

As you read, look inside, around, and beyond these words to figure out what they mean.

- **gloom**
- **feast**

1   The king called me to his throne
and said, "That dragon must be slayed!"
I bowed and played the brave, strong knight,
but in truth . . . I was afraid.

2   As I dressed in shining armor
and sharpened sword and lance,
a voice inside me whispered,
"You haven't got a chance!"

3   I climbed upon my faithful horse
and rode off into the gloom.
I hoped I'd see my home again
on the other side of doom.

4   I rode into the mountains
and faced the dangerous beast.
The dragon licked its lips and said,
"A man, a horse—a feast."

5   I raised my lance to charge it,
thinking, What else can I do?
Then the trees behind it crashed and fell
as a giant marched in view!

6   The earth beneath began to shake,
his huge figure blocked the sun.
Then the giant shouted happily,
"Why, I've found you, little one!"

7   As he bent down to catch the dragon,
I began to understand:
The dragon was the giant's pet,
scooped up in one huge hand.

8   The giant turned to me and said,
"Your people will want proof
that you bravely faced my dragon,
so I'll give you this baby tooth."

9   He reached into the dragon's mouth
and wiggled out a monster fang,
then tossed it through the air at me.
It hit my shield—clang!

10   The people cheered when I returned
and waved the dragon's sword-like tooth.
But I found I was afraid again—
Afraid to tell the truth!

▶ **Think** Use what you learned from reading the selection to respond to these questions.

1 Reread the first stanza of the poem.

> **The king called me to his throne**
> **and said, "That dragon must be slayed!"**
> **I bowed and played the brave, strong knight,**
> **but in truth . . . I was afraid.**

How do stanzas 2 and 3 build on this opening?

  A They show the knight deciding to be brave.

  B They show that the knight doesn't think he'll survive.

  C They show that the knight plans to ride home instead.

  D They show others telling the knight he is doomed.

2 Stanzas 4–10 each add something new to the story. Write the correct stanza number on each line to show when the event occurs and how the story builds.

_____ The giant realizes the knight needs proof.

_____ A giant appears.

_____ The giant sees the dragon.

_____ The giant tosses the knight a dragon tooth.

_____ The knight meets the dragon.

_____ The knight is afraid to tell what happened.

_____ The knight realizes the dragon is a pet.

3 Stanza 6 begins, "The earth beneath began to shake." What happens in stanza 5 that explains why the earth is shaking?

  A The dragon attacks the knight and his horse.

  B The knight charges the dragon with his lance.

  C A giant marches toward the knight and dragon.

  D Some trees are cut down in the forest nearby.

4 This question has two parts. First, answer Part A. Then answer Part B.

Part A
How do stanzas 6 and 7 change how the knight feels in stanza 5?

  A In stanza 5, the knight is only worried about the dragon. In stanzas 6 and 7, he runs from both the dragon and the giant.

  B In stanza 5, the knight is trying to figure out what else he can do. In stanzas 6 and 7, he comes up with a new plan.

  C In stanza 5, the knight is afraid of the dragon and giant. In stanzas 6 and 7, he realizes the dragon is the giant's pet.

  D In stanza 5, the knight is getting ready to charge the dragon. In stanzas 6 and 7, he realizes the giant will slay the dragon.

Part B
Underline **one** detail in stanza 6 and **one** detail in stanza 7 that support your answer in Part A.

  6 **The earth beneath began to shake,
  his huge figure blocked the sun.
  Then the giant shouted happily,
  "Why, I've found you, little one!"**

  7 **As he bent down to catch the dragon,
  I began to understand:
  The dragon was the giant's pet,
  scooped up in one huge hand.**

5 What does the giant do in stanza 9?

    A He makes the trees crash and fall to the ground.

    B He blocks out the sun as he walks along.

    C He throws the "monster fang" to the knight.

    D He makes the earth shake as he marches.

6 In stanza 10, why is the knight afraid again?

    A He is afraid he might be sent to fight another dragon.

    B He worries that the people won't like the real story of what happened.

    C He is afraid that the giant will appear and tell the truth.

    D He is afraid the tooth isn't enough proof that he has slain the dragon.

7 Reread the second stanza.

> **As I dressed in shining armor**
> **and sharpened sword and lance,**
> **a voice inside me whispered,**
> **"You haven't got a chance!"**

Which three words help you understand that a "lance" is a type of weapon?

    A dressed, armor, sword

    B armor, sharpened, sword

    C shining, armor, chance

    D dressed, shining, chance

Write

8 **Short Response** At the beginning of the poem, you think you will be reading about a knight fighting a dragon. How do stanzas 6 through 9 change the story?

_____

_____

_____

_____

_____

_____

_____

Learning Target

You've seen how stanzas of a poem build on each other to explore an idea or tell a story. Explain how you can use this understanding to get the most out of reading a poem.

Lesson 16
Point of View

Learning Target

As you read, determine if your point of view of a story is the same as or different from that of the narrator and characters.

▶ **Read** **Characters** are the people or animals in a story. Each character has a **point of view,** or feeling, about what is happening in the story. The **narrator** tells the story from the outside and describes events and actions in the story. The narrator also has a point of view.

As you are reading the story, you will have your own point of view. **Comparing** and **contrasting** your point of view from the characters' and narrator's points of view will help you better understand text. As you read, ask yourself questions to help you figure out your point of view, such as *Who is telling the story? What do the characters think? What do I think?*

Look at the family in the cartoon below. Do all these people feel the same way about green bean ice cream? Is Dad's point of view different from the childrens'?

It's my new delicious recipe for green bean ice cream!

▶ **Think** Using what you see in the cartoon, complete the first row by describing how the girl, the dad, and the boy feel about green bean ice cream. In the second row, describe each character's point of view.

Points of View

The Girl's Actions	The Boy's Actions	The Dad's Actions
• is smiling • seems to be enjoying the ice cream		
The Girl's Point of View thinks the ice cream is great	**The Boy's Point of View**	**The Dad's Point of View**

▶ **Talk** Take turns with your partner, describing each character's point of view. What is your point of view about green bean ice cream? Is your point of view the same as or different from the characters'?

⊙ **Academic Talk**
Use these words and phrase to talk about the text.
- **narrator**
- **characters**
- **point of view**
- **comparing**
- **contrasting**

> **Read**

Genre: Modern Fantasy

Night-Flying Friends

by Sean Vincent

1   Last week, I was perched peacefully on my favorite branch in a tall oak tree, watching everything with my big owl eyes. Suddenly I became aware of a strange creature flying crazily through the air nearby, swooping this way and that. What was his problem?

2   Then the creature flew toward my branch, landed next to me, and hung upside-down by his feet. That's when I saw that he was a young brown bat. Before I could say anything, he started chattering. He talked a mile a minute about all the bugs he'd just eaten and where he'd been flying. Then he said, "By the way, my name's Max! Good talking with you." A moment later, he let go of the branch and flapped off. Had I said a word?

3   "My name is Alec," I hooted after him. Not that I cared if he knew.

4   The next night, though, I found myself hoping Max would come back. True, his strange ways troubled me. He liked to eat mosquitoes and flies, after all. But we are both creatures of the night, and we can both fly. And it would be good to have someone to talk with. When I finally saw him, I swooped through the air toward him. "Hey, Max," I said, "Want to stop by my branch after dinner?"

5   "Sounds good!" he said. Then we flew through the night together, our first flight as friends.

> **Close Reader Habits**
>
> **Underline** details that show Max's and Alec's points of view.

Explore How is your point of view about the characters in "Night-Flying Friends" different from each character's view of each other?

Think

> A character's point of view can change during a story. Watch for details that show this might be happening.

1 What are Alec's and Max's points of view toward each other? Using evidence from the passage, complete the chart.

Points of View	
Alec's Actions	**Max's Actions**
Alec's Point of View	**Max's Point of View**

Talk

2 Talk to your partner about how Max's and Alec's points of view are the same and different. Do they change at the end of the story? Then talk about your point of view about each character.

Write

3 **Short Response** What is your point of view about each of the characters? Is your point of view the same as or different from those of Max and Alec? Support your answer with details from the text. Use the space provided on page 262 to write your answer.

> **HINT** What do Alec and Max realize about each other? What do you think?

The Stable Boy and the Prince

by John Martinsson

1   Sam offered the apple he'd found to the horse, Shadowfax. He stroked the horse's huge head and wished for a moment that Shadowfax could talk. Six months had passed since Sam had been taken from his village to work at the king's stables, and it had been a very lonely time for him.

2   Just then, the prince came riding past. Prince Oliver was about the only other boy his age that Sam ever saw. As the prince passed, Sam knelt and bowed his head. But as he looked down, he saw a huge snake coiling up in the prince's path. The prince's horse reared back and then bolted.

3   With hardly a thought, Sam jumped on Shadowfax and raced after Prince Oliver, who was struggling to stay in the saddle. But no horse was faster than Shadowfax. Sam reached the prince and grabbed his horse's reins.

4   The prince thanked Sam for his efforts. As they rode back to the castle, the prince spoke pleasantly with Sam. When they reached the stables, Sam said, "I hope we can talk again. It's so good to speak with someone my own age."

5   The prince fell silent. Then he said, "Remember your place. I am a prince, and you are just a stable boy."

6   Sam bowed and returned to the barn. "I'll never have a friend here," he whispered. Shadowfax walked over and rubbed his face against him. Sam hugged the horse. "What am I saying, my friend?" he said. "I've got you."

Close Reader Habits

What does the prince think of the stable boy? **Underline** details that show his point of view.

▶ **Think**

1 What is Sam's point of view about working at the king's stables?

  A He is excited because he can ride Shadowfax.

  B He is lonely because he has no friends.

  C He feels lucky to have such an important job.

  D He is bored because he has only a horse to talk with.

> How characters act and what they think and say can be clues to their points of view.

2 This question has two parts. Answer Part A. Then answer Part B.

Part A
What is Prince Oliver's point of view toward Sam?

  A He would like to be friends with the boy who rescued him.

  B He thinks Sam should not have spoken to him.

  C He likes Sam, but feels he can't be friends with a stable boy.

  D He feels sad that he is too old to be friends with Sam.

Part B
Underline phrases or sentences in both paragraphs that support your answer to Part A.

   The prince thanked Sam for his efforts. As they rode back to the castle, the prince spoke pleasantly with Sam. When they reached the stables, Sam said, "I hope we can talk again. It's so good to speak with someone my own age."

   The prince fell silent. Then he said, "Remember your place. I am a prince, and you are just a stable boy."

▶ **Talk**

3 Why was Sam so eager to talk with the prince again?

▶ **Write**

4 **Short Response** What is your own point of view toward the prince? Explain why you feel that way, using details from the story. Use the space provided on page 263 to write your answer.

> **HINT** Look for details about what the prince says and does.

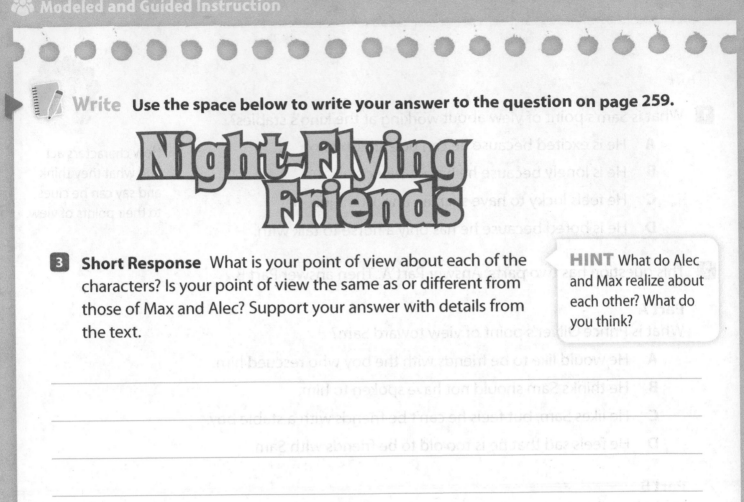

📝 **Write** **Use the space below to write your answer to the question on page 259.**

Night-Flying Friends

3 **Short Response** What is your point of view about each of the characters? Is your point of view the same as or different from those of Max and Alec? Support your answer with details from the text.

> **HINT** What do Alec and Max realize about each other? What do you think?

_____

_____

_____

_____

_____

_____

_____

> Don't forget to check your writing.

Write Use the space below to write your answer to the question on page 261.

The Stable Boy
and the Prince

4 **Short Response** What is your own point of view toward the prince? Explain why you feel that way, using details from the story.

> **HINT** Look for details about what the prince says and does.

_____

_____

_____

_____

_____

_____

_____

Check Your Writing

☐ Did you read the prompt carefully?

☐ Did you put the prompt in your own words?

☐ Did you use the best evidence from the text to support your ideas?

☐ Are your ideas clearly organized?

☐ Did you write in clear and complete sentences?

☐ Did you check your spelling and punctuation?

▶ **Read**

Genre: Realistic Fiction

Basketball Ballet

by Lori Anastasia, *Highlights*

WORDS TO KNOW
As you read, look inside, around, and beyond these words to figure out what they mean.

- **wrestling**
- **ballet**

1   "There's a new kid in our class," I told my friend Aidan as we hung up our coats at the back of the classroom.

2   "How do you know?" Aidan asked.

3   "He moved in next door to me," I said, sitting down at my desk. "Mom and I brought muffins over yesterday."

4   "Class, please welcome Brady Walker," Ms. Simpson said, while my new neighbor stood beside her.

5   "Brady, tell the class something about yourself," Ms. Simpson said.

6   "I'm from California," said Brady. "I have a dog that eats all my stuff."

7   Everyone giggled. His dog sounds just like mine, I thought.

8   "I like baseball and basketball, and I take dance class."

9   "Dance class," Aidan yelled. "That's for girls!"

10   The whole class laughed, and Brady's face turned bright red.

11   "That's enough," Ms. Simpson said.

12   At lunch, Brady walked over to an empty seat at my table.

13   "Hi, Emilio," Brady said to me. "Thanks again for those awesome muffins. Can I sit here?"

14   I was about to say yes, but Jordan put his foot on the chair. "This seat is taken," he said. "Sit with the girls."

15   Aidan laughed.

16   Brady walked away and sat by himself.

17   That afternoon, Brady sat by himself on the bus. I felt bad for him, so I thought about sitting with him, but I didn't want to get picked on.

18   I remembered how everyone teased me when I knit a scarf for Ms. Simpson. I didn't like being teased, so I gave up knitting. But what would have happened if I'd stood up for myself?

19   When I got home, I made a peanut butter and pickle sandwich. My dog, Gus, was barking by the living-room window. I walked over to see why, and Brady was shooting baskets in his driveway. He was really good!

20   I went back into the kitchen to get my sandwich, but it was gone. Gus stood by the counter with a tiny pickle hanging from his mouth.

21   The next day, we had gym with Coach Kelley.

22   "Today we're playing basketball," Coach Kelley announced. "Emilio and Natalie will be captains. Emilio, you pick first."

23   I looked around the room and noticed Brady, and it felt like giant robots were wrestling inside my stomach. I didn't want to get laughed at, but I knew what I had to do.

24   "I choose Brady," I said.

25   "What?" Aidan yelled. "He can't play basketball."

26   A giant smile spread across Brady's face, and he ran up and stood beside me.

27   "Why did you pick me?" he asked.

28   "I wasn't a good friend yesterday," I said. "Plus, I know you're good at basketball."

29   We started playing, and Brady made ten baskets and stole the ball from Aidan four times.

30   "Wow," Aidan said to Brady, "where did you learn those moves?"

31   Brady smiled. "Ballet class."

32   Aidan looked at me, then at Brady. "Could you teach me?"

33   Brady, Aidan, and I started hanging out together all the time after that. Usually, we were in Brady's driveway, practicing our basketball ballet.

Use what you learned from reading the selection to respond to these questions.

▶ Think

1. Describe each character's point of view toward Brady from paragraph 1 to paragraph 16 of the story. In the third column, write details from the story that support your choice.

Character	Point of View Toward Brady	Details
Emilio		
Aidan		
Jordan		

2. Why doesn't Emilio sit with Brady on the bus after school?

   A He always sits with Aidan on the bus.

   B He feels bad for Brady and doesn't want to bother him.

   C Emilio doesn't want to get picked on.

   D He thinks Brady should sit with a girl.

3. Why is it hard for Emilio to choose Brady for his basketball team?

   A He fears that Aidan and others will laugh at him for choosing Brady.

   B He has an upset stomach and doesn't want anyone else to know.

   C He is the only one who knows that Brady is good at basketball.

   D He worries that Brady might want to become friends with him.

4 This question has two parts. First, answer Part A. Then answer Part B.

Part A
What changes Emilio's point of view about how he should treat Brady?

    A The class behaves badly when Brady is introduced.

    B Emilio remembers once being teased himself.

    C Aidan realizes Brady is good at basketball.

    D The coach chooses Emilio to be team captain.

Part B
Which detail from the story **best** supports your answer to Part A?

    A "The whole class laughed, and Brady's face turned bright red."

    B "I didn't want to get laughed at, but I knew what I had to do."

    C "I didn't like being teased, so I gave up knitting."

    D "'I wasn't a good friend yesterday,' I said."

5 Use the dictionary entry to help you answer the question that follows.

> **basket**
>
> **1.** container made of sticks or twigs: *We put the apples in a basket.*
>
> **2.** amount that a basket can hold: *That is a basket of food.*
>
> **3.** basketball hoop: *The court had two baskets.*
>
> **4.** score made in basketball: *Babs made a basket for the team.*

Which meaning matches how *baskets* is used in this sentence from "Basketball Ballet"?

    Brady made ten baskets and stole the ball from Aidan four times.

    A meaning 1

    B meaning 2

    C meaning 3

    D meaning 4

6 This question has two parts. First, answer Part A. Then answer Part B.

Part A
How does Aidan's point of view of Brady change by the end of the story?

   A He thinks Brady is strange to enjoy ballet.

   B He admires Brady and becomes his friend.

   C He worries that Brady will start dancing.

   D He thinks that Brady won't teach him.

Part B
Underline details from the story that support your answer in Part A.

- " 'Sit with the girls.' Aidan laughed."

- " 'What?' Aidan yelled. 'He can't play basketball.' "

- " 'Wow,' Aidan said to Brady, 'where did you learn those moves?' "

- "Aidan looked at me, then at Brady. 'Could you teach me?' "

- " 'Dance class,' Aidan yelled. 'That's for girls!' "

7 Why does Emilio get to choose players for a basketball team?

   A The team is playing with his ball.

   B Coach Kelley named him team captain.

   C He was the first student in the gym.

   D He asked the coach to let him choose them.

▶ Write

8 **Short Response** What is your own point of view of Brady? Is it more like Emilio's or more like Aidan's? Use details from the story to support your answer.

_____

_____

_____

_____

_____

_____

 Learning Target

You've seen that your own point of view and those of the characters in the story may not be the same. Explain why determining point of view will help you understand the stories you read.

○○○○○○○○○○○○○○○○○○○○○○○○

_____

_____

_____

_____

_____

▶ **Read**

Read the poem. Then answer the questions that follow.

Squirrel

by Mary Ann Hoberman, *A Little Book of Little Beasts*

1   Grey squirrel
           Small beast
      Storing up a winter's feast,
      Hides a hundred nuts at least.

5   Nook and cranny stocked with seed
      Tucked away for winter's need.
      Acorns stuck in hole and crack.
      Will he ever get them back?

      When the snow is piled up high
10   And the year is at December,
      Can he really still remember
      Where he hid them in September?

      I have watched him from my window
      And he always seems to know
15   Where the food he hid is waiting
      Buried deep beneath the snow.

      And I wonder
           (Do you wonder?)
      How he knows where he must go.

Think

1 This question has two parts. First, answer Part A. Then answer Part B.

Part A

How does the poet use the word "feast" in line 3 of the poem?

    A to describe a large amount of food

    B to describe a special kind of nut

    C to describe how the nuts are safely stored

    D to describe where the nuts are stored

Part B

Which phrase from the poem **best** supports the answer to Part A?

    A "Small beast"

    B "Storing up"

    C "a hundred nuts"

    D "Nook and cranny"

2 Read these lines from the poem.

    Nook and cranny stocked with seed
    Tucked away for winter's need.

Why does the poet use the words "Tucked away"?

    A to show that the seeds are warm in the nooks and crannies

    B to show that the seeds will fall off the tree into the winter snow

    C to show that the seeds are safely put away, to eat in the winter

    D to show that the seeds will grow in the nooks and crannies

3 Which **best** describes the speaker's point of view about the squirrel?

    A She thinks the squirrel is clever.

    B She thinks the squirrel is annoying.

    C She thinks the squirrel is silly.

    D She thinks the squirrel is selfish.

4 In each empty box in the chart, write the sentence from the box below that **best** describes what happens in three of the poem's stanzas. Not all of the sentences will be used.

Stanza	Sentence that Describes the Stanza
Stanza 1	
Stanza 3	
Stanza 4	

The speaker wonders if the squirrel will find the acorns later.

The squirrel hides food for winter.

The snow begins to fall and starts to cover the squirrel's food.

The speaker watches the squirrel find his food.

5 How does stanza 4 answer the questions the speaker asks in stanzas 2 and 3? Use details in the poem in your answer.

_____

_____

_____

_____

Read

Read the play. Then answer the questions that follow.

Campfire Songs

by Bernie Paw

Characters

Bear
Raccoon
Bobcat

Act I, Scene 1

(**Bear**, **Raccoon**, *and* **Bobcat** *are walking through the forest looking for something to do.*)

Bear: Well, now that we've all had our dinner, what are we going to do for fun? (*He looks bored, walking slowly with head down.*)

Raccoon: I've had all the nuts I need for a week. What else is there to do around here? (*He kicks a stone and sends it flying.*)

Bobcat: I'm full of meat! It sure is a boring night in the forest.

Raccoon: Hey, what's happening over there in the clearing? (*He looks curious, his whiskers shaking.*) Ah, some humans. They're sitting around a fire. It might be fun to watch them and see what they do. Humans can do some strange things!

Bobcat: (*shaking her head and smiling*) What are they eating? (*She looks through some bushes.*) What kind of food is that? (*She laughs.*)

Act I, Scene 2

(The campsite is growing darker except for a campfire that is burning brightly like a candle. The animals are hidden behind some large bushes, watching with interest.)

Bear: (*staring through bushes, scratching his head*) Well, look at that, what are those weird puffy little white squares the boy is putting on a stick into the fire? Why do you suppose they would do that?

Raccoon: I don't know. Why are they using little odd-shaped sticks with five pointy ends to eat their food? Why don't they just use their paws like us? (*He makes a disgusted face at the people.*)

Bear: Well, if that don't beat all! The man is putting his fresh fish over the fire on some kind of a flat rock. Why do you suppose they need to burn perfectly fresh fish on a fire? (*He seems confused, shaking his head side to side.*)

Bobcat: (*rolls her eyes*) Look at the meat, it's on top of the fire and they're burning that, too! (*She laughs loudly, rolling on the ground holding her sides.*)

Act I, Scene 3

(The animals continue to watch the humans and then see another odd thing in the camp.)

Bear: (*lays down on his belly and pushes more bushes out of his way*) Look, look there! What's that funny box the woman is holding in her hands with strings? Can you hear those sounds she is making when she touches it?

*(The campers start to sing along with the guitar music. At first, **Bear**, **Bobcat**, and **Raccoon** look startled. Their eyes are opened wide, big as saucers. They continue to listen to the music and singing. As they listen, they begin to smile.)*

Raccoon: Hmm. This is starting to sound kind of nice. Almost as pretty as Owl's hoot and Wolf's howl.

(The animals lean on each other, eyes closed, and begin to slowly sway back and forth to the music. All three begin to yawn.)

Bobcat: *(sleepily)* Well, humans sure are strange, but they can make the sweetest sounds.

Bear: *(almost asleep, but still swaying to the music)* Hm. Hmm.

Raccoon: And here we thought there would be nothing interesting to do tonight.

*(One by one, **Bear, Bobcat,** and **Raccoon** curl up next to each other and fall asleep to the music.)*

▶ Think

6 Read this line from Scene 2.

Bear: Well, if that don't beat all!

What does this line tell about Bear?

    A He is surprised.

    B He wants to fight.

    C He hears a tapping sound.

    D He suddenly feels very tired.

7 Use the dictionary entry to answer the question.

sway (swā) *v.* **1.** to try to get others to see things a certain way **2.** to move slowly from side to side **3.** to keep changing one's opinion **4.** to rule or control something or someone

Which meaning matches how "sway" is used in this sentence?

The animals lean on each other, eyes closed, and begin to slowly sway back and forth to the music.

    A meaning 1

    B meaning 2

    C meaning 3

    D meaning 4

8 Read these lines from Scene 2 of the play.

Bobcat: (*rolls her eyes*) Look at the meat, it's on top of the fire and they're burning that, too! (*She laughs loudly, rolling on the ground holding her sides.*)

What does *"rolls her eyes"* show about Bobcat in these lines?

    A Bobcat is unhappy that the meat is burning.

    B Bobcat is curious to know why the humans are ruining their dinner.

    C Bobcat thinks the humans are doing something dangerous.

    D Bobcat thinks that burning meat is strange and funny.

9 In Scene 1, the animals think it will be fun to watch the humans because "humans can do some strange things." In Scene 2, what do the animals discover about humans that they think is strange? Use details from the play to support your answer.

_____

_____

_____

_____

_____

_____

_____

_____

_____

_____

10 What is the animals' point of view about the humans by the end of the play?

   A   They think the humans are too silly.

   B   They think the humans are too noisy.

   C   They think that some things the humans do are funny, but also frightening.

   D   They think that some things the humans do are strange, but also nice.

✏️ **Write**

11

Extended Response   At the beginning of the play, the animals feel bored. However, their feelings change during the play. Tell how the animals feel in Scene 1, Scene 2, and Scene 3 to show how their feelings change. Use details from the play to support your answer.

In your answer, be sure to
- tell how the animals feel in Scene 1, Scene 2, and Scene 3
- explain why their feelings change during the play
- use details from the play to support your answer

Check your writing for correct spelling, grammar, capitalization, and punctuation.

_____

_____

_____

_____

_____

_____

_____

_____

_____

_____

_____

_____

_____

©Curriculum Associates, LLC   Copying is not permitted.

Integration of Knowledge and Ideas in Informational Text

How is a good reader like a wise shopper? A wise shopper wants to see the real item. The words that describe it are just not enough. Here's an example—you want to buy a backpack. You want to see it, feel it, and try it on. Reading the words on the tag isn't good enough. Good readers look at the pictures when they read. The pictures help them understand what they learn from the words. A wise shopper wants to compare items. One backpack might feel better than another. Or the price might be better. Good readers want to compare, too. They compare two passages in order to get more information about a topic.

In this unit, you'll learn to use maps and photographs to help you understand what you read in a passage. You will also read and compare two passages about the same topic. You'll see how they are alike and different. By doing this, you'll get more information about the topic.

✓ Self Check

Before starting this unit, check off the skills you know below. As you complete each lesson, see how many more skills you can check off!

I can:	Before this unit	After this unit
use the maps in a text to help me understand the passage.	☐	☐
use the pictures in a text to help me understand the passage.	☐	☐
describe the way sentences and paragraphs use cause and effect and sequence.	☐	☐
describe the way sentences and paragraphs compare ideas.	☐	☐
compare and contrast the most important ideas in two texts on the same topic.	☐	☐

page 284

page 291

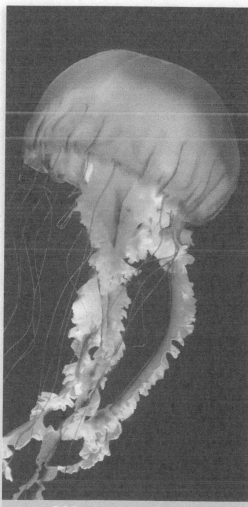

page 300

page 305

page 319

page 336

Lesson 17
Connecting Words and Pictures in Informational Text

Learning Target

Using information from both the pictures and the words in a text will help you understand what you read.

▶ **Read** Texts use words and **illustrations,** or pictures, to provide information in a passage. Illustrations can also include photographs or **maps.** Maps are drawings that show the cities, roads, rivers, and other details of an area.

By thinking about both the words and the pictures, you will better understand what you are reading. You can use the information from both the words and the pictures to tell what you've learned.

Look at this page. It is from a booklet about campgrounds at Pleasant Lake. What do you learn from both the words and the map?

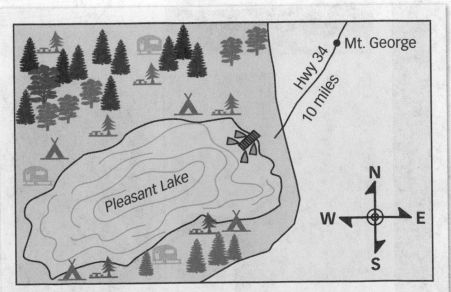

At Pleasant Lake you can enjoy boating, fishing, water skiing, and swimming. The lake is located 15 minutes from Mt. George. Campsites are available. **Call 111-1212 now!**

▶ **Think** Look again at the page from the booklet. Complete this chart to show what you learn from both the words and the map.

What the Words Tell	What the Map Shows
• what you can do at Pleasant Lake	

▶ **Talk** What do you learn from the words that was not on the map? What details did you learn from the map that were not in the words?

⊚ **Academic Talk**
Use these words to talk about the text.
• illustrations   • maps

The Invention That Dogs Are BARKING About

1   Do you know what your dog is saying when it barks? Now you can find out. A toy company in Japan has invented a tool that can tell you! One part of the device "listens" to the dog's bark. Then it sends the information to the owner's handheld speaker. The speaker plays a message telling how your dog is feeling. It can show six different feelings, including joy, sadness, excitement, and fear.

2   The gadget comes with some "extras," too. For example, it has dog-training tips and a health checklist. It also has a "Bow Wow Diary." It can even record barks when the dog is home alone!

Close Reader Habits

Underline sentences that describe the two parts of the device. Then **circle** the two parts of the device in the photo.

Explore How do the words and the photograph help you understand how the device works?

Think

> Illustrations can help you understand the words in the article. Combine information from both as you read.

1 Complete the chart with details from the words and the photo.

What the Words Tell	What the Photograph Shows

Talk

2 Paragraph 2 says that the device comes with "extras." What extras does this device come with? Tell which of these you think dog owners would find most useful, and why.

Write

3 **Short Response** Use the photo to describe what the handheld piece looks like and what you think each part does. Use the space provided on page 288 to write your answer.

> **HINT** Reread the words to help you understand what you are seeing in the photo.

▶ **Read**

The **Amazing** Canal

by Dell Sutcliff

1   The canal is one of the greatest inventions the world has ever known. A canal is a passage that uses water. It creates a shortcut allowing boats to travel through a land area. Without the canal, boats would have to travel around huge areas of land. Some of the oldest canals were built in Egypt nearly 4,000 years ago.

2   The Panama Canal is one of the most famous modern canals. It was completed in 1914. The canal stretches 51 miles across the Isthmus of Panama. It connects the Atlantic and Pacific Oceans. Before the canal was built, ships had to go around the tip of South America. The canal made the trip much shorter, faster, and safer.

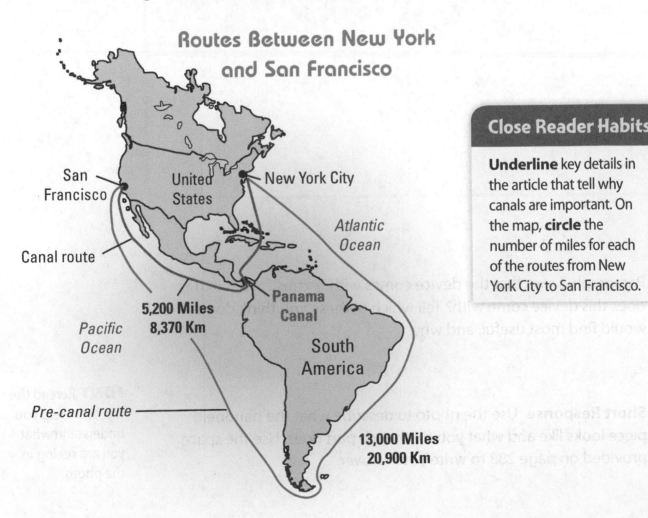

Routes Between New York and San Francisco

San Francisco

United States

New York City

Atlantic Ocean

Canal route

Panama Canal

5,200 Miles
8,370 Km

Pacific Ocean

South America

Pre-canal route

13,000 Miles
20,900 Km

Close Reader Habits

Underline key details in the article that tell why canals are important. On the map, **circle** the number of miles for each of the routes from New York City to San Francisco.

▶ Think

1 According to the map and the text of the passage, what does the Panama Canal connect?

> Read the title and labels on a map to understand what information it shows.

    A Atlantic Ocean and Pacific Ocean

    B North America and South America

    C Egypt and the United States

    D New York City and the tip of South America

2 Based on the map and the text, what did you learn about canals?

    A After the Panama Canal was built, most people still traveled around the tip of South America.

    B The Panama Canal created a shorter but more dangerous route.

    C Canals help people and goods get from one place to another more easily.

    D Portions of canals stretch across large bodies of water.

▶ Talk

3 Why are canals such a great invention? Find details in the text and map that help you understand this. Talk about your ideas with your partner.

> **HINT** Look at the map for details that support the text.

▶ Write

4 **Short Response** The author says that the canal is one of the greatest inventions the world has known. Write a paragraph telling why the author may have said this. Use one detail from the text and one detail from the map to support your answer. Use the space provided on page 289 to write your answer.

▶ 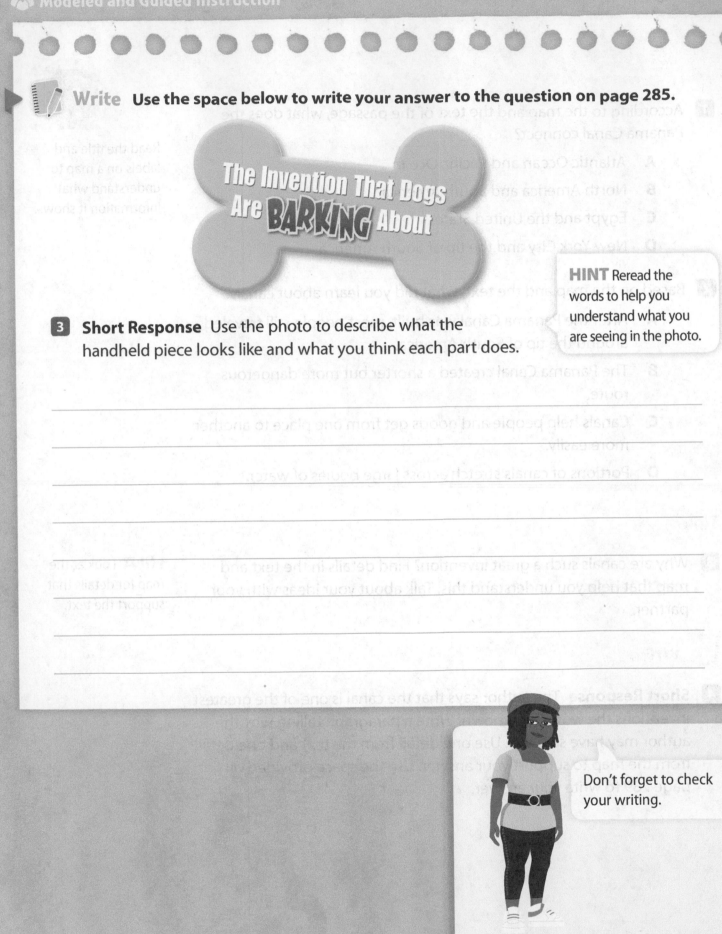 Write **Use the space below to write your answer to the question on page 285.**

The Invention That Dogs
Are **BARKING** About

HINT Reread the words to help you understand what you are seeing in the photo.

3 **Short Response** Use the photo to describe what the handheld piece looks like and what you think each part does.

_____

_____

_____

_____

_____

_____

_____

_____

Don't forget to check your writing.

Write Use the space below to write your answer to the question on page 287.

The Amazing Canal

4 **Short Response** The author says that the canal is one of the greatest inventions the world has known. Write a paragraph telling why the author may have said this. Use one detail from the text and one detail from the map to support your answer.

_____

_____

_____

_____

_____

_____

_____

_____

Check Your Writing

☐ Did you read the prompt carefully?

☐ Did you put the prompt in your own words?

☐ Did you use the best evidence from the text to support your ideas?

☐ Are your ideas clearly organized?

☐ Did you write in clear and complete sentences?

☐ Did you check your spelling and punctuation?

Read

Riiip!
Thanks, George!
by Hannah Ford

WORDS TO KNOW

As you read, look inside, around, and beyond these words to figure out what they mean.

- burs
- fibers
- fabric

1   Riiip! That familiar sound is what we might hear when we undo our shoes or open our backpacks. It's Velcro™! One side is fuzzy. The other side is prickly. It sort of feels like . . . a prickly plant? Well, that's because a prickly plant was the inspiration for Velcro.

2   George Mestral, the man who invented Velcro, lived in a country in Europe called Switzerland. One day, he was hiking in the Jura Mountains near his home. When he came home, he found lots of sticky burs on his pants and socks. *What makes these stick?* he wondered. He decided to look at them under a microscope.

3   Close up, George saw that each little spike on the bur ended in a hook. When he looked at the fibers of his pants and socks, he noticed they were little loops. The hooks from the burs got caught on the little loops. That got George thinking. *These things have real sticking power. Imagine if they could stick things together in a useful way!*

4   After many years of experimenting, George was able to re-create the sticking power of the little burs. He made two pieces of fabric: one piece that was covered in prickly hooks, the other covered in soft, fuzzy loops. Put them together and they hung on tight! With a hearty tug, riiip! They came apart!

5   George was eager to share his invention. A lot of people told him it was silly. George knew better. He knew that his invention could take the place of many fasteners. Zippers, buttons, pins, and shoelaces would all become a thing of the past, he claimed. In 1951, he patented his invention. He named it "Velcro," a combination of the words *velour* ("velvet") and *crochet* ("hook"). He began manufacturing it, sure that it would have thousands of uses. He was right.

6   Velcro's first big fan was NASA. Astronauts had lots of bulky equipment to put on and take off. Velcro proved to be a strong, easy-to-pull-off fastener for space suits. It could hold tools in place so they wouldn't float away. Skiers also wore bulky suits. They liked how Velcro fasteners held tight and opened easily. Sneaker makers saw Velcro straps as kid-friendly. Even toddlers could fasten and unfasten their straps!

7   From something most people find annoying, George Mestral gave us a wonderful convenience. The next time you hear that riiip, thank him!

▶ Think Use what you learned from reading the selection to respond to
these questions.

1 This question has two parts. First, answer Part A. Then answer Part B.

Part A
How did George Mestral come up with the idea for Velcro?

   A He looked at the unusual fasteners used on hiking clothes.

   B He saw special fabrics that were fuzzy on one side and prickly
on the other.

   C He had been asked to invent a new kind of fastener.

   D He noticed that burs were sticking to his pants and socks after
a hike.

Part B
Which sentence from the passage **best** supports your answer to Part A?

   A "Close up, George saw that each little spike on the bur ended
in a hook."

   B "After many years of experimenting, George was able to
re-create the sticking power of the little burs."

   C "He named it 'Velcro,' a combination of the words *velour*
('velvet') and *crochet* ('hook')."

   D "Even toddlers could fasten and unfasten their straps!"

2 According to both the photographs and the text of the passage, how
is a bur similar to Velcro?

   A Both grow on a plant.

   B Both are brownish in color.

   C Both have tiny hooks on the ends.

   D Both are shaped like tiny zippers.

3 Reread paragraph 4 and look again at the photographs. Which **two** of the following details explain how Velcro is made?

    A   It is made with spikes and hooks pulled from burs.

    B   It uses two different pieces of fabric.

    C   It uses the same fibers that socks are made from.

    D   It has prickly hooks on one side and loops on the other.

    E   It is made from velvet.

    F   It has special fasteners that act like laces.

    G   It uses hooks called "crochets."

4 What is one reason that astronauts first started to use Velcro?

    A   It held tools in place so they wouldn't float away.

    B   It allowed astronauts to wear sneakers.

    C   It allowed astronauts to walk inside a spaceship.

    D   It helped astronauts walk safely on the moon.

5 Why was Velcro popular with skiers?

_____

_____

_____

_____

6 Read these sentences from paragraph 5.

> **He knew that his invention could take the place of many fasteners. Zippers, buttons, pins, and shoelaces would all become a thing of the past, he claimed.**

What are **two** ways to figure out the meaning of *fasteners*?

   A Use the meaning of *invention*, which means something similar.

   B Use the examples in the next sentence, which are all objects used to join things together.

   C Think about the meaning of *fasten*, which means "to hold in place."

   D Think about the meaning of *fast*, which means "quick."

   E Break the word *fasteners* down into two smaller words.

7 Why would Velcro be **most** useful on clothing meant for children?

   A Children usually wear bulky clothing.

   B Velcro makes a ripping sound that children enjoy.

   C Velcro straps are easy to fasten and unfasten.

   D It can be used to hold caps and gloves in place.

8 Which sentence does the photograph of the astronaut on page 291 help you understand?

   A "He knew that his invention could take the place of many fasteners."

   B "Velcro's first big fan was NASA."

   C "It could hold tools in place so they wouldn't float away."

   D "Astronauts had lots of bulky equipment to put on and take off."

Write

9 **Short Response** Write a paragraph explaining how Velcro works. Use details from both the text and the photographs in your answer.

 **Learning Target**

Now that you've read articles that contain text and pictures, explain how both are important to understanding a topic.

Lesson 18
Describing Connections Between Sentences and Paragraphs

Learning Target

When you describe how ideas in sentences or paragraphs are connected, you will better understand what the author is trying to explain.

▶ **Read** You know that a paragraph is a group of sentences. Paragraphs and sentences both contain ideas that connect to each other in some way. Sometimes the **connection** is a cause-and-effect relationship. A **cause** is the reason something happens. An **effect** is what happens as a result. Words such as *because, so, as a result,* and *since* often signal this kind of connection.

Authors also connect sentences and paragraphs by showing that things happen in a **sequence,** or order. Look for signal words such as *first, then,* and *finally* in sentences to see how ideas and events in a sequence are connected.

Read this cartoon. How are the ideas connected?

The Invention of the Sandwich

▶ **Think** Finish the charts to show two different ways the ideas in the cartoon are connected. Use the first chart to show a cause-and-effect connection. Use the second to show a sequence.

Cause and Effect

Why It Happened (Cause)	What Happened (Effect)
One day, the Earl of Sandwich was too busy to eat.	

Sequence

1	2	3

▶ **Talk** Retell the story of the invention of the sandwich. Use signal words to show cause and effect or sequence.

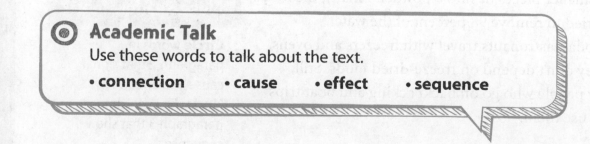

⊙ **Academic Talk**
Use these words to talk about the text.
- **connection**
- **cause**
- **effect**
- **sequence**

> Read

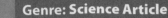

Space Food

by Claire Daniels

1   Astronaut food has changed over the years. In the early days of space exploration, astronauts traveled in small spacecraft, where there was little room for food. Fresh foods in early space travel were not practical. They spoiled, took up too much space, and were too heavy.

2   As a result, astronauts in space ate freeze-dried foods. Freeze-dried foods don't spoil. They don't weigh much, and they don't take up much space. Add water and you have "fresh" peas, mashed potatoes, steak, or macaroni and cheese. There is even freeze-dried ice cream!

3   Foods are freeze-dried in a food plant. First, vegetables and fruits are washed and cut up. Foods like meats and pasta are cooked. Second, the food is frozen to −40 degrees Fahrenheit. Then workers grind the food into smaller pieces or into a powder. Finally, the foods are dried to remove 98 percent of the water.

4   Today, astronauts travel with freezers and ovens, so they don't depend on freeze-dried foods. Still, many people who go on backpacking and boat trips often use them.

Close Reader Habits

Circle words in paragraph 2 that signal cause and effect.

Underline words in paragraph 3 that show sequence.

How are sentences and paragraphs connected in "Space Food"?

Think

> Look for what happened and why it happened to understand the events.

1 Finish the cause-and-effect chart with details from the first two paragraphs of "Space Food."

Cause and Effect

Why It Happened (Cause)	What Happened (Effect)

Talk

2 Talk with your partner about what it must be like to eat in space. What were some of the benefits of freeze-dried foods for the astronauts?

Write

3 **Short Response** In your own words, explain how freeze-dried foods are made. Use signal words correctly to show the sequence of the steps. Use the space provided on page 302 to write your answer.

> **HINT** Words such as *first, then,* and *finally* can signal sequence.

Lesson 18 Describing Connections Between Sentences and Paragraphs

Read

From
Eat This Spoon!

by Elizabeth Preston

1   Imagine you're at a picnic, enjoying some ice cream and fruit salad. Then you top off your meal by eating your spoon.

2   That's the vision of a company in India. They want to replace plastic forks and spoons with edible ones made out of food. This could cut down on how much plastic people use and throw away.

3   The company uses a simple recipe to create its spoons. It starts with flour made from a grain called sorghum, with wheat and rice flours mixed in. Workers knead the flour with water to make a dough. Then they shape it into spoons. They bake the spoons until they're hard.

4   An edible spoon is sturdy enough to handle cold ice cream or hot soup. You can also munch on one as a snack. The spoons are meant to be used only one time. They are not washed and reused. But if you're too full to eat your spoon after your meal, you can put it in a compost pile, or just throw it in the dirt. It should decompose in a week—unless bugs or animals eat it first!

> ### Close Reader Habits
>
> How are the ideas in paragraph 2 connected? **Circle** any signal words you see.

► **Think**

1 Reread paragraph 3 from "Eat This Spoon."

> The company uses a simple recipe to create its spoons. It starts with flour made from a grain called sorghum, with wheat and rice flours mixed in. Workers knead the flour with water to make a dough. Then they shape it into spoons. They bake the spoons until they're hard.

> Look for words that help you understand the order of events.

Which words in the paragraph signal a sequence?

A uses, made from, make

B starts, then, until

C with, in, into

D knead, shape, bake

► **Talk**

2 Where did the writer show a cause-and-effect connection in paragraph 4? What is the cause and what is the effect? Hint: What happens if you throw an edible spoon in the dirt?

► **Write**

3 **Short Response** Describe how the author uses a cause-and-effect connection in paragraph 4 to support her point that edible spoons are better than plastic spoons. Use the space provided on page 303 to write your response.

> **HINT** Reread paragraphs 2 and 4 to find ways that edible spoons are different from plastic ones.

Write Use the space below to write your answer to the question on page 299.

Space Food

3 **Short Response** In your own words, explain how freeze-dried foods are made. Use signal words correctly to show the sequence of the steps.

> **HINT** Words such as *first, then,* and *finally* can signal sequence.

_____

_____

_____

_____

_____

_____

_____

_____

> Don't forget to check your writing.

Write Use the space below to write your answer to the question on page 301.

Eat This Spoon!

3 **Short Response** Describe how the author uses a cause-and-effect connection in paragraph 4 to support her point that edible spoons are better than plastic spoons.

> **HINT** Reread paragraphs 2 and 4 to find ways that edible spoons are different from plastic spoons.

_____

_____

_____

_____

_____

_____

_____

Check Your Writing

☐ Did you read the prompt carefully?

☐ Did you put the prompt in your own words?

☐ Did you use the best evidence from the text to support your ideas?

☐ Are your ideas clearly organized?

☐ Did you write in clear and complete sentences?

☐ Did you check your spelling and punctuation?

Patriotic Pizza

by Karin Gaspartich, *Highlights*

1 Two thousand years ago, Greeks baked flat disks of bread and used the bread like a plate. They would first eat the food on top of the bread. Then they would eat the bread "plate."

2 People started to put toppings on the flat bread before it went into the oven. This was an early form of today's pizza.

3 In Italy, many centuries later, people also ate a form of pizza. It was considered food for the poor. Most people had flour, water, oil, and spices. They could use these ingredients to make a simple pizza.

4 Working-class people of Naples had short breaks for meals. They needed cheap food that could be eaten quickly. Pizza made by local vendors was a perfect solution. It could even be eaten without plates and forks.

A Queen's Favorite Pizza

5 In 1889, Queen Margherita and King Umberto I of Italy took a vacation in the seaside town of Naples, Italy. The queen saw people strolling outside eating pizza. She wanted to try some pizza for herself.

6 Raffaele Esposito was a popular pizza maker in town. He was chosen to make a pizza for the queen. Esposito wanted his pizza to be extra special. So he made a pizza using the colors of the Italian flag: red, green, and white. Red tomatoes, green basil (an herb), and white mozzarella cheese went on his patriotic pizza.

7 Esposito baked his creation, and it was delivered to the queen. She loved it. She sent a note of praise and thanks. Raffaele named it Pizza Margherita in honor of the queen. Soon everyone wanted to try it.

8 Around that time, workers began leaving Italy to live in America. Pizza bakers brought their talent and recipes with them. Gennaro Lombardi opened the first pizzeria in New York City in 1895. Early pizzerias had no chairs. People just went in, ordered their pizza, and left with it.

9 Pizza became popular with American workers, too. It was tasty and easy to eat on the go. Before long, pizza was one of the most popular foods in the United States.

10 Perhaps you could invent your very own pizza. Have fun . . . And finish your plate!

Make a mini Margherita pizza!

Ask an adult to help you with this recipe.
You will need:

- 3 English muffins
- 1 tomato, sliced
- 10 fresh basil leaves, cut in half
- 3/4 cup of shredded mozzarella cheese
- toaster oven (or conventional oven)

1. With an adult's help, preheat the oven to 350 degrees Fahrenheit.
2. Split the English muffins with a fork. On each half, put some mozzarella cheese, a slice of tomato, and a few pieces of basil.
3. Place the mini pizzas on a tray, and ask an adult to put them in the oven. Cook the pizzas for 10 minutes or until the cheese is melted.
4. Ask an adult to take your mini pizzas out of the oven. Share them.

▶ **Think** Use what you learned from reading the selection to respond to these questions.

1 This question has two parts. First, answer Part A. Then answer Part B.

Read these two sentences from paragraph 6.

> **Esposito wanted his pizza to be extra special. So he made a pizza using the colors of the Italian flag: red, green, and white.**

Part A
Which of the following describes the relationship between these two sentences?

    A The first sentence explains the reason for what is described in the second sentence.

    B The sentences compare the shape of the pizza to the Italian flag.

    C The second sentence gives the cause of what is described in the first sentence.

    D The sentences describe the steps to make a Margherita pizza.

Part B
Why did Esposito make this special pizza? Write your response.

_____

_____

_____

_____

_____

_____

_____

_____

2 Number these sentences to show the correct sequence of events in the history of the pizza.

_____ People began to put food on flat bread before it went into the oven, making the first pizza.

_____ In 1889, Queen Margherita made pizzas popular in all of Italy.

_____ American workers made pizza one of the most popular foods in the United States.

_____ Centuries later, a type of simple pizza was made as a food for the poor.

_____ In 1895, Gennaro Lombardi opened the first pizzeria in New York.

_____ The Greeks put food on baked bread that they used like plates.

3 Paragraphs 8 and 9 describe the arrival of pizza in America. Which sentence **best** describes the connection between the two paragraphs?

A It is a sequence that describes how the first pizzerias were built in America and how they changed over time.

B It is a cause-and-effect connection showing how pizzas came to America and why they became popular with American workers.

C It is a sequence explaining how Gennaro Lombardi became a well-known pizza maker in New York City.

D It is a cause-and-effect connection explaining why workers left Italy and came to the United States.

4 How did the writer organize the details in the recipe?

    A She used signal words to show sequence.

    B She showed the ingredients first to signal cause and effect.

    C She numbered the steps to show sequence.

    D She used cause and effect to show the results of using the oven.

5 Read these sentences from paragraph 6.

> **Raffaele Esposito was a popular pizza maker in town. He was chosen to make a pizza for the queen.**

What is the meaning of *popular* in this context?

    A rich

    B new

    C in demand

    D unknown

6 Which detail tells why pizza became popular with workers in America?

    A "Around that time, workers began leaving Italy to live in America."

    B "Pizza bakers brought their talent and recipes with them."

    C "Gennaro Lombardi opened the first pizzeria in New York City in 1895."

    D "It was tasty and easy to eat on the go."

▶ Write

7 **Short Response** Explain how to make a mini Margherita pizza. Write your explanation as a paragraph and use signal words to make the order of steps clear. You do not need to list the ingredients.

_____

_____

_____

_____

_____

_____

_____

 Learning Target

Now that you understand different ways the ideas in sentences and paragraphs can be connected to each other, tell why identifying these connections is important.

_____

_____

_____

_____

_____

Lesson 19
Describing Comparisons

Learning Target

Describing the connections between ideas in a text will help you understand what the author is explaining.

▶ **Read** Authors work carefully to show **connections** among ideas in their writing. This means that they make sure readers understand *how* sentences and paragraphs are connected and *why* the connections are important.

Sometimes a writer shows connections by making a **comparison** between facts and ideas. Comparing means showing how two or more things are alike and different. Signal words such as *like, as, also,* and *both* show how things are alike. Signal words such as *however, but, different,* and *unlike* show how things are different.

Read the following paragraph about toothbrushes. How does the comparison help you understand the subject?

Like people today, ancient peoples wanted to keep their teeth clean. They also used toothbrushes. However, their brushes were very different. Our toothbrushes are plastic with nylon bristles. But the first toothbrushes were made of twigs with crushed ends.

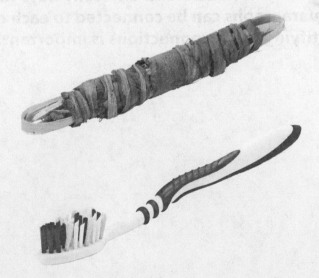

▶ **Think** Read the paragraph again. Then finish the chart to see how the writer used comparisons to connect ideas.

Sentences	Signal Words	Purpose of Comparison
"Like people today, ancient peoples wanted to keep their teeth clean."	Like	
"They also used toothbrushes. However, their brushes were very different."		
"Our toothbrushes are plastic with nylon bristles. But the first toothbrushes were made of twigs with crushed ends."		

▶ **Talk** How do the comparisons in the paragraph help you understand more about toothbrushes?

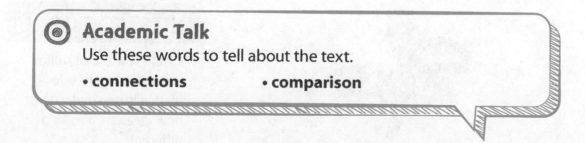

◉ **Academic Talk**
Use these words to tell about the text.
• **connections**   • **comparison**

Lesson 19 Describing Comparisons **311**

▶ **Read**

Ancient Toothpaste

by Tom Wiggins

1   People have always liked to have clean, white teeth. Today, we just squeeze some toothpaste onto a brush and start scrubbing. The toothpaste is made from sodium fluoride, which keeps our teeth strong. It also contains a whitener and flavoring. But toothpaste used to be very different.

2   The first tooth cleaner was made in Egypt over 1,600 years ago. Like today's tooth cleaners, it was a paste. Unlike today's toothpaste, it contained mint and dried iris flower. It also contained rock salt and pepper grains. And instead of using toothbrushes, the Egyptians rubbed the paste on their teeth with a finger.

3   Egyptian toothpaste also came in only one flavor: mint. Even with the mint, it tasted unpleasant and strong. Today, our toothpaste comes in many tasty flavors. We can choose from mint, cherry, and even bubblegum!

4   Like our toothpaste, ancient toothpaste did clean the teeth. However, it was not very pleasant to use. It was painful on the gums. It sometimes made them bleed. Egyptians must have cared a lot about their teeth to keep cleaning them even with all those problems!

Close Reader Habits

Circle words that signal comparisons. How do they help you understand how ideas are alike and different?

Explore

How do comparisons help connect the ideas in "Ancient Toothpaste"?

Think

1 Finish the chart to see how comparisons help connect ideas in the article. Add your own sentences in the last row.

> Time words can make comparisons. Look for words such as *now/then* and *before/after*.

Sentences	Signal Words	Purpose of Comparison
"Like today's tooth cleaners, it was a paste. Unlike today's toothpaste, it contained mint and dried iris flower."		
"Egyptian toothpaste also came in only one flavor: mint. . . . Today, our toothpaste comes in many tasty flavors."		

Talk

2 What ideas did you add to the last row of the chart? How are those ideas connected to each other and to other ideas in the article?

Write

3 **Short Response** How would you feel if you suddenly had to brush your teeth like the Egyptians did? Include comparisons from the article to explain your thinking. Use the space provided on page 316 to write your answer.

> **HINT** Think about how you'll organize your writing to show comparisons.

Read

THE GREAT INCA ROAD

by Hilary Dumitrescu

1   Roads are difficult to build and expensive to take care of. However, a great civilization needs great roads. Roads connect people to the goods they need to live. They allow the government to send help where it is needed. Even the most ancient civilizations understood the need for good roads.

2   High in the Andes mountains, the Incan Empire thrived for hundreds of years. When Spanish explorers arrived in the 16th century, they were amazed by the roads they found. Even the longest Roman road, the Via Appia, was not as long as the Incas' Royal Way. The Incan road was 3,500 miles long! Like the Via Appia, the Royal Way connected the capital to other parts of the empire. More roads connected to it. All in all, the Inca roads stretched for 23,000 miles.

3   Unlike the Romans, the Incas did not have wheels or carts. Instead, they rode llamas. These sturdy animals carried people and goods all over the empire. Messengers known as *chasquis* ran along the Inca Road. They carried messages from the king to all of his people.

4   The Inca Road passed through high mountains. To safely cross the deep mountain ravines, the Incas built amazing hanging bridges. These bridges were not made out of steel like modern bridges. Instead, they were woven out of plant fibers! But the Spanish found that the bridges were strong enough to carry soldiers and horses safely.

Close Reader Habits

How does the author use comparisons to help you understand the topic? **Underline** the two civilizations whose roads are compared in paragraph 2.

▶ **Think**

1 The roads of different groups of people are compared in this passage. Which groups are they?

  A   the Spanish and the Incas

  B   the Spanish and the Romans

  C   the Incas and the Romans

  D   the Incas, the Spanish, and the Romans

> Another way to spot comparisons is to look for the same details about two different subjects.

2 Which **two** sentences from the passage compare and contrast two important roads?

  A   "Even the most ancient civilizations understood the need for good roads."

  B   "When Spanish explorers arrived in the 16th century, they were amazed by the roads they found."

  C   "Even the longest Roman road, the Via Appia, was not as long as the Incas' Royal Way."

  D   "Like the Via Appia, the Royal Way connected the capital to other parts of the empire."

  E   "These bridges were not made out of steel like modern bridges."

  F   "Unlike the Romans, the Incas did not have wheels or carts."

  G   "But the Spanish found that the bridges were strong enough to carry soldiers and horses safely."

▶ **Talk**

3 How does the author make a connection between paragraphs 2 and 3? Talk about it with a partner.

▶ **Write**

4 **Short Response** Paragraph 4 compares two types of bridge. How does the comparison help you understand why Incan bridges were so amazing? Use the space provided on page 317 to write your answer.

> **HINT** Don't just look at signal words. Look for sentences that show how the bridges are the same or different.

✏️ **Write** **Use the space below to write your answer to the question on page 313.**

Ancient Toothpaste

3 **Short Response** How would you feel if you suddenly had to brush your teeth like the Egyptians did? Include comparisons from the article to explain your thinking.

> **HINT** Think about how you'll organize your writing to show comparisons.

_____

_____

_____

_____

_____

_____

_____

_____

_____

_____

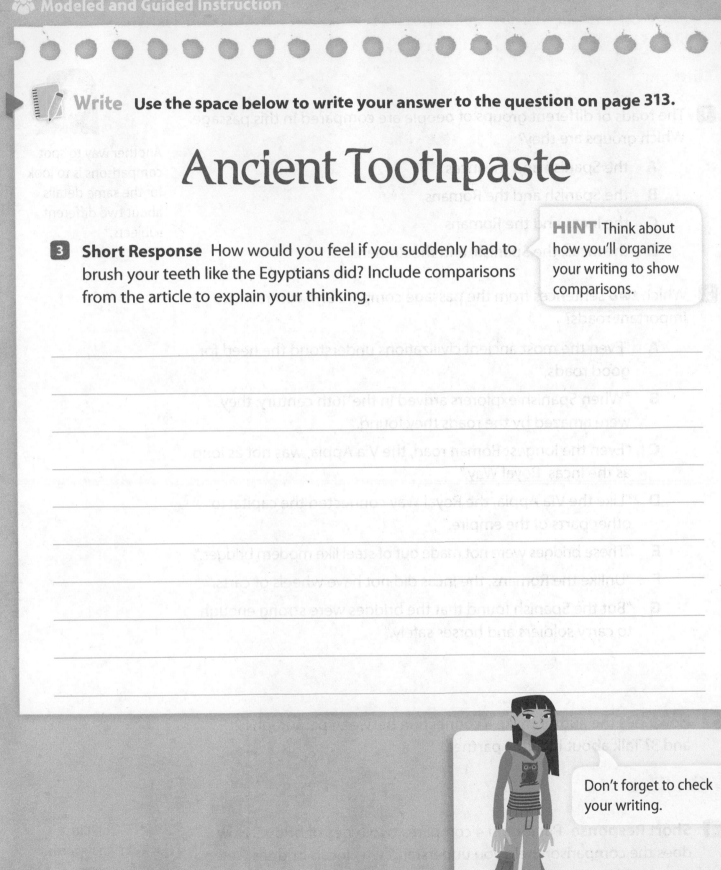

> Don't forget to check your writing.

Write Use the space below to write your answer to the question on page 315.

4 **Short Response** Paragraph 4 compares two types of bridge. How does the comparison help you understand why Incan bridges were so amazing?

HINT Don't just look at signal words. Look for sentences that show how the bridges are the same or different.

_____

_____

_____

_____

_____

_____

_____

_____

Check Your Writing

- ☐ Did you read the prompt carefully?
- ☐ Did you put the prompt in your own words?
- ☐ Did you use the best evidence from the text to support your ideas?
- ☐ Are your ideas clearly organized?
- ☐ Did you write in clear and complete sentences?
- ☐ Did you check your spelling and punctuation?

Read ▶

FROM

Writing on a Wasp's Nest

BY KACEY HARTUNG, *Appleseeds*

WORDS TO KNOW

As you read, look inside, around, and beyond these words to figure out what they mean.

- **mixture**
- **recipe**
- **ingredients**

1   You're outside on a warm spring day. You hear a buzzing sound over your head. On a nearby tree branch, you see a nest shaped like an upside-down umbrella. Wasps! Are you scared, or do you try to get a better look? Now think about this: A nest like that one led to the invention of something you would have a hard time living without—paper!

2   Before paper was invented, the ancient Chinese wrote on pieces of silk cloth. But silk was expensive. The empress (or queen) of China wanted something to write on that would be cheaper and easier to make than silk. So she asked a palace worker named T'sai Lun to find a new material to write on. This happened about 1,900 years ago.

3   According to the story, T'sai Lun remembered seeing an empty wasp's nest as a boy. The nest was made of a strong, lightweight material. T'sai Lun knew that if he could create a material like the wasp's nest, he would solve the empress's problem.

4   The job wasn't easy. It took T'sai Lun three years to come up with the perfect mixture: tree bark, scraps of fishing nets, and water. He boiled and beat the mixture into mush. Today we call the mush "pulp." Then he stretched a piece of cloth across a wooden frame and dipped it into the pulp. When he lifted the frame, a thin layer of pulp remained on top of the cloth. After drying in the sun, the layer formed kog-dz, which means "paper made from bark of mulberry tree."

5   The Chinese were proud of T'sai Lun's invention and tried to keep the recipe for kog-dz a secret. Slowly, traders from China brought kog-dz to Japan, northern Africa, and Europe. As the use of kog-dz spread, the ingredients changed. In Europe, the people used cloth rags instead of tree bark. The rags worked well, but there were not enough to make all the paper that people wanted.

6   Today, paper is still made in the same basic way that T'sai Lun made it thousands of years ago. Wood is cut into small pieces, then broken down into pulp by large grinding machines. The pulp is sprayed onto a wire screen and heated until the paper is dry.

7   We make different papers for different uses: soft tissue, stiff cardboard, colorful construction paper, smooth paper for computers, and glossy paper for magazines. They look and feel different, but they are all made from wood.

8   Would you have thought that a wasp's nest could lead to a product we use every day? Before you run from those wasps, thank them for sharing their "recipe" for paper and changing our lives. Then you can run—after all, you don't want to get stung!

A worker dips a frame into pulp to make a large sheet of paper.

Think Use what you learned from reading the selection to respond to these questions.

1 As explained in paragraph 2, how did the new writing material need to be different from the silk cloth that was being used?

    A It needed to be stronger and heavier than silk.

    B It had to be cheaper and easier to make than silk.

    C It had to be more colorful than silk.

    D It had to be made from the bark of trees.

2 As described in paragraph 5, how was papermaking in Europe different from papermaking in China?

    A In Europe, there were more rags available than tree bark.

    B In Europe, paper was made from a wasp's nest instead of tree bark.

    C In Europe, paper was made from cloth rags instead of tree bark.

    D In Europe, the rags worked much better than tree bark.

3 Read this sentence from paragraph 3.

    The nest was made of a strong, lightweight material.

What is the **best** way to figure out the meaning of *lightweight*?

    A The word *light* means that it has something to do with color.

    B The context means that it is similar in meaning to *strong*.

    C It's made of the words *light* and *weight*, so it means "not heavy."

    D Since the material is used to make a nest, it means "grassy."

4 This question has two parts. First, answer Part A. Then answer Part B.

Part A
How is paragraph 6 connected to one of the other paragraphs in the article?

    A It compares how paper is made today to the description of how T'sai Lun made it in paragraph 4.

    B It compares T'sai Lun's paper to the types of papers described in paragraph 7.

    C It shows how writing materials have changed from what was described in paragraph 2.

    D It shows how T'sai Lun's paper is different from the wasp's nest described in paragraph 3.

Part B
Which detail from the article **best** supports your answer to Part A?

    A "The empress (or queen) of China wanted something to write on that would be cheaper and easier to make than silk."

    B "As the use of kog-dz spread, the ingredients changed."

    C "Today, paper is still made in the same basic way that T'sai Lun made it thousands of years ago."

    D "We make different papers for different uses. . . ."

5 Read the following sentence from paragraph 7.

    They look and feel different, but they are all made from wood.

What is being compared in this sentence? Explain how the sentence connects to the one that came before it.

_____

_____

_____

_____

_____

6 Which sentence **best** describes the connection between paragraphs 3 and 4?

    A Paragraph 4 shows how hard it was to come up with a writing material similar to the wasp's nest described in paragraph 3.

    B Paragraph 3 shows how the wasp's nest reminded T'sai Lun of the recipe he came up with in paragraph 4.

    C Paragraph 4 shows how the tree bark T'sai Lun used was similar to the wasp's nest he remembered in paragraph 3.

    D Paragraph 3 describes the thin layer of pulp that T'sai Lun tried to make in paragraph 4.

Write

Comparisons are used throughout this article to help readers understand more about the history of paper. Reread the article. Underline every comparison you find.

7 **Plan Your Response** Create a list of the comparisons you found. What key ideas does each comparison help explain? Write that idea next to the comparison.

8 **Write an Extended Response** Choose **two** comparisons from the list you made. Tell how those comparisons help connect or explain ideas in the article.

_____

_____

_____

_____

_____

_____

_____

_____

_____

_____

_____

_____

_____

_____

_____

_____

_____

_____

_____

 ## Learning Target

You've seen how comparisons can be used to connect or explain ideas in a passage or article. Tell how these comparisons and connections can help you understand what you read.

_____

_____

_____

_____

Lesson 20
Comparing and Contrasting Two Texts

Learning Target

Looking at how two texts on the same topic are alike and different can give you a better understanding of the topic.

▶ **Read** When you read two texts on the same topic, remember to compare and contrast their most **important points** and **key details.** When you **compare,** you look at how the texts are alike. When you **contrast,** you look at how they are different.

Read the ad and the news story. How are they alike? How are they different?

All New for 1983!
The DynaTAC 8000X

Wish you could make a phone call anytime, anyplace? Now you can, with your own handheld cellular phone!
- Save favorite numbers.
- Talk for up to 60 minutes.
And at only 28 ounces, this phone can go anywhere you can.

➤ *Order yours today!*

Cellular Phones Approved for Sale

September 21, 1983

Today, a company received FCC approval to sell the DynaTAC 8000X. This phone will be the first handheld cellular phone to be offered to the public. It offers 60 minutes of talk time and weighs 28 ounces. The initial price will be $3,995.

▶ **Think** Think about what you've learned so far about comparing and contrasting two texts on the same topic. How are they the same? How are they different? Use the *Venn diagram* below to organize your ideas.

Ad Only

- shows what the phone looks like

Both Ad and News Story

- DynaTAC 8000X

News Story Only

- offered to the public

▶ **Talk** Read the ad again and look at the details. Which details show that the ad is written for people who might want to buy the phone?

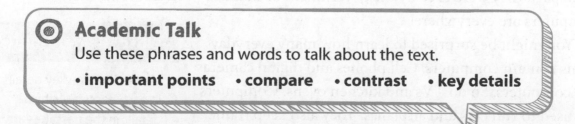

◉ **Academic Talk**
Use these phrases and words to talk about the text.
- **important points** • **compare** • **contrast** • **key details**

Lesson 20 Comparing and Contrasting Two Texts   **325**

▶ **Read**

A Short History of Computers
by Spencer Kay

1   In 1833, a man named Charles Babbage came up with the idea of the modern computer. But there was one problem. He couldn't figure out how to make one.

2   A hundred years later, computers became a reality. In 1939, the first computers were invented to help countries fight wars. Then, around 1950, companies began using computers to help run their businesses. These computers were so huge that they filled large rooms.

3   In 1981, the first PC, or personal computer, was sold. It fit on a desktop and had a keyboard and a screen. Since then, computer use has exploded. Computers are everywhere today. Computers have become faster, smarter, and smaller. They are so small that we hold them in our hands!

Computers Today
by Aparna Singh

1   Fifty years ago, few people knew much about computers. For the most part, they were used by the government or in businesses. But today computers are everywhere!

2   You might be surprised to learn how many everyday items contain computers. Cell phones and digital cameras use computers. So do TVs and kitchen ovens. Computers are used to run cars and airplanes. They also keep traffic lights blinking and trains on schedule.

> ## Close Reader Habits
>
> **Underline** the key details in each passage. Which details in the passages are alike? Which are different?

How are the two articles about computers alike and different?

> Looking for key details in each text will help you find information that's alike and different.

Think

1 Complete the Venn diagram to show how the two articles give information about computers that is alike and different.

A Short History of Computers | Both | Computers Today

Talk

2 Get together with a partner and talk about how the information in each article is alike and different. What did you learn about computers by reading both articles?

Write

3 **Short Response** Why has the use of computers increased so much over the last fifty years? Find reasons in **both** articles. Use the space provided on page 332 to write your answer.

> **HINT** Beginning in 1981, what changed about computers and how they were used?

History of TELEVISION

by Marcus Fink

1   David Sarnoff had an idea. If sound could travel over the radio, why couldn't pictures? In 1939, he showed the world it was possible. Broadcast television was born.

2   No one person can claim that he or she invented television. People in several countries were inventing it about the same time. But even though television was invented, there was a catch. No one knew what to do with it. Sarnoff did, and he knew where to introduce it.

3   In 1939, Sarnoff showed the first television broadcast at the New York World's Fair. People crowded around the tiny sets to watch the black-and-white pictures. The first show was of President Franklin D. Roosevelt, who gave a speech. That same year, television sets went on sale. The first ones were small—only 5-inch by 12-inch screens.

4   Television companies began showing programs. In 1939, the first baseball game was put on television. Stations began to broadcast news shows, children's shows, comedies, and dramas. Today there are hundreds of channels and many more kinds of programs.

5   The number of TV sets in use also keeps growing. In 1946, there were about 6,000 televisions sets in use in the United States. In 1951, there were 12 million. As more people watched, more shows were added. By 1962, around 49 million U.S. households had televisions in the home. Today, 99 percent of homes have a television. Some even have three or more!

Close Reader Habits

Underline the most important idea in each paragraph. Then look for key details that support each idea.

Should We Watch TV?

by Zak Shimek

1   What do you do in your free time? If you say, "watch television," you are not alone. About 99 percent of American households own a television. The airwaves are flooded with all kinds of programs. There are hundreds of channels to choose from.

2   And there's so much to see! You can watch a tiger hunt in the jungle—something you might never see in person. You can visit the bottom of the ocean or cruise in outer space from your sofa. You can learn how to do new things, such as cook. TV is also a good way to relax. Watching a funny show can be relaxing.

3   But do Americans watch too much television? One study said that the average person watches four hours each day. If that person lived to be 65 years old, he or she would have watched TV for nine years!

4   Watching television doesn't require effort. All you have to do is sit and watch. When children watch TV, they are not playing and running. They aren't playing games or solving problems. Also, children who watch a lot of TV tend to eat more junk food, including chips and soda. So watching a lot of TV can be bad for your health.

5   Watching a little television each day isn't harmful. It might even make you smarter. But if you are watching four hours a day, think about doing something else!

Close Reader Habits

In "Should We Watch TV?", **underline** important ideas that are like those in "History of Television." **Draw a wavy** line under important ideas that are new.

▶ **Think**

1 Which choice **best** describes why the author wrote "History of Television"?

   A   to tell why David Sarnoff was important to TV

   B   to show how television has grown since 1939

   C   to describe the types of programs available on TV

   D   to prove that people watch too much television

> When you compare two texts, think about each author's reason for writing.

2 This question has two parts. Answer Part A. Then answer Part B.

Part A
What is one of the most important ideas of "Should We Watch TV?"

   A   Television shows will make you smarter.

   B   Watching too much TV can be harmful.

   C   The number of TVs in homes is increasing each year.

   D   A wide variety of programs is available on TV.

Part B
What are **two** details from "Should We Watch TV?" that support your answer to Part A?

   A   "The airwaves are flooded with all kinds of programs."

   B   "About 99 percent of American households own a television."

   C   "One study said that the average person watches four hours each day."

   D   "Watching a little television each day isn't harmful."

   E   "Watching television doesn't require effort."

   F   "So watching a lot of TV can be bad for your health."

3 Which of the following ideas is found in **both** passages?

    A Watching television might make you smarter.

    B Too many Americans watch too much television.

    C The first television screens were only 5 inches by 12 inches.

    D Most households in America have a television.

4 Which sentence **best** describes the difference between the two passages?

    A The first passage shows the benefits of television; the second passage shows the problems with television.

    B The first passage describes the invention of television; the second passage explains why television is so popular.

    C The first passage explains the importance of TV; the second passage describes how TV can be used in education.

    D The first passage describes the history of television; the second passage explores whether watching TV is good or bad.

Talk

5 In which passage would you find information about how TVs have changed? Which one would you use to learn how TV has affected us? Refer to details from each passage when talking about your answers.

Write

6 **Short Response** What are two things you learned in "Should We Watch TV?" that you didn't learn in "History of Television"? Use the space provided on page 333 to write your answer.

> **HINT** Reread "Should We Watch TV?" Look again at the sentences you underlined or marked with a wavy line.

📝 **Write** Use the space below to write your answer to the question on page 327.

A Short History of Computers

Computers Today

> **HINT** Beginning in 1981, what changed about computers and how they were used?

3 **Short Response** Why has the use of computers increased so much over the last fifty years? Find reasons in **both** articles.

_____

_____

_____

_____

_____

_____

_____

> Don't forget to check your writing.

Write Use the space below to write your answer to the question on page 331.

History of TELEVISION

Should We Watch TV?

> **HINT** Reread "Should We Watch TV?" Look again at the sentences you underlined or marked with a wavy line.

6 **Short Response** What are two things you learned in "Should We Watch TV?" that you didn't learn in "History of Television"?

_____

_____

_____

_____

_____

_____

_____

_____

_____

Check Your Writing

☐ Did you read the prompt carefully?

☐ Did you put the prompt in your own words?

☐ Did you use the best evidence from the text to support your ideas?

☐ Are your ideas clearly organized?

☐ Did you write in clear and complete sentences?

☐ Did you check your spelling and punctuation?

▶ **Read**

Genre: Magazine Article

Goodbye, Books?

WORDS TO KNOW

As you read, look inside, around, and beyond these words to figure out what they mean.

- skeptical
- access

by Jamie Joyce,
Time for Kids

1   Cushing Academy used to have 20,000 books in its library. But over the summer, this small Massachusetts high school began to replace printed books with electronic books, or e-books. Why? "The school wanted to put its focus on 21st-century learning," Tom Corbett, the library's executive director, told TFK. Few students were using library books to do their school assignments. Most did their research online. Transforming the library seemed like the best way to meet students' needs. Without a print collection to care for, Corbett says librarians can now concentrate on helping students use the online collection in new and better ways. They can also work with teachers to bring technology into the classroom.

More Books, More Reading

2   Teacher Nancy Boyle says her students still enjoy regular books. But they're also testing out the Kindle, an electronic reader. So far, it's been a success. "It's great," Boyle told TFK. "The kids are reading more."

3   Sixteen-year-old Meghan Chenausky was skeptical at first. "I love the feeling of books," she told TFK. "I really thought I was going to be missing out when I started using a Kindle. But now I absolutely love using it. It's so convenient. You can have so many books right at your fingertips."

Meet an E-Reader

4   Can your backpack fit 1,500 books? An e-reader can. Most e-readers are pencil-thin and weigh less than a pound. They can download an e-book in 60 seconds. Don't understand the meaning of a word? Click on it to get the definition. Is the print too small? An e-reader can adjust the size.

5   E-readers aren't cheap, but it costs the school just $5 or $10 to download an e-book on as many as six e-readers. "Now, students have access to a million titles," Corbett says.

6   Still, regular books have one big advantage over e-readers: They don't use electricity. E-readers have to be charged, like cell phones.

Genre: Persuasive Essay

E-Readers: No Substitute for Books
by Linda Timm

1   It's a cold, stormy day, and lightning has knocked out the power in your neighborhood. No problem! You'll just grab a snack, curl up with a good book, and read for hours. You pull out your e-reader, press the button . . . and the screen remains dark. The battery is dead. And since there's no electricity, there's no way to recharge the device. Guess you're out of luck.

2   This is just one example of how impractical e-readers are. Sure, an e-reader can store thousands of books. But what good is that if you can't use the reader whenever you need to? Running out of power is only one of the issues. E-readers can also break. Drop one, and the screen may crack or the reader may just stop functioning. You have to purchase a new book AND a new device. If you drop a printed book, though, you can just pick it up and keep reading.

3   E-readers also make reading itself more difficult. Sentences may break across lines in awkward ways. Or, one sentence may get stretched across a page, leaving huge spaces between words. It's also hard to find parts you want to reread. Even with search tools, it's difficult to "flip" back and forth as you would with a printed book. Note-taking can also take longer and be more frustrating.

4   Still, some schools are beginning to buy e-readers for students in place of books. School leaders feel they can get more books for less money that way. But e-readers are expensive, so how much money will schools have to spend to replace readers that students lose or break? Also, one research study showed that some people don't learn as well from e-readers. They don't understand as much, and they don't remember what they read. So are e-readers really good for students?

5   Sometimes the simplest choice is the best one. Printed books are inexpensive, recyclable, and portable. They are easy to distribute, easy to care for, and easy to replace. And the best part? Printed books will NEVER run out of power!

Think Use what you learned from reading the passages to respond to these questions.

1 This question has two parts. First, answer Part A. Then answer Part B.

Part A
Which sentence **best** describes how the main ideas of these two passages are different?

    A "Goodbye, Books?" is about the new library at Cushing Academy, while "E-Readers: No Substitute for Books" is about a library that uses only printed books.

    B "Goodbye, Books?" tells how e-readers are good for students and schools, while "E-Readers: No Substitute for Books" tells why e-readers should not replace printed books.

    C "Goodbye, Books?" explains why printed books are no longer useful, while "E-Readers: No Substitute for Books" explains why printed books are still good.

    D "Goodbye, Books?" is about the low cost of e-readers, while "F-Readers: No Substitute for Books" is about the low cost of printed books.

Part B
Choose **one** detail from **each** passage that supports your answer to Part A.

    A "Cushing Academy used to have 20,000 books in its library." ("Goodbye, Books?")

    B "So far, it's been a success. 'It's great,' Boyle told TFK. 'The kids are reading more.'" ("Goodbye, Books?")

    C "Still, regular books have one big advantage over e-readers: They don't use electricity." ("Goodbye, Books?")

    D "Sure, an e-reader can store thousands of books." ("E-Readers: No Substitute for Books")

    E "Still, some schools are beginning to buy e-readers for students in place of books." ("E-Readers: No Substitute for Books")

    F "Also, one research study showed that some people don't learn as well from e-readers." ("E-Readers: No Substitute for Books")

2 Which **two** ideas can be found in **both** passages?

    A   E-books are inexpensive to use.

    B   Printed books are inexpensive and recyclable.

    C   Few students use library books to do assignments.

    D   E-readers can store more than a thousand books.

    E   E-readers can make the reading process more difficult.

    F   Schools are buying e-readers for students to use.

3 Reread these sentences from paragraph 1 of "Goodbye, Books?"

> **Few students were using library books to do their school assignments. Most did their research online. Transforming the library seemed like the best way to meet students' needs.**

Given the context, what does *transforming* mean?

    A   changing

    B   closing

    C   rebuilding

    D   emptying

▶ 📓 Write

Should schools use e-readers instead of printed books? Reread both passages. Put a plus sign (+) next to facts that support the use of e-readers. Put a minus sign (–) next to facts that describe problems with e-readers.

4 **Plan Your Response** Make a two-column chart. Put facts that support e-readers in one column. Put facts that show problems with e-readers in the second column. Study your chart.

5 **Write an Extended Response** Explain whether or not schools should use e-readers instead of printed books. Use details from both passages to support your ideas. Your chart can help you choose your evidence.

_____

_____

_____

_____

_____

_____

_____

_____

_____

 Learning Target

Now that you've compared and contrasted passages, explain
how reading two or more texts on the same topic can help you
understand the topic better. Use examples from some of the
passages you read to make your point clear.

_____

_____

_____

_____

_____

▶ Read

Genre: Science Article

Read the science articles. Then answer the questions that follow.

Signs in the Sky

by Michelle August

A halo around the moon can mean that rain is coming.

1   Today, every news channel has a weather person. They can predict the weather for days, or even weeks in advance. The science of meteorology involves using special devices to track weather systems. However, long before people had this kind of technology, they could predict the weather by observing the natural world.

2   For as long as people have grown their own food, they have wanted to predict the weather. Knowing the signs that told of coming rain or storms was important for survival. Over many centuries, human beings learned to watch the sky for signs of coming weather. They even made up special sayings to help them remember the signs. Today, scientists have discovered something fascinating. Some of those old-fashioned sayings were right!

***Red sky in the morning, sailors take warning. Red sky at night,
sailors' delight.***

3   This is a weather saying that is at least half right. Storm systems
usually move from west to east. A red sunset in the west usually means
that a high pressure system, or dry weather, is coming. Sunrises, on the
other hand, can be red for a variety of reasons. Today, weather
satellites track the movement of storms. But it is still fun to remember
the old saying!

***Ring around the moon, rain's
coming soon.***

4   Sometimes the moon appears to
have a ring around it. This occurs
when there are high clouds in the sky
that contain water and ice. When the
moonlight shines through the tiny
pieces of ice, a halo appears. That
same water and ice can soon fall as
rain. This old saying is another one
that "rings" true!

***When clouds appear like rocks and
towers, the earth's refreshed with
frequent showers.***

5   Have you ever seen clouds that
look thin and spread out? These
are called cumulus clouds and rarely
carry rain. Other clouds are called
cumulonimbus clouds. Strong
winds cause these clouds to grow
tall like towers. Heavy water in the
clouds makes them look dark like rocks.
These clouds almost always bring storms.

Storm clouds like these can bring wind and rain.

6   Today, we have all kinds of technology to predict the weather.
Weather satellites travel into space and weather software tracks storm
patterns. But if all else fails, just look at the sky. The signs are out there!

MAPPING
Sunshine and Rain

by Krista O'Connell

1   Weather is important to all people. A farmer's field can be ruined if the weather is hot and dry. A picnic can be spoiled by rain. People like to know what the weather will be like tomorrow, three days from now, and even next week. This is now possible thanks to the science of meteorology.

The Weather Map

2   One of the tools used to predict the weather is a weather map. Scientists use special machines to create these maps. These machines are used to collect information about conditions in the sky.

What Weather Maps Can Tell Us

3   A weather map might look complicated. But the truth is that most people can make weather predictions using a map like the sample one at the top of the next page. You just need to know what the shapes, symbols, and letters mean. Look at the map as you read along.

4   First, a weather map shows the places where weather fronts are found. Two main types of fronts are warm fronts and cold fronts. Both form when cooler air and hotter air meet. The map shows the symbols for each type of front. Warm fronts often bring rain and clouds. Cold fronts bring clear skies and cooler weather.

5   Second, a weather map shows any weather systems in the area. These can be high pressure or low pressure systems. They are shown on the map by the letters H and L. Both types move from west to east. High pressure systems often result in nice, sunny weather. Low pressure systems are likely to cause rain.

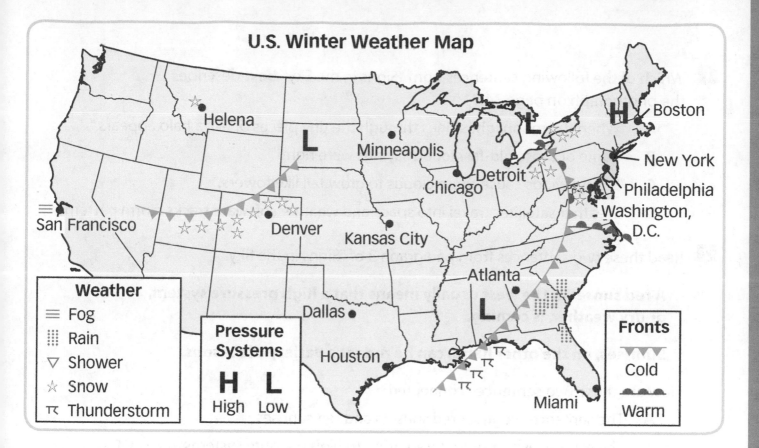

U.S. Winter Weather Map

Weather
≡ Fog
⦂⦂ Rain
▽ Shower
☆ Snow
⊼ Thunderstorm

Pressure Systems
H **L**
High   Low

Fronts
▼▼▼ Cold
⌒⌒⌒ Warm

6   Third, maps show what type of weather these fronts and systems will cause. The map shows that the cold front in Denver is expected to bring snow. The cold front between Atlanta and Miami will likely bring rain and thunderstorms.

Replacing Signs in the Sky with Sound Science

7   It's true that looking into the sky can give some clues about what the weather will be in the near future. Most of us have seen the dark clouds that fill the sky before a thunderstorm. The color of the sky and the look of the moon can provide other clues.

8   People no longer have to make a guess about the weather. There are now maps like the one above as well as other tools. These can help meteorologists[1] make very exact weather forecasts. They can also help predict the weather well before it ever arrives.

[1] **meteorologists:** scientists who study and predict weather

► **Think**

1 Which of the following sentences from "Signs in the Sky" **best** describes the photograph on page 341?

    A "When the moonlight shines through the tiny pieces of ice, a halo appears."

    B "Some of those old-fashioned sayings were right!"

    C "Strong winds cause these clouds to grow tall like towers."

    D "Weather satellites travel into space and weather software tracks storm patterns."

2 Read these two sentences from paragraph 3 of "Signs in the Sky."

> **A red sunset in the west usually means that a high pressure system, or dry weather, is coming.**
>
> **Sunrises, on the other hand, can be red for a variety of reasons.**

How are these two sentences connected?

    A The sentences contrast red sunsets and red sunrises.

    B The sentences compare dry weather to high pressure systems.

    C The sentences explain steps in a process.

    D The sentences explain the reasons for sunsets and sunrises.

3 Based on the photograph on page 340 and the text of "Signs in the Sky," explain why the moon appears to have a ring around it. Use details to support your answer.

_____

_____

_____

_____

_____

4 Place these ideas from "Signs in the Sky" in the correct order by writing 1, 2, 3, and 4 on the lines next to them.

_____ The clouds fill with heavy water.

_____ The clouds bring storms to the area.

_____ Strong winds come and make cumulonimbus clouds grow like tall towers.

_____ The heavy water makes them look like dark rocks.

5 On the map, look at the low pressure system next to Denver. Now reread paragraph 6 of "Mapping Sunshine and Rain." What kind of weather is expected in Denver because of this low pressure system?

    A fog

    B snow

    C rain

    D thunderstorms

6 Read the sentences from paragraph 4 of "Mapping Sunshine and Rain."

    Both form when cooler air and hotter air meet.

    Warm fronts often bring rain and clouds.

    Cold fronts bring clear skies and cooler weather.

How are these sentences connected?

    A The sentences describe how warm fronts cause cold fronts.

    B The sentences describe three steps in a process.

    C The sentences compare and contrast clouds and cooler weather.

    D The sentences compare and contrast warm fronts and cold fronts.

7 Read this sentence from paragraph 2 of "Mapping Sunshine and Rain."

These machines are used to collect information about conditions in the sky.

What does the word *conditions* mean in this sentence?

    A what machines are in the sky

    B what maps say about the sky

    C what weather is going on in the sky

    D what things are collected from the sky

8 How does the map in "Mapping Sunshine and Rain" help the reader understand the passage?

    A by showing the kinds of weather that happen around fronts

    B by showing how a weather map is made by special machines

    C by showing why high pressure systems form in some areas and not others

    D by showing how a winter weather map is different from a summer weather map

9 How are paragraphs 4–6 of "Mapping Sunshine and Rain" connected?

    A They tell the steps of how to read a weather map.

    B They tell the effects of both warm and cold fronts.

    C They tell how different maps compare with each other.

    D They tell why weather systems are formed in certain areas.

10 Which key detail can you find in **both** passages?

    A A ring around the moon shows that rain is coming.

    B Weather systems move from west to east.

    C Warm fronts often bring rain and clouds.

    D A star symbol is used to stand for snow.

11 This question has two parts. First, answer Part A. Then answer Part B.

Part A

How are the main ideas of "Signs in the Sky" and "Mapping Sunshine and Rain" alike?

    A They are both about tools a meteorologist uses.

    B They are both about tracking pressure systems.

    C They are both about old-fashioned weather sayings.

    D They are both about predicting weather.

Part B

Find a sentence in "Signs in the Sky" and a sentence in "Mapping Sunshine and Rain" with details that support the answer to Part A. Write the sentences on the lines below.

_____

_____

_____

_____

12 Which fact can a person learn by reading **both** passages?

    A Rain and clouds are the result of warm fronts.

    B Weather maps are better than sayings for predicting weather.

    C Red sunrises tell people that bad weather is coming.

    D Predicting weather is important for growing crops.

📝 **Write**

13 **Extended Response** How are the main ideas of "Signs in the Sky" and "Mapping Sunshine and Rain" different? Be sure to include key details from the text and the photos of both passages to support your answer.

In your answer, be sure to
- identify the main idea of "Signs in the Sky."
- identify the main idea of "Mapping Sunshine and Rain."
- use key details from each passage to explain how the main ideas are different.

Check your writing for correct spelling, grammar, capitalization, and punctuation.

_____

_____

_____

_____

_____

_____

_____

_____

_____

_____

_____

_____

UNIT 6

Integration of Knowledge and Ideas in Literature

Have you ever read more than one story or book that has the same character? Maybe you've read some of the *Magic Tree House* books, or maybe *Homer Price* or *Judy Moody*. In each story, the characters have a new problem or adventure. The same characters appear in each book. But where the stories take place, and what happens, changes. When you read these books, you share an adventure with the characters. You don't just read the words in the story, but you look at the pictures, too. From the pictures, you learn more about what the characters think and feel. You predict what the characters might do next. Reading books in a series makes reading an adventure.

In this unit, you will practice looking at the details in pictures. In the pictures, you'll find clues about the characters, the setting, and the message of each story. You'll read several stories about one character. And you'll notice what is alike and different about the stories. One thing's for sure—it will be an adventure!

✓ Self Check

Before starting this unit, check off the skills you know below. As you complete each lesson, see how many more skills you can check off!

I can:	Before this unit	After this unit
explain how pictures in a story help me understand the story's characters.	☐	☐
explain how pictures in a story help me understand the story's setting.	☐	☐
explain how pictures in a story help me understand the mood of a story.	☐	☐
compare and contrast the settings of stories written by the same author about the same characters.	☐	☐
compare and contrast the plots and themes of stories written by the same author about the same characters.	☐	☐

page 356

page 362

page 370

page 376

page 378

page 384

Lesson 21
Connecting Words and Pictures

Learning Target

By looking at the illustrations in a story, you can learn more about the characters, where the story takes place, and the feeling the author creates.

▶ **Read** Everyone loves stories with pictures. But pictures, or **illustrations,** are more than just decoration. Illustrations work with the words to help you understand how characters look. They provide details about the **setting,** or where the story takes place. They can also show you what's happening and add to the **mood,** or feeling, that the story creates in the reader. For example, the mood of a story can be frightening, serious, or funny.

Look at the illustration and the text beneath it. What do you learn from both?

This was no ordinary door. Somehow this door led Mia into the world of the video game she had just been playing. Its bright colors and smooth shapes were inviting. Best of all, Jorex seemed to be waiting for her. But Mia had to wonder: if she went in, would she ever get out?

▶ **Think** Reread the text and look at the illustration. What details do both provide that help you understand the characters, the setting, and the mood? Add what you notice to the chart.

	Text	Illustration
Details About Characters	Mia the game character	
Details About Setting	world of the video game	
Details That Create Mood		

▶ **Talk** How would you describe the mood of this story? Which details from the text and the illustration help create that mood?

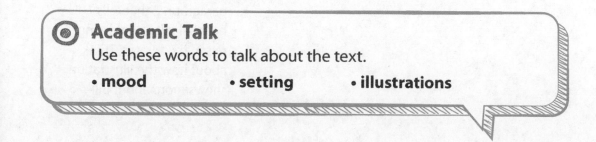

◎ **Academic Talk**
Use these words to talk about the text.
- **mood**
- **setting**
- **illustrations**

WHEN PECOS BILL WAS YOUNG

BY WALT BISCO

1   Right from the day he was born, Pecos Bill was not much like other kids. He had eighteen older brothers and sisters. When he was just a baby, he jumped on a horse and rode it alongside his family's covered wagon as they traveled West. Oh, and Bill also wrestled bears! Bill's family was sure he would lead an amazing life.

2   One time, the wagon went over a big bump, and Bill was launched into the air and far, far away. After he landed on the soft ground, a mother coyote spotted Bill. She took Bill back to her den and raised him as one of her own. For a long time, Bill didn't know he *wasn't* a coyote.

Close Reader Habits

Underline a sentence in paragraph 2 that tells how Bill felt about being raised by coyotes. Think about how the illustration shows more about Bill and his coyote family.

Explore

How do the text and the illustration work together to tell about Pecos Bill and the coyotes?

▶ **Think**

The mood of a story is how it makes you feel. Both words and illustrations can add to the mood.

1 Finish the chart with details from the story and the illustration that tell you more about Bill and his coyote family.

	Text	Illustration
Details About Characters		
Details About Setting		
Details That Create Mood		

▶ **Talk**

2 How does Bill feel about being raised by coyotes? Talk with a partner about details in the text and the illustration that helped you decide.

▶ **Write**

3 **Short Response** How would you describe the mood of the Pecos Bill story? What details help create that mood? Use the space provided on page 358 to write your answer.

HINT In the illustration, how do Bill and the coyotes seem to feel about each other?

Guided Practice

> **Read**

Genre: Tall Tale

Paul Bunyan and the Tallest Tree

1   Paul Bunyan was the tallest, strongest lumberjack who ever lived. One day his boss told him to chop down the tallest tree in the forest. The tree was easy to find because it was the only one taller than Paul.

2   Paul swung his ax—*thunk!* The ax sliced halfway through the tree, and two tons of sawdust fell at Paul's feet. "One more swing," thought Paul. He swung his ax again at the same place—*thunk!*—but the tree didn't fall.

3   Paul stood back and stared up at the tree, and that was when he understood the problem. This wasn't just the tallest tree in the forest; it was the fastest-growing, as well!

4   Paul returned with his spare ax and swung them both, one with his left hand, one with his right. *Thunk!* The blades chopped right through the trunk and met in the middle. The pine came tumbling to the ground, causing an earthquake when it fell. Paul Bunyan was tall and strong, but he was smart, too!

Close Reader Habits

How do the words and illustration help you understand why Paul has trouble cutting down the tree? **Underline** sentences that describe the problem. **Circle** the part of the illustration that shows what Paul saw after he swung his ax the second time.

▶ **Think**

1 This question has two parts. Answer Part A. Then answer Part B.

Part A

Why didn't the tree fall after Paul made his second cut?

A The trunk of the tree was too thick for Paul to chop all the way through.

B The tree was taller than Paul so he couldn't reach high enough.

C The tree had huge branches that blocked Paul's swing.

D The tree grew too quickly for Paul to make a second cut at the same place.

> If you combine details from the text with what you see in an illustration, you'll have a better understanding of what you're reading.

Part B

How does the illustration support your answer to Part A?

A It shows the first cut is high above the second.

B It shows that the tree is so tall we can't even see the top.

C It shows that the tree trunk is much wider than those of other trees.

D It shows that Paul couldn't get close enough to the tree to swing his ax.

▶ **Talk**

2 How does the illustration help you understand the height of both Paul and the tree he is cutting?

▶ **Write**

3 **Short Response** Imagine you want to draw an illustration showing Paul's solution to his problem. What would the illustration include? Use the space provided on page 359 to write your answer.

> **HINT** Use details from the text to help you decide what you'd show in the illustration.

✏️ **Write** Use the space below to write your answer to the question on page 355.

WHEN PECOS BILL WAS
YOUNG

3 **Short Response** How would you describe the mood of the Pecos Bill story? What details help create that mood?

> **HINT** In the illustration, how do Bill and the coyotes seem to feel about each other?

_____

_____

_____

_____

_____

_____

_____

> Don't forget to check your writing.

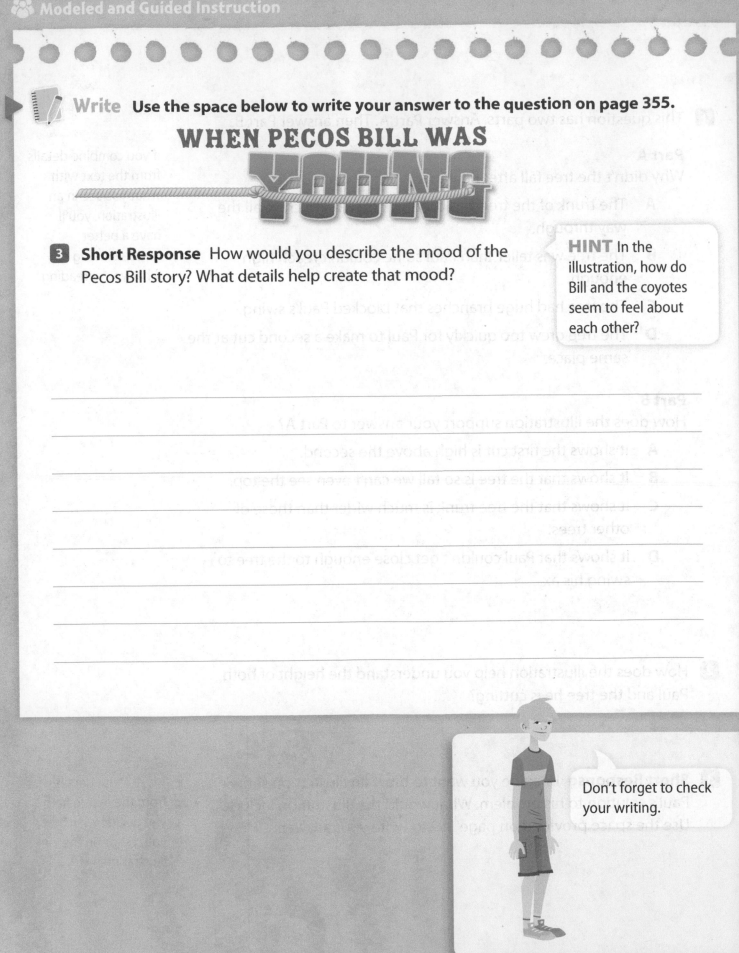

✏️ **Write** **Use the space below to write your answer to the question on page 357.**

Paul Bunyan and the Tallest Tree

3 **Short Response** Imagine you want to draw an illustration showing Paul's solution to his problem. What would the illustration include?

> **HINT** Use details from the text to help you decide what you'd show in the illustration.

_____

_____

_____

_____

_____

_____

_____

_____

Check Your Writing

☐ Did you read the prompt carefully?

☐ Did you put the prompt in your own words?

☐ Did you use the best evidence from the text to support your ideas?

☐ Are your ideas clearly organized?

☐ Did you write in clear and complete sentences?

☐ Did you check your spelling and punctuation?

▶ **Read**

Stormalong
by Mary Pope Osborne, *American Tall Tales*

WORDS TO KNOW

As you read, look inside, around, and beyond these words to figure out what they mean.

• **fathoms**
• **Yankee clipper**
• **bowsprit**

1   One day in the early 1800s a tidal wave crashed down on the shores of Cape Cod in New England. After the wave had washed back out to sea, the villagers heard deep, bellowing sounds coming from the beach. When they rushed to find out what was going on, they couldn't believe their eyes. A giant baby three fathoms tall—or eighteen feet!—was crawling across the sand, crying in a voice as loud as a foghorn.

2   The villagers put the baby in a big wheelbarrow and carried him to town. They took him to the meeting house and fed him barrels and barrels of milk. As ten people patted the baby on the back, the minister said, "What will we name him?"

3   "How about *Alfred Bulltop Stormalong*!" a little boy piped up.

4   "And call him Stormy for short."

5   The baby smiled at the boy, then let out a giant burp that nearly blew the roof off the meeting house.

6   "Stormy it is!" everyone cried.

7   By the time Stormy was twelve, he was already six fathoms tall—or thirty-six feet! "I guess you're going to have to go out into the world now," his friends said sadly. "Maybe you should go to Boston. It's a lot bigger than Cape Cod."

8   "A sailor's life is the only one for me," he said, staring longingly at Boston Harbor. "The sea's my best friend. It's with her that I belong." And with his back to Boston, Stormy strode toward the biggest Yankee clipper docked in the harbor, *The Lady of the Sea*.

9   "Blow me down!" said the captain when Stormy stood before him. "I've never seen a man as big as you before."

10   "I'm not a man," said Stormy. "I'm twelve years old."

11   "Blow me down again!" said the captain. "I guess you'll have to be the biggest cabin boy in the world then. Welcome aboard, son."

12   The sailors were a bit shocked when the captain introduced the thirty-six-foot giant as their new cabin boy. But the day soon came when all the sailors of *The Lady of the Sea* completely accepted Stormy's awesome size. It happened one morning when the clipper was anchored off the coast of South America.

13   "Hoist the anchor!" the captain shouted after a few hours of deep-sea fishing. But when the crew pulled on the great chain, nothing happened. The sailors heaved and hoed, and still could not move the anchor off the bottom of the ocean.

14   "Let me take care of it!" Stormy boomed. Then the cabin boy stuck a knife between his teeth, climbed onto the bowsprit, and dived into the sea.

15   After Stormy disappeared, terrible sounds came from the water. The ship began pitching and tossing on wild, foaming waves. It seemed that all aboard were about to be hurled to a wet grave, when suddenly the sea grew calm again—and Stormy bobbed to the surface.

16   "What happened?" cried the crew.

17   "Just a little fight with a two-ton octopus," said Stormy.

18   "Octopus!"

19   "Aye. He didn't want to let go of our anchor."

20   "What'd you do to him?" the others cried.

21   "Wrestled eight slimy tentacles into double knots. It'll take a month o' Sundays for him to untie himself."

22   From then on Stormy was the most popular sailor on board.

▶ Think   Use what you learned from reading the selection to respond to these questions.

1 This question has two parts. First, answer Part A. Then answer Part B.

Part A
Based on the illustrations, which word **best** describes the mood of the story?

    A serious

    B funny

    C frightening

    D sad

Part B
Which **two** lines from the story support the choice you made in Part A?

    A "One day in the early 1800s a tidal wave crashed down on the shores of Cape Cod in New England."

    B "The baby smiled at the boy, then let out a giant burp that nearly blew the roof off the meeting house."

    C "'Blow me down again!' said the captain. 'I guess you'll have to be the biggest cabin boy in the world then.'"

    D "After Stormy disappeared, terrible sounds came from the water."

    E "The ship began pitching and tossing on wild, foaming waves."

2 In the illustration on page 361, what is happening to the ship?

    A The ship begins to tilt because of Stormy's weight.

    B The ship begins to sink when Stormy fights the octopus.

    C The ship is tilting because the anchor is too heavy.

    D The ship is being blown over by a strong wind.

3 What are **three** details you learned about clipper ships from the illustration on page 362?

_____

_____

_____

4 Look at the illustration on page 362. Based on the illustration and the text, what are *tentacles?*

    A large eyes

    B small disks

    C long arms

    D long chains

5 Reread the following paragraphs from the story. Underline details that are shown in the illustration on page 362.

> **"What happened?" cried the crew.**
> **"Just a little fight with a two-ton octopus," said Stormy.**
> **"Octopus!"**
> **"Aye. He didn't want to let go of our anchor."**
> **"What'd you do to him?" the others cried.**
> **"Wrestled eight slimy tentacles into double knots. It'll take a month o' Sundays for him to untie himself."**

📝 **Write** How did the illustrations increase your enjoyment of "Stormalong"? Look again at the illustrations. Think about what each one adds to the story.

6 **Plan Your Response** Reread paragraphs 14–22. Then look at the illustration on page 362. In a two-column chart, record details you learned from the text and details you learned from the illustration.

7 **Write an Extended Response** Explain how the illustration of Stormy's fight with the octopus added to what you read in the story. Use details from both the text and the illustration in your answer.

_____

_____

_____

_____

_____

_____

_____

_____

_____

_____

_____

_____

_____

 ## Learning Target

You've read stories in which the words and the illustrations are both important. Explain how illustrations can add to your enjoyment and understanding of a story.

_____

_____

_____

_____

_____

Lesson 22
Comparing and Contrasting Stories

Learning Target

When you read several stories that an author has written about the same characters, you can compare and contrast the themes, settings, and plots.

▶ **Read** Sometimes an author will write about the same characters in different books. The **characters** might be the same, but when you **compare** and **contrast** the stories, you'll find many differences.

Each story by the same author will have its own **plot,** or set of events. The stories may also have different **settings,** where the action takes place. You can also compare the **themes,** which are messages or lessons the stories offer.

Look at the two book covers from a series called *The Adventures of Super Cat!* Think about what is similar and what is different in the covers.

Book 1

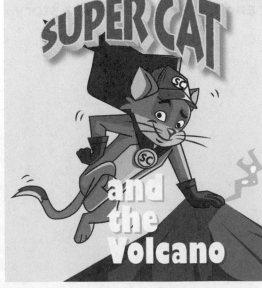

Book 2

▶ **Think**   Finish this chart to compare and contrast the two books.

	Book 1	Book 2
Characters	Super Cat kitten	
Setting		a volcano
Plot	Super Cat rescues a lost kitten.	
Theme		Use your powers to help others.

▶ **Talk**   Which details from the chart would you expect to be the same for
another book in the Super Cat series?

⊙ **Academic Talk**
Use these words to talk about the text.
- **characters**
- **plot**
- **settings**
- **compare**
- **contrast**
- **themes**

The Fox and the Goat

Adapted from The Aesop for Children

1   A Fox fell into a well and could not get out again. After a long time, a thirsty Goat came by. The Goat thought the Fox had gone down to drink, so he asked if the water was good.

2   "The finest in the country," said the Fox, "jump in and try it."

3   The Goat jumped in and began to drink. The Fox quickly jumped on the Goat's back and leaped out of the well.

4   The Goat now saw what trouble he had gotten into and begged the Fox to help him out. But the Fox was already on his way to the woods.

5   "If you had as much sense as you have beard," he said as he ran, "you would have been more cautious about finding a way to get out again before you jumped in."

6   *Moral: Look before you leap.*

The Wolf and the Crane

Adapted from The Aesop for Children

1   A Wolf had been feasting, and a bone had stuck in his throat. He could get it neither up nor down, and of course he could not eat.

2   So away he hurried to the Crane. He was sure that she, with her long neck and bill, would be able to reach the bone and pull it out. "I will reward you," said the Wolf, "if you pull that bone out for me."

3   The Crane was very uneasy about putting her head in a Wolf's throat. But she did what the Wolf asked her to do. When the Wolf felt that the bone was gone, he started to walk away.

4   "But what about my reward!" called the Crane.

5   "What!" snarled the Wolf, whirling around. "Isn't it enough that I let you take your head out of my mouth without snapping it off?"

6   *Moral: Expect no reward for serving the wicked.*

Close Reader Habits

Circle the main characters in each fable.
Underline the moral, or lesson, that is stated at the end of each story.

Explore How are the two fables by the storyteller Aesop alike and different?

▶ **Think**

To find the theme of a story, ask what lesson or message the author wants to share.

1 Complete the chart to show how the two fables are alike and different.

	"The Fox and the Goat"	"The Wolf and the Crane"
Characters		
Plot		
Theme		

▶ **Talk**

2 What are three ways that the two stories are alike?

▶ **Write**

3 **Short Response** Describe how the two fables are alike and different. Be sure to use details about characters, setting, and theme from each story. Use the space provided on page 374 to write your answer.

HINT Think about how you can organize your writing to show how things are the same and how they are different.

from
The Home of the Winds

retold from
Homer's *The Odyssey* by Alfred J. Church

1   The next day Ulysses and his companions set sail. After a while they came to the floating island where the King of the Winds had his home. For a whole month the king made him welcome.

2   When Ulysses wished to go home, the king did what he could to help him. He took the hide of an ox, very thick and strong. He put in it all the winds that would keep Ulysses from getting to his home, and he fastened it to the deck of his ship. Then he made a gentle wind blow from the west. For nine days it blew, till the ships were very near to the island of Ithaca.

3   But just before dawn on the tenth day, Ulysses, who had stayed awake all the time, fell asleep. The crew of his ship said to each other: "See that great bag of ox hide. It must have something very precious inside it—silver and gold and jewels. Why should the chief have all these good things to himself?"

4   So they cut the bag open, and all the winds rushed out and blew the ship away from Ithaca. Ulysses woke up at the noise, and at first thought that he would throw himself into the sea and die. Then he said to himself, "No! It is better to live," and he covered his face and lay still, without saying a word to his men. And the ships were driven back to the island of the King of the Winds.

Close Reader Habits

What are the key elements, or parts, of this story? **Circle** the main characters. **Underline** the two settings where the story takes place.

FROM ULYSSES AND THE SIRENS

RETOLD FROM HOMER'S *THE ODYSSEY* BY ALFRED J. CHURCH

1 The first place they came to was the Island of the Sirens. The Sirens were mermaids who sang so sweetly that no sailor who heard them could pass on his way, but was forced to go to them. But when he came near, the Sirens flew upon him and tore him to pieces.

2 Now Circe had warned Ulysses about these dreadful creatures, and told him what he ought to do. So he closed the ears of his companions with wax so tightly that they could hear nothing. As for himself, he made his men tie him with ropes to the mast of the ship. "And see," he said, "that you don't loose me, however much I may beg and pray."

3 As soon as the ship came near to the island, the wind ceased to blow. The men took down the sails and began to row.

4 Then the Sirens saw the ship and began to sing. Ulysses, where he stood bound to the mast, heard them. And when he understood what they said, he forgot all his caution. They promised just the thing that he wanted. For he was a man who thought he could never know enough about other countries and the people who dwelt in them. And the Sirens said that they could tell him all this.

5 Then he made signs with his head to his men that they should loose him. But they remembered what he had told them and rowed on. So they got safely past the Island of the Sirens.

Close Reader Habits

How is this story similar to and different from the one you just read? **Circle** the main characters. **Underline** the two places that are mentioned.

▶ **Think**

1. Complete this chart to show how key elements of the stories are the same and different.

> An *epic* is a series of adventures that a hero has over a long period of time. To get the most out of an epic, compare those adventures and how the hero acts in each one.

	"The Home of the Winds"	"Ulysses and the Sirens"
The two settings in each story		
Magical parts		
The actions of the crew		
The result of the crew's actions		

2. In what **two** ways are the settings of the stories alike?

    A Both stories take place on or near unusual islands.

    B Both stories take place in the home of a king.

    C Both stories take place on land far from the sea.

    D Both stories take place near Ulysses's home of Ithaca.

    E Both stories take place in part on Ulysses's ship.

3. Which of these **best** explains how the actions of Ulysses's crew in "The Home of the Winds" are different from their actions in "Ulysses and the Sirens"?

    A In "The Home of the Winds," the crew obeys Ulysses.

    B In "The Home of the Winds," the crew is not loyal to Ulysses.

    C In "The Home of the Winds," the crew saves Ulysses from disaster.

    D In "The Home of the Winds," the crew leaves Ulysses.

4 This question has two parts. Answer Part A. Then answer Part B.

Part A

Based on the two stories, which sentence **best** describes the kind of man Ulysses is?

   A   He is a poor leader but a good and thoughtful man.

   B   He is a strong leader who watches out for his crew.

   C   He is a weak man who depends on others to help him.

   D   He is a good man who is learning how to be brave.

Part B

Choose **one** detail from **each** story that supports your answer to Part A.

   A   "When Ulysses wished to go home, the king did what he could to help him." ("Winds")

   B   "Ulysses woke up at the noise, and at first thought that he would throw himself into the sea and die." ("Winds")

   C   "Then he said to himself, 'No! It is better to live,' and he covered his face and lay still, without saying a word to his men." ("Winds")

   D   "So he closed the ears of his companions with wax so tightly that they could hear nothing." ("Sirens")

   E   "And when he understood what they said, he forgot all his caution." ("Sirens")

   F   "Then he made signs with his head to his men that they should loose him." ("Sirens")

Talk

5 What themes, or lessons, could you draw from each story? How similar or different are those themes?

Write

6 **Short Response** One theme from *The Odyssey* could be that a leader like Ulysses has to be able to depend on his men. Use details from **both** stories to compare and contrast how they teach that lesson. Use the space provided on page 375 to write your answer.

> **HINT** Review the chart on page 372, especially the part that shows the crew's actions and the result of those actions.

▶ 📓 **Write** Use the space below to write your answer to the question on page 369.

The **Fox** and the **Goat**

The **Wolf** and the **Crane**

> **HINT** Think about how you can organize your writing to show how things are the same and how they are different.

3 **Short Response** Describe how the two fables are alike and different. Be sure to use details about characters, setting, and theme from each story.

_____

_____

_____

_____

_____

_____

> Don't forget to check your writing.

Write Use the space below to write your answer to the question on page 373.

The Home of the Winds

ULYSSES AND THE SIRENS

6 **Short Response** One theme from *The Odyssey* could be that a leader like Ulysses has to be able to depend on his men. Use details from both stories to compare and contrast how they teach that lesson.

> **HINT** Review the chart on page 372, especially the part that shows the crew's actions and the result of those actions.

_____

_____

_____

_____

_____

_____

_____

Check Your Writing

☐ Did you read the prompt carefully?

☐ Did you put the prompt in your own words?

☐ Did you use the best evidence from the text to support your ideas?

☐ Are your ideas clearly organized?

☐ Did you write in clear and complete sentences?

☐ Did you check your spelling and punctuation?

▶ **Read**

from The CYCLOPS

retold from Homer's *The Odyssey* by Alfred J. Church

> **WORDS TO KNOW**
> As you read, look inside, around, and beyond these words to figure out what they mean.
>
> • **pens**
> • **shepherd**

1   One of Ulysses's many adventures was in the country of the Cyclops or Round-eyed People. While exploring the country, he and his men came to a cave. Inside there were pens for sheep and baskets full of cheeses. Ulysses's men said to him: "Let us go away before the master comes back." But Ulysses would not listen to them. He wanted to see what kind of man this shepherd might be.

2   In the evening the Cyclops came home. He was a great giant, with one big eye in the middle of his forehead. He drove his flocks inside and then closed up the mouth of the cave with a rock so big that twenty wagons could not carry it.

3   When the giant saw the men, he grabbed up two of them and swallowed them. Then he lay down among his sheep and slept.

4   Ulysses thought: "Shall I slay this monster as he sleeps? But no; if I do this, we will be trapped. Who shall be able to roll away the great rock that is against the mouth of the cave?"

5   The giant left early the next morning, but kept the sheep and the men in the cave by rolling the rock back in place. All day, Ulysses and his men worked on a plan to escape the cave. In the evening, the giant came back. He grabbed two more men and swallowed them. When he had finished, Ulysses came to him with a special drink in his hand and said, "Drink, Cyclops, now that you have eaten."

6   The Cyclops took the glass and drank. "Give me more," he said, "and tell me your name."

7   Then Ulysses said: "My name is No Man."

8   When the giant fell asleep, Ulysses threw the spear he and his men had made into the giant's one eye. The giant leapt up and cried out so loudly that the Round-eyed people on the island came to see what had happened.

9   "Is someone hurting you?" they asked.

10   The giant bellowed, "No Man is hurting me!"

11   "Well," said the Round-eyed people, "if no man is hurting you, then it must be the gods that do it. We cannot help you against them."

12   Now Ulysses had made a plan to escape the cave. He took the biggest sheep and tied the men underneath their bellies. For himself, he clung to the belly of a sheep with both hands. When morning came, the flocks went out of the cave. The giant, now blind, felt them as they passed, but he did not feel the men.

Genre: Epic

from THE DANGEROUS WAY

RETOLD FROM HOMER'S *THE ODYSSEY* BY ALFRED J. CHURCH

WORDS TO KNOW

As you read, look inside, around, and beyond these words to figure out what they mean.

- **whirlpool**
- **linger**

1   There was a narrow place between the mainland and an island. On the one side there was a cave, in which there lived a terrible monster named Scylla. On the other side, there was a dreadful whirlpool called Charybdis. If a ship ever got into that, it was sucked down to the bottom of the sea and never came up again.

2   Circe had told Ulysses what he should do. "It will be better," she had said, "to go near Scylla than to go near Charybdis. Scylla will pounce down upon your ship when it comes within her reach. She will take six men, one for each of the six heads that she has. But if you go too near to Charybdis, your whole ship will be swallowed up. It is better to lose six men than have all of them drown."

3   When Ulysses had said, "May I not take shield and spear and fight with this monster?" Circe had answered, "You are wonderfully bold. You would fight with the gods themselves. But be sure that you cannot fight with Scylla. She is too strong for any man. And while you linger she will take six more men. No. Fly from the place as fast as you can."

4   So now he told the steersman to steer the ship as near as he could to the side of the strait near Scylla's cave. Nevertheless, they went very close to the whirlpool. It was a wonderful sight. At one time, you could see to the very bottom of the sea. And at another time, the water seemed to boil up almost to the top of the cliffs.

5   Now, Ulysses had said nothing to his men about the monster on the other side. He was afraid that if they knew about her they would not go on with their voyage. So they all stood and watched the whirlpool. Then, suddenly, there came down upon the ship Scylla's dreadful heads. She caught up six of the crew, the bravest and strongest of them all. Ulysses heard them cry to him to help them, but he could do nothing. And this, he said afterwards, was the very saddest thing that happened to him in all his troubles.

▶ **Think** Use what you learned from reading each selection to respond to these questions.

1 This question has two parts. First, complete Part A. Then answer Part B.

Part A
Put an **X** to show which statements are **true** in each story.

	"The Cyclops"	"The Dangerous Way"
Ulysses and his crew face a monster.		
Ulysses makes a poor choice that puts his crew in danger.		
Ulysses gets advice on how to deal with the monster.		
Ulysses saves most of his crew with a clever trick.		
Ulysses saves most of his crew by making a difficult decision.		

Part B
What are the biggest differences between the two stories?
Summarize them here.

_____

_____

_____

_____

2 Which words **best** describe Ulysses in both stories?

    A selfish and moody

    B brave and clever

    C adventurous but foolish

    D sad but determined

3 Below, underline **one** sentence in **each** excerpt that helps show the difference in how Ulysses responds to a threat to his crew.

> **While exploring the country, he and his men came to a cave. Inside there were pens for sheep and baskets full of cheeses. Ulysses's men said to him: "Let us go away before the master comes back." But Ulysses would not listen to them. ("The Cyclops")**
>
> **When Ulysses had said, "May I not take shield and spear and fight with this monster?" Circe had answered, "You are wonderfully bold. You would fight with the gods themselves." ("The Dangerous Way")**

4 Read the following sentence from "The Dangerous Way."

> **Then, suddenly, there came down upon the ship Scylla's dreadful heads.**

If the word *dread* means "to think about with great fear," what does the word *dreadful* mean in this context?

    A frightened

    B ugly

    C terrifying

    D dangerous

Write You have read the stories "The Cyclops" and "The Dangerous Way" about Ulysses. Think about how they are the same and how they are different.

5 **Plan Your Response** For each story that you read, list whom Ulysses meets, what problem he faces, and how he solves the problem.

6 **Write an Extended Response** Describe what is the same and different in "The Cyclops" and "The Dangerous Way." Use details about the characters, setting, and plot from each story in your answer.

_____

_____

_____

_____

_____

_____

_____

_____

_____

_____

_____

_____

_____

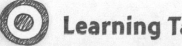 **Learning Target**

In this lesson you've compared and contrasted stories that have
the same or similar characters. What can this help you
understand about the characters and stories?

_____

_____

_____

_____

▶ **Read**

Read the folktales. Then answer the questions that follow.

Anansi Tries to Steal All the Wisdom in the World

a folktale from West Africa

1   Anansi the spider knew that he was not wise. He was a sly trickster who could use his wit to fool many different people. But he knew that he did not have much wisdom.

2   Then one day he had a clever thought. "If I can get all of the wisdom in the village and put it in a hollow gourd," he thought, "I will be very wise indeed. In fact, I will be the wisest of all!"

3   So he found a hollow gourd and began to carry out his plan. He went from door to door to collect the village's wisdom. People chuckled at poor Anansi, for they knew that more than any other creature, he needed wisdom. So each person put a bit of wisdom in his gourd and wished him well.

4   Soon the gourd was overflowing with wisdom and could hold no more. Now Anansi needed to find a place to store it. "I am certainly the wisest person in the world. But if I don't find a good hiding place for my wisdom, I am sure to lose it."

5   He looked around and spotted a very tall tree. "Ah," Anansi said, "I will hide my wisdom high in that tree. Then I will never have to worry about someone stealing it from me!"

6   Anansi set out to climb the towering tree with the heavy gourd tied to the front of his belly where it would be safe. As he climbed, however, the gourd full of wisdom kept getting in the way. He tried and tried, but he could not climb very high.

7   Just then, Anansi's youngest son walked by. "What are you doing, Father?" asked the little spider.

8   "I am climbing this tree with my gourd full of wisdom," Anansi replied.

9   "But Father," said the son, "wouldn't it be much easier if you tied the gourd behind you instead of in front?"

10   Anansi sat there quietly for a very long time. Then he said, "Shouldn't you be going home now?"

11   After his son left, Anansi moved the gourd so that it was behind him. Then he proceeded up the tree without a problem. When he reached the top, he cried out, "I collected so much wisdom that I am the wisest person ever, and still my baby son is wiser than me. Here! Take back your wisdom!"

12   He lifted the gourd high over his head and spilled its contents into the wind. The wisdom blew far and wide and settled across the land. And this is how wisdom came back to the world.

Anansi and the LION

a folktale from West Africa

1   Anansi the spider caught some fish and cooked them. He put them in a sack to take into the forest, where he could eat them all himself. "These will taste delicious," he chuckled.

2   Anansi hadn't gone very far when he met Lion, and Lion asked him, "Well, brother Anansi, what have you got there?"

3   "Oh . . . just some old bones that I'm going to bury in the mountains."

4   Lion walked away, but then he started thinking. "I know that Anansi is a great trickster. He probably has something in that sack he doesn't want me to see. I will follow him to see what he's up to."

5   When Anansi got into the woods, he set his sack down, took out one fish, and ate it. He didn't think anyone else was around, so he took out another fish. But just then, Lion came up and said, "Well, brother Anansi, those don't look like bones to me. That was a pretty tale you told me."

6   "Oh! brother Lion, I am so glad you have come. Never mind what I told you—it was only my fun. Come and join me."

7 So Lion sat down and began to eat, and before Anansi had eaten one fish, Lion had almost emptied the sack. Anansi said to himself, "Greedy fellow, eating up all my fish!"

8 "What did you say, sir?"

9 "I said you do not eat fast enough," Anansi replied, for he was afraid of what Lion might do. Soon, all the fish were gone.

10 While Anansi didn't complain, he did want to get back at Lion for eating most of his fish. He had a clever thought. "Which of us do you think is the stronger?"

11 Lion said, "Why, I am, of course."

12 Then Anansi said, "We will tie one another to that tree, and we shall see who is the stronger."

13 Now they agreed that Lion should tie Anansi first, and he tied him with some very fine string, and not very tight. Anansi twisted himself two or three times, and the string broke.

14 Then it was Anansi's turn to tie Lion, and he took some very strong rope. Lion said, "You must not tie me tight, for I did not tie you tight."

15 And Anansi said, "Oh, no, to be sure, I will not!" But he tied him as tight as ever he could and then told him to try and get loose.

16 Lion tried and tried, but he could not get loose.

17 Anansi thought, "That is what he gets for eating my meal, and now it's time for me to leave." So Anansi took up his empty sack and left Lion behind, tied to the tree.

▶ **Think**

1 Look at the picture on page 383 that goes with "Anansi Tries to Steal All the Wisdom in the World." What does the picture tell you about the way Anansi feels in this part of the story?

    A He is proud because he got what he wanted.

    B He is excited to see his young son.

    C He is sad and unhappy because someone might steal from him.

    D He is angry because he can't climb faster.

2 Which word from "Anansi Tries to Steal All the Wisdom in the World" do both pictures help you understand?

    A village

    B hollow

    C gourd

    D contents

3 Read the paragraph from "Anansi Tries to Steal All the Wisdom in the World." Underline the sentence that explains what has caused Anansi to do what he is doing in the picture on page 384.

> **After his son left, Anansi moved the gourd so that it was behind him. Then he proceeded up the tree without a problem. When he reached the top, he cried out, "I collected so much wisdom that I am the wisest person ever, and still my baby son is wiser than me. Here! Take back your wisdom!"**

4 Read this sentence from "Anansi and the Lion."

    "These will taste delicious," he chuckled.

What does the author's use of "chuckled" in this sentence tell about Anansi?

    A He is silly.

    B He is happy.

    C He is careful.

    D He is clever.

5 This question has two parts. First, answer Part A. Then answer Part B.

Part A
What is happening in the picture on page 385?

    A Anansi is offering to share his fish with Lion.

    B Anansi is telling Lion about his bag of bones.

    C Anansi has a contest of strength with Lion.

    D Anansi is upset that Lion has eaten most of the fish.

Part B
Which sentence from "Anansi and the Lion" **best** supports the answer to Part A?

    A "'Oh! brother Lion, I am so glad you have come.'"

    B "While Anansi didn't complain, he did want to get back at Lion for eating most of his fish."

    C "When Anansi got into the woods, he set his sack down, took out one fish, and ate it."

    D "Lion tried and tried, but he could not get loose."

6 Which of the following statements is true about Anansi in **both** stories?

    A Anansi thinks he is foolish.

    B Others think Anansi is foolish.

    C Anansi thinks he is clever.

    D Others think Anansi is clever.

7 Which sentence describes one way the two stories are **alike**?

    A They both have a happy ending.

    B They both explain why something happens in nature.

    C They both tell how animals get along with each other.

    D They both have a character who wants something all to himself.

8 A trickster is a type of character that likes to play tricks on others. Why is Anansi called a trickster in both stories? Use details from both stories and the pictures to support your answer.

_____

_____

_____

_____

_____

_____

_____

9 Which statement is true about the setting in **both** stories?

    A A tree is an important part of the setting.

    B A village is an important part of the setting.

    C The mountains are an important part of the setting.

    D The sky is an important part of the setting.

🔖 **Write**

10 **Extended Response** In both stories, which characters are greedy? What do they want? Do they finally get what they want? Use details from each story to support your answer.

In your answer, be sure to
- tell which characters are greedy in each story
- tell what the greedy characters want in each story
- tell whether or not the greedy characters finally get what they want
- use details from both stories in your answer

Check your writing for correct spelling, grammar, capitalization, and punctuation.

_____

_____

_____

_____

_____

_____

_____

_____

_____

_____

_____

Glossary of Words to Know

A

access a way of getting: *We have access to hundreds of movies on cable TV.*

ancient extremely old: *The ancient city was almost hidden by vines.*

B

ballet a graceful type of dance often used to tell a story: *The dancers in the ballet moved like swans.*

barge a flat-bottomed boat: *A barge carried supplies down the river.*

boulder a large rock: *There were huge boulders on either side of the trail.*

bowsprit a long pole that extends from the front of a ship: *The first thing we saw was the ship's bowsprit coming around the cliffs.*

bur a prickly seed case: *After I walk in the field, my clothes are always covered with burs.*

C

century a period of one hundred years: *That library was built over a century ago.*

ceremony a formal event that is part of a special occasion: *We will be going to my cousin's graduation ceremony this week.*

chore a small job that has to be done: *One of her chores was loading the dishwasher.*

coast the part of land near the sea: *Seashells wash up on the ocean coast.*

commission to place an order for something to be made: *The town council commissioned a statue for the war memorial.*

corral a pen for animals on a farm or ranch: *The horses are trained in the largest corral.*

current water moving in a definite direction: *A strong current can pull a swimmer away from shore.*

D

device a thing used to do a job or task: *A cell phone is one kind of electronic device.*

difficult hard to do: *Racing uphill is difficult even for strong runners.*

disbelief refusal to accept that something is true: *Lara stared at him in disbelief.*

dismantle to take apart: *The movers dismantled the bookcase before loading it on the truck.*

doubts worries or concerns about something: *We all had doubts about our plan.*

E

exploration the act of traveling through an area to learn about it: *Their exploration of the island led them to a waterfall.*

Glossary of Words to Know

F

fabric a woven or knitted material: *That red fabric will be used to make a cape.*

fathom six feet; used to describe the depth of water: *The harbor was eight fathoms deep.*

feast a large meal, usually for a celebration: *The cooks prepared a great feast to honor the new king.*

fellow a word used to describe someone from the same group: *Mark joined his fellow athletes on the field.*

fiber a thin thread of material: *That cloth is made from cotton fibers.*

function the special purpose for which something exists: *The kidney's main function is to clean the blood.*

fuss unusual amount of excitement or complaint: *One customer made a terrible fuss over the salesperson's mistake.*

G

gloom partial or total darkness: *The gloom of the forest made it hard to find our way.*

glossy shiny: *We used glossy paint on the old furniture.*

granite a very hard rock: *The statue was made of solid granite.*

groomed given a neat and tidy appearance: *Her two dogs are always well groomed.*

H

halter a strap put around the head of an animal to guide it: *Jake slipped the halter over the nervous horse's head.*

I

immediately right away: *The play began immediately after the lights went down.*

ingredient one of the things used to make a food or product: *We're missing some of the ingredients we need to make the cake.*

interactive something that requires two or more people or things to connect with each other: *Many teachers use interactive games in the classroom.*

L

linger to stay in a place: *Do not linger at the store, but come right home.*

lope to run in a relaxed way: *Three giraffes loped across the empty plain.*

Glossary of Words to Know

 M

massive extremely large: *A massive stone blocked the entrance.*

mixture something made by combining two or more ingredients: *Paste is a mixture of flour and water.*

 O

object something that can be seen or touched: *The most interesting objects were made from recycled trash.*

 P

pedestal the base on which a statue is placed: *The statue was put on a large stone pedestal.*

pen a closed off area where animals are kept: *The goats were herded into several large pens.*

pizzeria a restaurant that serves mainly pizzas: *My favorite pizzeria offers a dozen different types of pizza.*

portable easy to carry: *The campers used a small portable stove.*

 R

radiation a powerful form of energy: *High levels of radiation can make a person ill.*

recipe instructions for making a food or product: *My dad has a great recipe for chili.*

 S

scaffold a raised wooden platform: *The painter stood on a scaffold to reach the ceiling.*

shepherd a person who takes care of sheep: *The shepherd counted every sheep and lamb.*

skeptical showing doubt about something: *The police were skeptical of the woman's story.*

slunk moved in a way that did not attract attention: *Embarrassed by his mistake, he slunk away from the group.*

stall **1.** an enclosed area where a farm animal is kept: *Workers clean the horse's stall twice each day.* **2.** A booth where goods are sold at a market: *We bought fresh tomatoes at the vegetable stall.*

survive to stay alive: *Some animals survive harsh winters by hibernating.*

 T

thrive to grow successfully: *Those plants thrive in wet, shady areas.*

trot to move faster than walking but not as fast as running: *The pony trotted down the stone path.*

 U

unusual different or strange: *I collect rocks with unusual shapes.*

V

vendor a person who sells something: *Fruit and vegetable vendors called out to the passing shoppers.*

volunteer to work without being paid: *Lin volunteers at the food pantry once a week.*

W

whirlpool a place in a river or sea where the water spins around very fast: *The raft was caught in a whirlpool and pulled under the water.*

wondrous amazing: *The inside of the cave was truly wondrous.*

wrestling fighting that involves throwing or forcing another person to the ground: *The brothers were always wrestling with each other.*

Y

Yankee clipper a fast sailing ship from the nineteenth century: *Yankee clippers were used to get cargo from one place to another quickly.*

Language Handbook

Table of Contents

Lesson 1 Nouns 398

Lesson 2 Pronouns 400

Lesson 3 Verbs 402

Lesson 4 Adjectives. 404

Lesson 5 Adverbs. 406

Lesson 6 Plural Nouns 408

Lesson 7 Abstract Nouns. 410

Lesson 8 Simple Verb Tenses 412

Lesson 9 Regular Verbs 414

Lesson 10 Irregular Verbs. 416

Lesson 11 Subject–Verb Agreement. 418

Lesson 12 Pronoun–Antecedent Agreement. 420

Lesson 13 Comparative and Superlative
Adjectives and Adverbs 422

Lesson 14 Coordinating Conjunctions. 424

Lesson 15 Simple and Compound Sentences 426

Lesson 16 Subordinating Conjunctions and Complex Sentences 428

Lesson 17 Capitalization in Titles 430

Lesson 18 Punctuating Addresses. 432

Lesson 19 Punctuating Dialogue..434

Lesson 20 Possessive Nouns..436

Lesson 21 Possessive Pronouns..438

Lesson 22 Adding Suffixes 440

Lesson 23 Using Reference Works..442

Lesson 24 Choosing Words and Phrases for Effect.....................444

Lesson 25 Spoken and Written English 446

Lesson 26 Using Context Clues 448

Lesson 27 Prefixes and Suffixes...450

Lesson 28 Root Words 452

Lesson 29 Using a Dictionary or Glossary.............................454

Lesson 30 Literal and Nonliteral Meanings............................456

Lesson 31 Real-Life Connections...458

Lesson 32 Shades of Meaning 460

Lesson 33 Words for Time and Space....................................462

👥 Introduction   A **noun** is a word that names a person, place, or thing.

- A **common noun** names any person, place, or thing.
- A **proper noun** names a particular person, place, or thing. A proper noun begins with a capital letter.

	Common Nouns	**Proper Nouns**
Person	girl, teacher, president	Emily, Mr. Wong, Abraham Lincoln
Place	street, lake, country	Pine Street, Lake Mead, Mexico
Thing	cereal, month, holiday	Crispies, April, Thanksgiving

👥 Guided Practice

Underline the nouns in each sentence. Write *person*, *place*, **or** *thing* **above each noun to tell what it names.**

> **HINT** A proper noun can be more than one word. Each important word in a proper noun begins with a capital letter.

1 Aunt Lisa takes us to Oak Park.

2 The big slide is near Vine Street.

3 Nicole climbs the ladder quickly.

4 Alex loves the green and blue swing.

5 My little brother plays in the sand.

6 My sister pulls her wagon beside the pond.

7 Our Koby Kite flies high in the sky.

8 My aunt always brings a Fruitybar to share.

Independent Practice

For numbers 1–4, choose the correct word or words to answer each question.

1 Which words in this sentence are nouns?

Chase Pond is in the large park.

A Chase Pond, is

B the, park

C Chase Pond, park

D in, large

2 Which words in this sentence are nouns?

Mark and his sister often swim there.

A Mark, sister

B and, sister

C his, often

D Mark, swim

3 Which noun in this sentence names a person?

One day Meera saw a frog and a turtle.

A day

B Meera

C frog

D turtle

4 Which noun in this sentence names a place?

Ms. Patel and her friend enjoy having a picnic on the beach.

A Ms. Patel

B friend

C picnic

D beach

Lesson 2
Pronouns

👥 Introduction A **pronoun** is a word that can take the place of a noun. Use pronouns in your writing so you don't repeat the same noun over and over.

> She
> Sonya rides horses. ~~Sonya~~ is a very good rider.

- **Subject pronouns** take the place of the subject of a sentence. The **subject** is the part of the sentence that tells whom or what the sentence is about.

> He   They
> ~~Mr. Alvarez~~ gives riding lessons. ~~The lessons~~ are fun to learn.

- **Object pronouns** take the place of nouns that follow action verbs and words such as *to*, *in*, *at*, *on*, and *for*.

> him   them
> Horses love ~~Mr. Alvarez~~. Mr. Alvarez is kind to ~~horses~~.

	Subject Pronouns	Object Pronouns
Singular	I, you, he, she, it	me, you, him, her, it
Plural	we, you, they	us, you, them

👥 Guided Practice Circle the correct pronoun to take the place of the underlined word or words.

HINT Use a singular pronoun to replace a noun that tells about one person, place, or thing. Use a plural pronoun to replace a noun that tells about two or more people, places, or things.

1 <u>Sonya</u> has been riding for six years.

    Her   **It**   **She**

2 Mr. Alvarez found a gentle horse for <u>Sonya's brother</u>.

    he   **him**   **they**

3 Asa got in the saddle. He sat up straight in <u>the saddle</u>.

    him   **you**   **it**

4 Now <u>Sonya and Asa</u> go riding together.

    them   **they**   **she**

Independent Practice

For numbers 1–5, choose the correct pronoun to take the place of the underlined words in the sentence.

1 The horses are beautiful.

  A It

  B They

  C Them

  D We

2 The stable is my sister's favorite place.

  A Them

  B You

  C He

  D It

3 The riding teachers love my sister.

  A it

  B they

  C us

  D her

4 Mr. Chen gives fresh hay to the horses.

  A they

  B him

  C them

  D it

5 Mr. Chen owns the stable.

  A He

  B They

  C Him

  D Them

👥 Introduction A **verb** is a word that tells what someone or something *does* or *is*.

- Some verbs show action. An **action verb** tells what someone or something does.

  Squirrels eat nuts and leaves. I watch the squirrels in the tree.

- Some verbs do <u>not</u> show action. The verb *be* tells what someone or something is. The verb *be* has different forms. *Am, is,* and *are* are all forms of *be*.

Forms of *Be*	Examples
am	I am an expert on squirrels.
is	A tree is a good home for squirrels. Is it a safe place to hide? Yes, it is.
are	Most squirrels are brown or gray. They are so cute!

👥 Guided Practice **Underline the verb in each sentence. Write *A* above the verb if it is an action verb. Write *B* if it is a form of the verb *be*.**

HINT In a question, the verb **be** can come at the beginning of the sentence.

Example:
Is it furry?

1 Squirrels live in cities and in the country.

2 Are you afraid of squirrels?

3 I am not afraid of them.

4 I study different kinds of squirrels.

5 Indian giant squirrels grow as long as three feet!

6 A pygmy squirrel is five inches long.

7 Most gray squirrels eat acorns in fall and winter.

8 Is that a gray squirrel in the tree?

🧑 Independent Practice

For numbers 1–5, choose the word in each sentence that is a verb.

1 Some squirrels glide through the air.

  A Some

  B through

  C glide

  D air

2 They stretch their arms and legs.

  A They

  B arms

  C and

  D stretch

3 Their tails are flat and wide.

  A tails

  B Their

  C wide

  D are

4 Is that a squirrel or a bat?

  A squirrel

  B Is

  C that

  D bat

5 Mary wrote her report about those squirrels.

  A Mary

  B wrote

  C her

  D about

Adjectives

👥 Introduction

An **adjective** is a word that tells something about a noun. When you write, you can use adjectives to help your readers picture what you are describing.

Some adjectives tell *what kind*. They describe how something looks, feels, sounds, tastes, or smells. In the example below, *blue* describes the noun *ocean*. *Cold* describes *water*.

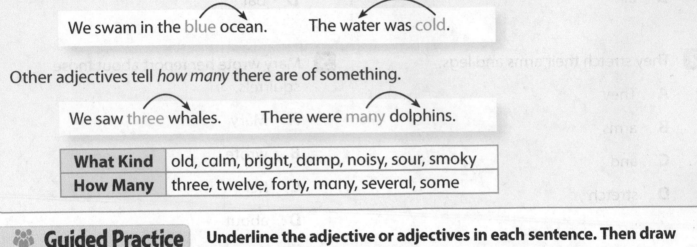

We swam in the blue ocean.　　The water was cold.

Other adjectives tell *how many* there are of something.

We saw three whales.　　There were many dolphins.

What Kind	old, calm, bright, damp, noisy, sour, smoky
How Many	three, twelve, forty, many, several, some

👥 Guided Practice

Underline the adjective or adjectives in each sentence. Then draw an arrow from each adjective to the noun that it tells about.

HINT Sometimes an adjective comes after the noun it describes. When this happens, other words usually come between the noun and adjective.

1 The Davis family goes to a beautiful beach in July.

2 The dunes at the beach are huge.

3 Maddy loves to feel the soft sand between her toes.

4 She likes to jump in the foamy waves.

5 The warm air smells salty from the ocean.

6 Little Chloe digs in the wet sand.

7 Yesterday, she found several shells.

8 Three shells were round.

Independent Practice

For numbers 1–3, choose the word in each sentence that is an adjective.

1 The cottage they stay in is two blocks from the ocean.

  A two

  B cottage

  C stay

  D ocean

2 Father takes the happy children to the beach.

  A to

  B happy

  C beach

  D children

3 The children like the smell of the tangy air.

  A The

  B like

  C smell

  D tangy

In numbers 4 and 5, what does the adjective in each sentence describe?

4 The hot sand burns in the sun.

  A how the sand looks

  B how the sand sounds

  C how the sand smells

  D how the sand feels

5 The water is salty.

  A how the water feels

  B how the water looks

  C how the water tastes

  D how the water sounds

Conventions of Standard English

Knowledge of Language

Vocabulary Acquisition and Use

Lesson 5
Adverbs

👥 Introduction
An **adverb** is a word that tells something about a verb, or action.

Many adverbs end in -ly and tell *how* or *in what way*. When you write, you can use adverbs to help your readers picture clearly what is happening.

The batter quickly ran to first base.   The umpire watched the runner closely.

- The adverb *quickly* describes the verb *ran*. It tells how the batter ran.

- The adverb *closely* describes the verb *watch*. It tells in what way the umpire watched.

👥 Guided Practice

Underline the adverb in each sentence. Draw an arrow from the adverb to the verb that it tells about.

HINT An adverb can come either before or after the verb it describes. A sentence might say *walked slowly*, or it might say *slowly walked*.

1 Jasmine nervously stood at home plate.

2 Her family shouted her name loudly.

3 She carefully rested the bat against her shoulder.

4 The pitcher gripped the ball tightly and then threw it.

5 Jasmine hit the ball sharply, and it soared toward left field.

6 A player tried to catch the ball but accidentally dropped it.

7 Jasmine easily slid into home base.

8 Her whole team cheered wildly!

Independent Practice

For numbers 1–3, choose the word in the sentence that is an adverb.

1 The crowd clapped excitedly when Jasmine hit the home run.

A crowd

B clapped

C excitedly

D hit

2 The coach told Jasmine that she had hit the ball perfectly.

A coach

B told

C ball

D perfectly

3 Jasmine's brother waved proudly and jumped from his seat.

A waved

B proudly

C jumped

D seat

For numbers 4 and 5, choose the word that the underlined adverb describes.

4 Jasmine smiled <u>shyly</u> when she saw her family.

A smiled

B saw

C Jasmine

D family

5 She <u>quickly</u> jogged back to the bench and sat down.

A jogged

B back

C bench

D sat

Plural Nouns

👥 Introduction
A **singular noun** is a noun that names one person, place, or thing. A **plural noun** names more than one person, place, or thing.

- You can form the plural of most nouns just by adding *-s*.

Singular	a frog	one pond	a turtle
Plural	six frogs	two ponds	some turtles

- To form the plural of a noun that ends in *ch*, *sh*, *ss*, or *x*, add *-es*.
- To form the plural of a noun that ends in a consonant and *y*, change the *y* to *i* and add *-es*.

Singular	bunch	brush	mess	box	fly	baby
Plural	bunches	brushes	messes	boxes	flies	babies

- Some plural nouns do not end in *s*. **Irregular plurals** change in special ways or do not change at all! You just have to remember these plural nouns.

Singular	man	mouse	goose	foot	deer	moose
Plural	men	mice	geese	feet	deer	moose

👥 Guided Practice

Write the plural of the noun in parentheses ( ) to complete each sentence.

HINT If a noun ends in *y* but there is a vowel before the *y*, do not change the *y* to *i*. Just add *-s*.

Example:
boy + **s** = **boys**

1 I went to pick _____ in the woods. (berry)

2 I heard a noise behind some _____. (rock)

3 I thought I would see a few _____. (deer)

4 Then six big birds came out of those _____. (bush)

5 At first I thought they were _____. (goose)

6 Then I realized that they were _____! (turkey)

Independent Practice

For numbers 1–3, choose the sentence in which the plural noun or nouns are spelled correctly.

1
A Two familys of mouse live in that stone wall.

B Two familyes of mices live in that stone wall.

C Two family of mouses live in that stone wall.

D Two families of mice live in that stone wall.

2
A Colorful butterflys flit through the air.

B Colorful butterflis flit through the air.

C Colorful butterflies flit through the air.

D Colorful butterflyes flit through the air.

3
A Some mooses drink from the pond.

B Some moose drink from the pond.

C Some moosies drink from the pond.

D Some meese drink from the pond.

For numbers 4 and 5, read each sentence and answer the question.

4 The wind blows through the branchses of the trees.

What is the correct plural of the underlined word?

A branchies

B branchys

C branches

D branchs

5 Are there any bears or foxses in this forest?

What is the correct plural of the underlined word?

A foxs

B foxes

C foxys

D foxies

Lesson 7
Abstract Nouns

👥 **Introduction** You know that a **noun** is a word that names a person, place, or thing.

- Most nouns name things you can see, touch, taste, smell, or hear. These are called **concrete nouns**.

  I love to look at pictures of my father when he was young.

- Some nouns name ideas, feelings, beliefs, or other things that you *cannot* see, touch, taste, smell, or hear. These are called **abstract nouns**.

  My father has many happy memories of his childhood.

Compare these examples of concrete and abstract nouns.

Concrete Nouns	food	hero	prize	seatbelt
Abstract Nouns	hunger	bravery	pride	safety

👥 **Guided Practice** Circle the abstract noun in each sentence. Then choose one noun you circled, and use it in a sentence about your own family.

HINT Ask yourself if each word you circled is an idea, a feeling, a belief, or something else that you cannot see, touch, taste, smell, or hear.

1 My grandparents teach us good values.

2 They show their love by giving us big hugs.

3 Grandma reminds us to treat our friends with kindness.

4 Grandpa tells us how important honesty is.

5 I am glad he shares his thoughts with us!

6 _____

_____

Independent Practice

For numbers 1–5, choose the abstract noun to complete each sentence.

1 My grandparents came to the United States with _____.

   A dishes

   B suitcases

   C hope

   D maps

2 In the United States, they would find _____.

   A trees

   B baseball

   C subways

   D freedom

3 They wanted their children to have a better _____.

   A house

   B life

   C school

   D car

4 My grandparents needed _____ to move to this country.

   A courage

   B money

   C passports

   D tickets

5 Here, they got lots of _____ from friends and family.

   A rides

   B clothing

   C furniture

   D help

Simple Verb Tenses

👥 Introduction
The **tense** of a verb helps readers know when something is happening.

- The **present tense** shows that something is happening *now*, or in the present.

  > I walk on the grass.

- The **past tense** shows that something happened *before*, or in the past. To form the past tense of most verbs, add *-ed* at the end.

  > In 1969, Neil Armstrong walk<u>ed</u> on the moon.

- The **future tense** shows what *is going to* happen in the future. To form the future tense, put *will* before the verb.

  > Maybe someday we <u>will</u> walk on Mars.

Look at the table below. Notice how the verbs change when the tense changes.

Present Tense	look	roam	discover
Past Tense	looked	roamed	discovered
Future Tense	will look	will roam	will discover

👥 Guided Practice
Write the correct tense of the verb to complete each sentence.

HINT Words and phrases such as *in 1958*, *today*, and *years from now* can help you decide which verb tense to use.

1 The NASA space program _____ in 1958.
start

2 In 1961, NASA _____ a capsule called *Freedom 7*.
launch

3 John Glenn _____ Earth in 1962.
orbit

4 Today, astronauts _____ on a space station.
stay

5 Years from now, we will _____ to other planets.
travel

👤 Independent Practice

For numbers 1–5, choose the sentence in which the tense of the verb is correct.

1
  A   Our class visited Johnson Space Center next Wednesday.

  B   Our class will visited Johnson Space Center next Wednesday.

  C   Our class visit Johnson Space Center next Wednesday.

  D   Our class will visit Johnson Space Center next Wednesday.

2
  A   Yesterday we learn about a space rover trip to Mars.

  B   Yesterday we learned about a space rover trip to Mars.

  C   Tomorrow we learned about a space rover trip to Mars.

  D   Yesterday we will learn about a space rover trip to Mars.

3
  A   The rover, named *Curiosity*, landed on Mars in August of 2012.

  B   The rover, named *Curiosity*, land on Mars in August of 2012.

  C   The rover, named *Curiosity*, will land on Mars in August of 2012.

  D   The rover, named *Curiosity*, will landed on Mars in August of 2012.

4
  A   Right now, videos from *Curiosity* show the surface of Mars.

  B   Right now, videos from *Curiosity* will showed the surface of Mars.

  C   In the future, videos from *Curiosity* showed the surface of Mars.

  D   In the future, videos from *Curiosity* show the surface of Mars.

5
  A   At the Space Center next week, I ask more about *Curiosity*.

  B   At the Space Center next week, I asked more about *Curiosity*.

  C   At the Space Center next week, I will ask more about *Curiosity*.

  D   At the Space Center next week, I will asked more about *Curiosity*.

Lesson 9
Regular Verbs

👥 Introduction
A verb in the past tense shows that something already happened. Most verbs are **regular verbs**. They each follow the same rules to form the past tense.

- For most regular verbs, add -ed to form the past tense.

  watch + **ed**   We watched the dancers on the stage.

- For verbs that end in silent e, just add -d.

  move + **d**   They moved gracefully across the floor.

- For verbs that end in a consonant and y, change the y to i before you add -ed.

  carry – **y** + **i** + **ed**   One dancer carried the other.

- For verbs that end in a short vowel sound and a consonant, double the consonant before you add -ed.

  flip + **p** + **ed**   Then he flipped her in the air!

👥 Guided Practice

Write the past tense of the verb to complete each sentence. Be sure to use correct spelling.

HINT If a verb ends in y but there is a vowel before the y, do <u>not</u> change the y to i. Just add -ed.

Example:
stay + **ed** = **stayed**

1 Yuki _____ in a dance show last night.
   perform

2 The dancers _____ to several different songs.
   dance

3 They _____ to the music.
   sway

4 Near the end, the music suddenly _____.
   stop

5 Yuki's teacher _____ behind the stage.
   hurry

Independent Practice

For numbers 1–5, choose the correct spelling of the past tense verb to complete each sentence.

1 My school _____ a talent show last week.

   A presentd

   B presented

   C presentted

   D present

2 I _____ my act every day for a month.

   A practicied

   B practiceed

   C practice

   D practiced

3 I _____ that I would make a mistake.

   A worreid

   B worryd

   C worried

   D worryed

4 For my act, I _____ four tomatoes.

   A juggled

   B juggleed

   C jugglled

   D juggld

5 The audience _____ loudly when I was done.

   A claped

   B clappd

   C clapped

   D clapedd

Irregular Verbs

Introduction Most verbs are regular. Regular verbs end in *-ed* when they show that something happened in the past. Some verbs are irregular. **Irregular verbs** change in special ways to show past time.

Present	Sometimes I make my own lunch.
Past	Yesterday I made a sandwich.

Another way to tell about the past is to use the helping verb *has*, *have*, or *had* with the past form of the main verb. Some irregular verbs change spelling when they are used with *has*, *have*, or *had*.

Present	Past	Past with *Has, Have,* or *Had*
begin	began	(has, have, had) begun
come	came	(has, have, had) come
eat	ate	(has, have, had) eaten
go	went	(has, have, had) gone
make	made	(has, have, had) made
see	saw	(has, have, had) seen
run	ran	(has, have, had) run
give	gave	(has, have, had) given

Guided Practice Circle the form of the verb that correctly completes each sentence.

HINT To know which past form of the verb to use, look for the helping verb *has*, *have*, or *had*. Sometimes the word *not* or another word comes between the helping verb and the main verb.

1 I have always _____ each day with a healthy breakfast.

    begun   **began**   **begin**

2 Yesterday Mom _____ me a bowl of oatmeal with fruit.

    given   **give**   **gave**

3 My dad has _____ yummy banana bread.

    made   **maked**   **make**

4 Grandma had not _____ yet, so she had some, too.

    eaten   **eat**   **ate**

👤 Independent Practice

For numbers 1–5, read each sentence. Then choose the word that replaces the underlined verb and makes the sentence correct.

1 Mom and I <u>go</u> to the store last week.

   A gone

   B goed

   C went

   D goned

2 We had <u>ran</u> out of healthy snacks.

   A run

   B runned

   C ranned

   D rund

3 At the store, we <u>see</u> a lot of cookies and candy.

   A seen

   B seened

   C sawed

   D saw

4 Mom has never <u>give</u> me snacks like those.

   A gave

   B gaven

   C given

   D gived

5 We <u>come</u> home with carrots and raisins.

   A camed

   B came

   C camen

   D comed

Subject–Verb Agreement

👥 Introduction The **subject** of a sentence tells whom or what the sentence is about. A subject can tell about one or more than one person, place, or thing. The verb in the sentence must **agree** with, or match in number, the subject. The subject can be singular or plural.

Singular	Plural
subject verb Kenji writes poems for a hobby.	subject verb His brothers write songs.

Follow these rules if the subject is a singular noun or the pronoun *he*, *she*, or *it*.

Add -*s* to the end of most verbs.	Tara collects old trains.
Add -*es* if the verb ends in *ch*, *sh*, *ss*, or *x*.	She washes the trains.
Change *y* to *i* before adding -*es* if the verb ends in a consonant and *y*.	She tries to fix them.

Do <u>not</u> add anything to the verb if the subject is a plural noun or the pronoun *I*, *you*, *we*, or *they*.

Sometimes I help Tara, too. The trains always look beautiful.

👥 Guided Practice **Cross out each verb that does not agree with its subject. Write the verb correctly above it.**

HINT If a verb ends in a vowel and *y*, just add -*s* if the subject is singular. Do <u>not</u> add anything if the subject is plural.

Example:
Tina **plays** sports.
We **play**, too.

Many people enjoys hobbies. My friend Simon likes baseball

cards. He keep them in a huge box. My sister Kim watch cartoons.

Then she draws her favorite characters. My grandparents travel

a lot. They saves coins from everywhere. Even our dog finds bones

and bury them in our yard.

Independent Practice

For numbers 1–5, read each sentence. Then choose the correct verb to agree with the subject.

1 My uncle _____ for a hobby.

   A fishs

   B fishies

   C fishes

   D fish

2 He _____ the fish home in a pail.

   A carrys

   B carries

   C carryes

   D carry

3 My sisters _____ to hike.

   A likes

   B likse

   C liks

   D like

4 They _____ for interesting flowers and rocks.

   A searchs

   B searches

   C search

   D searchse

5 Dora _____ the names of many rocks.

   A knows

   B knowes

   C knowz

   D know

Lesson 12
Pronoun–Antecedent Agreement

Introduction You know that pronouns take the place of nouns. Pronouns must **agree** with, or match in number, the noun they replace. The singular pronouns are *I, you, he, she, it, me, him,* and *her*. The plural pronouns are *we, you, they, us,* and *them*.

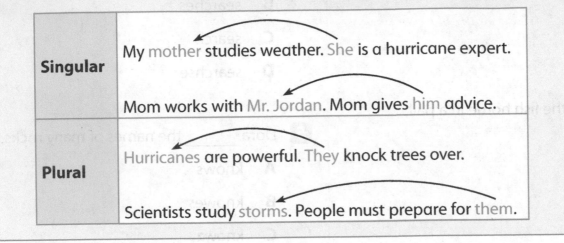

Singular	My mother studies weather. She is a hurricane expert.
	Mom works with Mr. Jordan. Mom gives him advice.
Plural	Hurricanes are powerful. They knock trees over.
	Scientists study storms. People must prepare for them.

Guided Practice Cross out each pronoun that does not agree with the noun it replaces. Write the correct pronoun above it.

HINT Use *he* or *him* when you are talking about a boy or a man. Use *she* or *her* when you are talking about a girl or a woman.

1 The weather interests Sara. Mom teaches him about it.

2 Mom knows about storms. She keeps track of it.

3 Grandpa remembers a bad storm. He tells about them.

4 The wind was 95 miles an hour. She was very strong.

5 Trees crashed down. It fell on the house.

6 Grandpa was on the porch. They yelled for Grandma.

7 Grandma heard Grandpa. She ran outside to find them.

8 My grandparents were safe. It stayed in a shelter.

Independent Practice

For numbers 1–5, read each sentence. Then choose the pronoun that agrees with the underlined noun.

1 <u>Mr. Jordan</u> reports the weather.
_____ gets help from my mother.

A She

B He

C It

D They

2 Mr. Jordan warned <u>people</u> about a hurricane and told _____ what to do.

A him

B her

C them

D it

3 <u>People</u> stayed safe because _____ listened to his advice.

A she

B he

C it

D they

4 <u>Mayor Maria Perez</u> called Mr. Jordan and my mom. _____ thanked them.

A She

B He

C It

D We

5 My mom enjoys working with <u>Mr. Jordan</u>. She has a lot of respect for _____ .

A she

B he

C her

D him

Lesson 13
Comparative and Superlative Adjectives and Adverbs

👥 Introduction When you write, you can use adjectives and adverbs to tell how things are alike or different.

- Add *-er* to most adjectives to compare two people, places, or things.
  Add *-est* to compare three or more people, places, or things.

cold + **er**	The lake is colder than the pond.
cold + **est**	Of all bodies of water, the ocean is the coldest place to swim.

- Use *more* with adverbs that end in *-ly* to compare two actions.
  Use *most* to compare three or more actions.

more + gracefully	Emma swims more gracefully than Madison.
most + gracefully	Ann swims the most gracefully of all the girls.

👥 Guided Practice Read each sentence. Circle the correct word or words to complete it.

HINT Never use *more* or *most* together with adjectives that end in *-er* or *-est*.

Correct:
fuller, fullest

Incorrect:
more fuller,
most fullest

1 The adults' pool is _____ than the children's pool.

     deepest   **deeper**   **more deeply**

2 My little brother swims _____ than I do.

     slowly   **more slowly**   **slowest**

3 The morning is the _____ time of all at the pool.

     most calmest   **more calm**   **calmest**

4 This lifeguard blows her whistle the _____ of all the guards.

     most loudly   **louder**   **more louder**

Independent Practice

For numbers 1–5, choose the correct word or words to complete each sentence.

1 Nikki built the _____ sand castle on the beach.

  A tall

  B most tallest

  C more tall

  D tallest

2 I saw a seahorse that was _____ than my fingernail.

  A most small

  B more smaller

  C smaller

  D smallest

3 Dan put on his snorkel _____ than his little brother did.

  A most carefully

  B more carefully

  C careful

  D carefully

4 Pari was the _____ swimmer of all of us.

  A stronger

  B strongest

  C more stronger

  D most strongest

5 Max held the little crab the _____ of all the children.

  A most gently

  B gentle

  C more gently

  D gently

Lesson 14
Coordinating Conjunctions

👥 Introduction
A **conjunction** is a word that is used to join other words, groups of words, or sentences. The words *and*, *but*, *or*, and *so* are conjunctions.

- Use *and* when you mean "also."

  Birds and dogs are my favorite animals.

- Use *but* when you want to show a difference.

  Mario's cat is playful, but Lila's cat likes to sleep.

- Use *or* when you want to show a choice.

  Dad says we can have a kitten or a puppy.

- Use *so* when you want to give a reason.

  I love animals, so I like having a lot of pets.

👥 Guided Practice

Write the conjunction *and*, *but*, *or*, or *so* to complete each sentence.

HINT Sometimes more than one conjunction can make sense in a sentence. Choose the conjunction that makes the meaning clearest.

1 Poodles _____ collies are both smart dogs.

2 I take my dog to the park, _____ he can get more exercise.

3 Shanti likes cats _____ not dogs.

4 Pedro wants a dog, _____ he does not want a big dog.

5 Kim walks her dog _____ then feeds him.

6 Should we name the puppy Ernie _____ Bert?

7 Our dog doesn't obey, _____ we need to send him to a dog trainer.

8 Pedro might get a dog today, _____ he will wait until tomorrow.

Independent Practice

For numbers 1–5, choose the best conjunction to complete each sentence.

1 Parrots are colorful _____ smart birds.

A and

B but

C or

D so

2 Most parrots live in jungles, _____ some of them live in homes as pets.

A and

B but

C or

D so

3 Parrots have strong, curved beaks, _____ they can crack open seeds.

A and

B but

C or

D so

4 Anisa wants a parrot _____ no pet at all.

A and

B but

C or

D so

5 I would like to have both a parrot _____ a parakeet.

A and

B but

C or

D so

Simple and Compound Sentences

👥 Introduction A **sentence** is a group of words that tells a complete thought.

- A **simple sentence** has one subject and one predicate. The **subject** tells whom or what the sentence is about. The **predicate** tells what the subject does or is.

> subject   predicate
> [Alfredo] [goes to art class on Tuesday and Thursday.]

- A **compound sentence** has two simple sentences joined together by the conjunction *and*, *but*, *or*, or *so*. There is usually a comma before the conjunction.

> simple sentence   simple sentence
> [Alfredo likes art class], but [his sister enjoys music class.]

- Combining two short sentences into a compound sentence can make your writing less choppy. It also helps you show that two ideas are connected.

> Alfredo painted a picture. His sister sang a song.

> Alfredo painted a picture, and his sister sang a song.

👥 Guided Practice

Combine each pair of simple sentences to make a compound sentence. Use the conjunction in parentheses ( ).

HINT Be sure to put a comma before the conjunction in each compound sentence you write.

1 Should we start class? Should we wait? (or)

_____

2 I finished my picture. Neil did not finish his. (but)

_____

3 Liz has a flute lesson soon. She must practice. (so)

_____

4 She made up a song. It sounded great! (and)

_____

👤 Independent Practice

For numbers 1–4, pick the choice that correctly combines the two simple sentences into a compound sentence.

1 Mr. Ramirez loves music. He is a great teacher.

   A   Mr. Ramirez loves music and he is a great teacher.

   B   Mr. Ramirez loves music, but he is a great teacher.

   C   Mr. Ramirez loves music, and he is a great teacher.

   D   Mr. Ramirez loves music, or he is a great teacher.

2 Anita was going to sing. She had a sore throat.

   A   Anita was going to sing, but she had a sore throat.

   B   Anita was going to sing, so she had a sore throat.

   C   Anita was going to sing, or she had a sore throat.

   D   Anita was going to sing, and she had a sore throat.

3 You may play the piano first. You may play the drums first.

   A   You may play the piano first, and you may play the drums first.

   B   You may play the piano first, so you may play the drums first.

   C   You may play the piano first, but you may play the drums first.

   D   You may play the piano first, or you may play the drums first.

4 We cannot hear the music. Please make it louder.

   A   We cannot hear the music, and please make it louder.

   B   We cannot hear the music, so please make it louder.

   C   We cannot hear the music, but please make it louder.

   D   We cannot hear the music so, please make it louder.

Lesson 16
Subordinating Conjunctions and Complex Sentences

👥 Introduction Simple sentences can be combined using different kinds of conjunctions.

- One way to combine simple sentences is to use a conjunction such as *after*, *because*, *when*, or *while*. When you combine two simple sentences with such conjunctions, you form a **complex sentence**.

simple sentence		simple sentence
[Yasmin did not stay for the game]	although	[she loves soccer.]

- In a complex sentence, the conjunction shows how the ideas in the two simple sentences go together.
- The conjunction can come at the beginning or in the middle of the sentence.

Conjunctions	When to Use	Examples
because	to explain or give a reason	Yasmin went home because she felt ill.
after, before, until, when, while	to show when things happen	She had a snack before she took a nap. When she woke up, she watched TV.
although, unless	to compare or to show an exception	She'll stay home Monday unless she feels better.

👥 Guided Practice **Combine each pair of simple sentences to make a complex sentence. Use the conjunction in parentheses ( ).**

HINT When you begin a sentence with a conjunction, use a comma after the first simple sentence.

Example:
Before you play soccer, you should stretch.

1 The soccer players have fun. They practice. (while)

_____

2 Kayla works hard. She wants to be a better player. (because)

_____

3 Milo was on the team. He got hurt. (until)

_____

Independent Practice

For numbers 1–4, first read the simple sentences. Then pick the choice that correctly combines the simple sentences into a complex sentence.

1 The game had already begun. We arrived.

   A The game had already begun because we arrived.

   B Although the game had already begun, we arrived.

   C The game had already begun when we arrived.

   D The game had already begun while we arrived.

2 It started to rain. The game was not called off.

   A Although it started to rain, the game was not called off.

   B Because it started to rain, the game was not called off.

   C It started to rain when the game was not called off.

   D It started to rain unless the game was not called off.

3 The Hawks won. They scored the most goals.

   A The Hawks won unless they scored the most goals.

   B The Hawks won before they scored the most goals.

   C After the Hawks won, they scored the most goals.

   D The Hawks won because they scored the most goals.

4 The game was over. We went out for pizza.

   A Until the game was over, we went out for pizza.

   B After the game was over, we went out for pizza.

   C The game was over unless we went out for pizza.

   D The game was over because we went out for pizza.

Capitalization in Titles

Introduction There is a special way to write the title of a book, magazine, newspaper, or movie.

- Always capitalize the first word, the last word, and all the important words in a title.
- Do <u>not</u> capitalize short words such as *a, an, the, and, of, for, in,* and *on* unless they are the first or last word of the title.

Book	*The Adventures of Peter Vine*
Magazine	*Fun for You and Me*
Newspaper	*The Daily News*
Movie	*Sara Drake and the Secret Cave*

Guided Practice Write each title correctly, adding capital letters where they are needed.

HINT Usually the title of a book, magazine, newspaper, or movie is shown in *italics*. But when you write one of these titles by hand, you should <u>underline</u> it instead.

1 *oliver in space* (movie)
2 *abby and the zebra* (book)
3 *explore and more* (magazine)
4 *the star county times* (newspaper)
5 *a dragon in town* (movie)
6 *lily the lucky ladybug* (book)
7 *diary of an amazing mouse* (movie)
8 *sports for healthy kids* (magazine)

1 _____

2 _____

3 _____

4 _____

5 _____

6 _____

7 _____

8 _____

Independent Practice

For numbers 1–5, choose the correct answer to each question.

1 How should the title of this movie be written?

   A *a Hog on a Log*

   B *A Hog On a Log*

   C *a Hog on a log*

   D *A Hog on a Log*

2 How should the title of this book be written?

   A *Sam The Storm chaser*

   B *Sam the Storm Chaser*

   C *Sam the storm Chaser*

   D *Sam The Storm Chaser*

3 How should the title of this magazine be written?

   A *The Planets And The Stars*

   B *The planets and the Stars*

   C *The Planets and the Stars*

   D *the Planets And the Stars*

4 How should the title of this newspaper be written?

   A *Weekly News for All*

   B *Weekly News For all*

   C *Weekly news for All*

   D *Weekly news For all*

5 How should the title of this book be written?

   A *And the Cat Wants in*

   B *And the Cat Wants In*

   C *and the Cat Wants in*

   D *And The Cat Wants In*

Punctuating Addresses

👥 Introduction
What is the name of the street where your school is? What city or town is it in? What is the name of the state where you live? When you put all of this information together, you get an **address**.

When you write an address, place a **comma (,)** between the name of the street and the city. Place another comma between the name of the city and the state.

The store is at 300 Craig Street, Durham, North Carolina.

👥 Guided Practice
Rewrite each address. Add commas where they are needed. Then finish the last sentence by writing your own address.

HINT The name of a street can also have the word *Road*, *Drive*, *Lane*, or *Avenue* at the end. The comma always comes after those words.

1 18 West Lane Orlando Florida

_____

2 2 Griggs Avenue Albany New York

_____

3 531 Front Street Monroe Wisconsin

_____

4 1538 Oakwood Drive Canton Ohio

_____

5 49 Jeffrey Road Athens Georgia

_____

6 My address is _____

_____

_____

👤 Independent Practice

For numbers 1–4, pick the choice that correctly punctuates the address underlined in the sentence.

1 My grandmother lives at 945 Peters Street Fresno California.

   A 945 Peters, Street Fresno, California

   B 945 Peters Street, Fresno, California

   C 945 Peters Street Fresno, California

   D 945 Peters Street, Fresno California

2 I sent the card to 310 Medford Road Concord North Carolina.

   A 310 Medford Road, Concord, North Carolina

   B 310, Medford Road, Concord, North Carolina

   C 310 Medford Road, Concord North, Carolina

   D 310 Medford Road Concord, North Carolina

3 The address on the envelope was 18 Arcola Lane Tucson Arizona.

   A 18 Arcola, Lane, Tucson, Arizona

   B 18 Arcola Lane, Tucson Arizona

   C 18 Arcola Lane, Tucson, Arizona

   D 18 Arcola Lane Tucson, Arizona

4 Hiro's family moved to 4 Charles Drive Bristol Rhode Island.

   A 4 Charles Drive Bristol, Rhode Island

   B 4 Charles Drive, Bristol Rhode Island

   C 4, Charles Drive, Bristol, Rhode Island

   D 4 Charles Drive, Bristol, Rhode Island

Punctuating Dialogue

👥 Introduction
When characters in a story talk to each other, this is a **dialogue**. When you write a dialogue, use **quotation marks** (" ") before and after each speaker's words.

> Mr. Simons said, "We're going on a field trip!"
>
> "Hooray!" the class shouted.

When a speaker's words come last in a sentence, use a **comma (,)** to separate the speaker's words from the rest of the sentence.

> Myra asked, "Where are we going?"
>
> Mr. Simons answered, "We are going to the Natural History Museum."

👥 Guided Practice

Read each sentence. Then rewrite the sentence on the line below, adding quotation marks and commas where needed.

HINT The end punctuation after a speaker's words should be *inside* the quotation marks.

Correct: "It's a dog, isn't it**?**"

Incorrect: "It's a dog, isn't it**"?**

1 I am so excited about our trip to the museum! Janie said.

_____

_____

2 Carlos asked Do you think it will be boring?

_____

_____

3 Then Justin explained It's a chance to go someplace new.

_____

_____

4 I think we'll have a great time! Tanisha added.

_____

_____

Independent Practice

For numbers 1–5, choose the sentence in each group that uses correct punctuation.

1 **A** "This museum is gigantic"! Anna exclaimed.

   B "This museum is gigantic!" Anna exclaimed.

   C "This museum is gigantic! Anna exclaimed."

   D This museum is gigantic! "Anna exclaimed."

2 **A** Celia said, "Everyone should visit this museum."

   B Celia said "Everyone should visit this museum."

   C Celia said, Everyone should visit this museum.

   D "Celia said" Everyone should visit this museum.

3 **A** Alberto asked. "What is this?"

   B Alberto asked, "What is this"?

   C Alberto asked "What is this"!

   D Alberto asked, "What is this?"

4 **A** I've never seen anything like it! Juanita replied.

   B I've never seen anything like it! "Juanita replied."

   C "I've never seen anything like it!" Juanita replied.

   D "I've never seen anything like it! Juanita replied."

5 **A** Billy announced, "It's a fossil footprint."

   B Billy announced. "It's a fossil footprint."

   C Billy announced "It's a fossil footprint".

   D "Billy announced, "It's a fossil footprint.

Lesson 20
Possessive Nouns

👥 Introduction Some nouns show that a person or animal owns something. A noun that shows ownership is called a **possessive noun**. For example, *the girl's hat* means that the girl owns or has the hat. *The tiger's fur* means that the fur belongs to the tiger.

- To form the possessive of a singular noun, add an **apostrophe (')** and then an *-s*.

seller + 's	The ticket seller's booth is at the front of the zoo.

- To form the possessive of a plural noun, add an apostrophe (') *after* the *-s*.

lions + '	The lions' area is near the back of the zoo.

👥 Guided Practice Write the possessive form of the noun in parentheses ( ) to complete each phrase.

HINT How can you tell if the possessive noun should be singular or plural? Look at the ending of the noun in ( ). Also look for clue words, such as *a*, *one*, *several*, and *few*.

1 a _____ key (zookeeper)

2 several _____ ears (bunnies)

3 one _____ flippers (penguin)

4 a few _____ tails (foxes)

5 three _____ brooms (cleaners)

6 a _____ tickets (guest)

7 some _____ nests (cranes)

8 an _____ egg (emu)

Independent Practice

For numbers 1–5, choose the correct way to write each underlined noun.

1 Several <u>workers</u> pails had food for the animals.

   A   worker's'

   B   workers

   C   worker's

   D   workers'

2 The workers put bottles in a few <u>babies</u> mouths.

   A   babies'

   B   babie's'

   C   babies

   D   babie's

3 The zookeeper pointed out three <u>ostriches</u> strong legs.

   A   ostriche's's

   B   ostriches

   C   ostriches'

   D   ostriche's

4 There was a big spray of water from an <u>elephants</u> trunk.

   A   elephants

   B   elephant's

   C   elephants's

   D   elephants'

5 We loved seeing one <u>peacocks</u> colorful feathers.

   A   peacocks'

   B   peacocks

   C   peacock's

   D   peacocks's

Lesson 21
Possessive Pronouns

Introduction You know that a possessive noun shows ownership. When a pronoun shows ownership, it is called a **possessive pronoun**.

- A possessive pronoun can take the place of a possessive noun.

> Her
> Lena had the idea for the bake sale. ~~Lena's~~ aunt made bread.

- A possessive pronoun can be singular or plural. It must agree with, or match, the noun it is replacing.

	Possessive Pronouns	Examples
Singular	my, your, his, her, its	Brett and his sister baked cakes.
Plural	your, our, their	The twins and their dad helped.

Guided Practice Write a possessive pronoun to take the place of the underlined word or words.

HINT The *possessive* pronoun *their* means "belonging to them." Use it when you want to show that two or more people own or have something.

1 Maria's colorful signs : _____ colorful signs

2 the tray's handles : _____ handles

3 Tim's and Lena's brownies : _____ brownies

4 Michael's yummy churros : _____ yummy churros

5 Pedro's and my cupcakes : _____ cupcakes

6 the bagel that belongs to you : _____ bagel

7 the basket that is mine : _____ basket

8 the pan that belongs to the two of you : _____ pan

👤 Independent Practice

For numbers 1–5, choose the pronoun that correctly completes the sentence by agreeing with the underlined word or words.

1 <u>Mr. Blanco</u> asked _____ son to set up the food tables.

   A his

   B her

   C our

   D its

2 <u>One table</u> was broken, so Jim fixed _____ wobbly legs.

   A her

   B our

   C its

   D their

3 <u>Mrs. Chin</u> put _____ punch bowl on the table.

   A his

   B her

   C its

   D their

4 <u>Sari and Lil</u> sold _____ tasty cookies right away.

   A her

   B its

   C his

   D their

5 <u>My dad and I</u> were proud of _____ healthy snacks.

   A your

   B our

   C her

   D their

Lesson 22
Adding Suffixes

👥 **Introduction** A **suffix** is a word part added to the end of a base word. Adding a suffix changes the meaning of a word.

> **base word** **suffix**
>
> walk + **ing** = walking

Follow these spelling rules when adding suffixes to base words.

When a Suffix Begins with a Vowel	
If the base word ends in a short vowel sound and one consonant, double the consonant.	ba**t** + **t** + ing = batting jo**g** + **g** + ed = jogged
If the base word ends in a silent *-e*, drop the *e*.	smil**e** – **e** + ing = smiling saf**e** – **e** + er = safer
When a Base Word Ends with a Consonant and *y*	
Change the *y* to *i* before adding most suffixes.	hap**py** – **y** + **i** + ness = happiness sil**ly** – **y** + **i** + est = silliest

👥 **Guided Practice** Add the suffix shown to each word. Write the new word.

HINT When you add *-ing* to a verb that ends in *y*, do not change the *y* to *i*.

Example:
try + **ing** = **trying**
fly + **ing** = **flying**

1 hike + ed _____

2 skip + ing _____

3 nice + er _____

4 hurry + ing _____

5 silly + ness _____

6 try + ed _____

7 dive + ing _____

8 funny + est _____

👤 Independent Practice

For numbers 1–5, read each question and choose the correct answer.

1 How would you spell the new word if you added the suffix *-ing* to "spin"?

  A   spineing

  B   spining

  C   spinning

  D   spinneing

2 How would you spell the new word if you added the suffix *-er* to "brave"?

  A   braveer

  B   bravver

  C   bravr

  D   braver

3 How would you spell the new word if you added the suffix *-ness* to "heavy"?

  A   heavyness

  B   heaviness

  C   heavyiness

  D   heavieness

4 How would you spell the new word if you added the suffix *-ed* to "smile"?

  A   smiled

  B   smield

  C   smild

  D   smilled

5 How would you spell the new word if you added the suffix *-est* to "rainy"?

  A   rainyest

  B   rainyiest

  C   rainest

  D   rainiest

Using Reference Works

👥 Introduction
What can you do if you aren't sure how to spell a word? A **dictionary** is a good place to look to find the correct spelling of an unfamiliar word.

- A dictionary lists words in alphabetical order. Each entry shows a word's pronunciation, part of speech, and meaning.
- **Guide words** at the top of each page show the first and last entry words on the page.

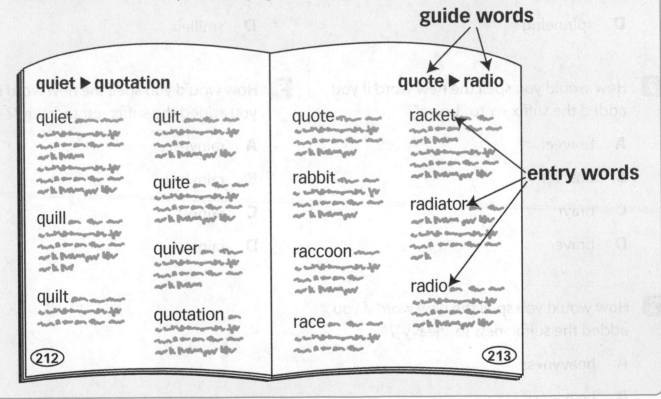

👥 Guided Practice
Use a dictionary to check the spelling of each underlined word. If the word is spelled wrong, write the correct spelling.

HINT Read the guide words at the top of the dictionary page to decide if the word you are looking for is on that page.

1 Do you <u>rememmber</u> your dreams? _____

2 <u>Sometims</u> dreams are funny. _____

3 Some dreams can be <u>scary</u>. _____

4 I had a <u>wierd</u> dream yesterday. _____

Independent Practice

For numbers 1–5, read each sentence. Then use the sample dictionary on page 442 to choose the correct spelling of the underlined word.

1 Last night a <u>rabit</u> hopped into my bedroom.

  A rabbet

  B rabbit

  C rabet

  D rabit

2 He sat still, but his whiskers began to <u>quivver</u>.

  A quiver

  B quivur

  C quivure

  D quivver

3 He said, "I must hide from a <u>racoon</u>!"

  A racoonn

  B raccon

  C racon

  D raccoon

4 The clanging <u>radeator</u> woke me up from my dream.

  A radeator

  B radeatur

  C radiator

  D radiatur

5 All of that clanging made quite a <u>rackit</u>.

  A rackitt

  B rackett

  C racket

  D raccket

Choosing Words and Phrases for Effect

👥 Introduction When writing, pick words and phrases that express your ideas and experiences in a lively, interesting way.

- Replace general words or phrases with more precise words or phrases.

  On Saturday
  ~~Last week~~ I went to a nice swimming party.

- Swap general verbs with more specific or descriptive verbs.

  attended
  On Saturday I ~~went to~~ a nice swimming party.

- Trade in weak adjectives for stronger or more interesting adjectives.

  an amazing
  On Saturday I attended ~~a nice~~ swimming party.

- The final sentence is much more precise and interesting to read than the first one.

  On Saturday I attended an amazing swimming party.

👥 Guided Practice **Circle the word or phrase that can best take the place of the underlined word or phrase. The goal is to make each sentence more precise and interesting.**

HINT When replacing a word or phrase, make sure you are changing the effect of the sentence but not its meaning.

1 The swimming party started <u>in the afternoon</u>.

    at noon   **later on**   **early**

2 When I arrived, the sun <u>was</u> over the pool.

    rose   **moved**   **blazed**

3 Everyone at the party was <u>very glad</u> to swim.

    ready   **surprised**   **excited**

4 The pool <u>was</u> a depth of 12 feet.

    measured   **seemed**   **had**

5 I walked to the edge and slowly <u>got</u> into the pool.

    went   **jumped**   **eased**

Independent Practice

For numbers 1–5, which word or phrase would replace the underlined words with more specific language? (The correct answer will not change the meaning of the sentence.)

1 At the pool party there was <u>good-tasting</u> food such as pizza.

   A delicious

   B salty

   C filling

   D cheap

2 I ate <u>a lot of</u> pizza.

   A some

   B a piece of

   C a few bites of

   D at least five slices of

3 Then I noticed that someone had brought <u>a dog</u> to the pool.

   A an animal

   B a golden retriever

   C a pet

   D a creature

4 A sign next to the pool <u>said</u> that pets were not allowed.

   A decided

   B wondered

   C warned

   D thought

5 The dog was <u>nice</u>, so the pool manager let it stay.

   A friendly

   B small

   C huge

   D smart

Spoken and Written English

👥 Introduction

When you speak with friends, you don't have to worry about every word and how it sounds. But when you write, you want your words to be exact and clear.

- When you speak, you often use single words and phrases. When you write, you should use complete sentences.

Spoken English	Written English
Dan: Want to see the stars tonight? **Ava:** Nah. Too many clouds. Maybe tomorrow.	Clear nights are the best time to see stars.

- When you speak, you often use slang such as *hey* or *can't*. When you write, you usually do not use slang or contractions.

Spoken English	Written English
Dan: That's a shooting star. **Ava:** Hey, there's another one. Whoa! There are so many I can't count them all!	During the meteor shower, more than 150 shooting stars came streaking across the sky.

👥 Guided Practice

Read each sentence with a partner. Which ones sound like spoken language? Write *spoken* or *written* next to each sentence. Tell your partner which clues helped you decide.

HINT To find spoken language, look for slang such as *yup* and *awesome*. Also, look for sentences that are not complete.

1 This is okay homework. _____

2 Yup, really good. _____

3 Learning about meteors is interesting. _____

4 The next meteor shower will be in August. _____

5 Awesome. Can't wait! _____

6 The number of shooting stars people see depends on where they stand. _____

Independent Practice

Dan and Ava are watching the sky again. Read what they say in numbers 1–4. Then rewrite the information as if it were a report about stars.

1 **Ava:** Stars are really cool, and constellations are even cooler.

   Dan: Right, they look like pictures of things.

   _____

   _____

2 **Ava:** Wow! That's the Big Dipper. Looks like a ladle. See its handle?

   Dan: Yeah, I see it. I can count all seven stars.

   _____

   _____

3 **Ava:** Check out the North Star. It's in the Little Dipper.

   Dan: Ever get lost? The North Star can help you find your way.

   _____

   _____

4 **Ava:** What are those bright stars? The ones over there.

   Dan: Don't know their names. They're part of another constellation.

   _____

   _____

Lesson 26
Using Context Clues

👥 **Introduction** Sometimes when you read, you will see a word you do not know. You can figure out its meaning by looking at the words around it. You can use **context clues**.

- Sometimes a sentence includes a definition of the word.

> **definition**
> Living in a frigid, or **extremely cold**, place can be difficult.

- A sentence might also give an example that explains a word.

> **example**
> Frigid temperatures in the Arctic can be as low as **58°F below zero**.

👥 **Guided Practice** Use context clues to figure out the meaning of each underlined word. Write the meaning. Then circle the words that were a clue.

HINT As you read, look for the words *such as*. These words might introduce an example that helps you figure out the meaning of an unknown word.

1 Animals <u>adapt</u> by changing in a way that allows them to live in a certain place.

2 The polar bear's furry snout and ears help it <u>survive</u>, or stay alive, in the cold Arctic.

3 The white fur of the Arctic fox lets it hide from <u>predators</u> such as wolves.

4 The Arctic bee has to <u>shiver</u>, or shake, to keep itself warm.

1 _____

2 _____

3 _____

4 _____

Independent Practice

Read the sentence below. Then use it to answer numbers 1 and 2.

The ground squirrel <u>hibernates</u>, sleeping for months during the winter.

1 What does the word <u>hibernates</u> mean?

   A hides in the ground

   B hides for a long, long time

   C sleeps because it has nowhere to go

   D sleeps to live through low temperatures

2 What words help you understand the meaning of <u>hibernates</u>?

   A "ground" and "squirrel"

   B "ground squirrel" and "months"

   C "sleeping" and "during the winter"

   D "months" and "winter"

Read the sentence below. Then use it to answer numbers 3 and 4.

The fur on polar bears helps them <u>repel</u>, or keep away, cold water.

3 What does the word <u>repel</u> mean?

   A to fight

   B to push something away

   C to make something warm

   D to soak up or take in

4 What words help you understand the meaning of <u>repel</u>?

   A "keep away"

   B "fur on polar bears"

   C "cold water"

   D "helps them"

Language Handbook Lesson 26 Using Context Clues **449**

Prefixes and Suffixes

👥 Introduction
Use your knowledge of word parts to figure out what new words mean.

- A **prefix** is a word part added to the beginning of a word. Adding a prefix changes the meaning of a base word.

Prefix	Meaning	Example	Meaning
dis-	"not" or "opposite of"	dislike	"to not like"
pre-	"before"	prewash	"to wash before"
un-	"not" or "opposite of"	untrue	"not true"

- A **suffix** is a word part added to the end of a word. Adding a suffix changes the meaning of a base word.

Suffix	Meaning	Example	Meaning
-able	"can be" or "able to"	trainable	"can be trained"
-ful	"full of" or "having"	skillful	"having skill"
-less	"without"	useless	"without use"

- Some words have both a prefix and a suffix: *uncomfortable*, *disagreeable*.

👥 Guided Practice

HINT A prefix or a suffix can have more than one meaning. Think about which meaning makes sense in the sentence.

Write the base word and the prefix or suffix that make up each underlined word. Then tell a partner what the underlined word means.

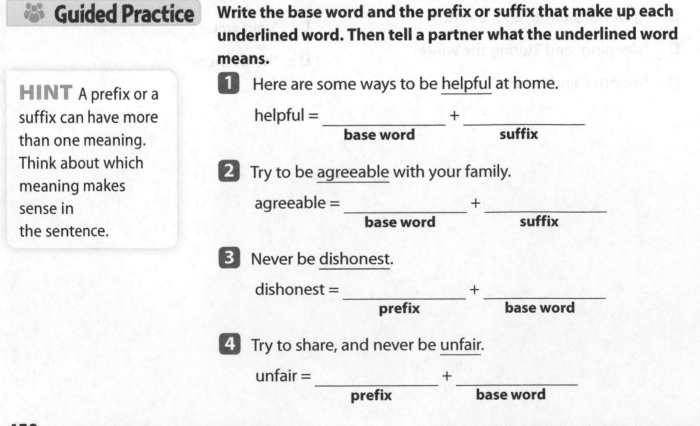

1 Here are some ways to be <u>helpful</u> at home.

helpful = _____ + _____
           base word   suffix

2 Try to be <u>agreeable</u> with your family.

agreeable = _____ + _____
             base word   suffix

3 Never be <u>dishonest</u>.

dishonest = _____ + _____
             prefix   base word

4 Try to share, and never be <u>unfair</u>.

unfair = _____ + _____
          prefix   base word

👤 Independent Practice

For numbers 1–5, read each sentence. Then choose the correct meaning of each underlined word.

1 Follow these <u>useful</u> safety tips.

   A   without use

   B   not used

   C   having use

   D   before using

2 Don't be <u>careless</u> when you carry something hot.

   A   without care

   B   full of care

   C   able to care

   D   having care

3 Let adults <u>preview</u> movies you want to see.

   A   not view

   B   view without you

   C   mostly view

   D   view before

4 Never <u>unbuckle</u> your seatbelt while in a moving car.

   A   buckle before

   B   do the opposite of buckle

   C   without a buckle

   D   full of buckles

5 You will find these safety tips are easily <u>doable</u>.

   A   able to be done

   B   not done

   C   having done

   D   mostly done

Root Words

👥 Introduction

Have you noticed that some words have the same parts? For example, the words *addition* and *additional* both have the **root word** *add*. This tells you that the words *addition* and *additional* are related to each other.

- Words with the same root have similar meanings.
- You can use a word you know to figure out the meaning of an unknown but related word.

> I visited my friend Kate. Her house has a new addition.
>
> Her family built the additional room for guests.

If you know that *add* means "to put together," you can figure out that *addition* means "something put together with something else," and *additional* means "extra" or "added."

👥 Guided Practice

Read the sentence or sentences beside each number. Find and circle the word related to the underlined word. Then tell a partner the meaning of each word you circled.

HINT Think about the meaning of the word part that is the same in both words. Use the underlined word to help you figure out the meaning of the word you circled.

1 Kate's dog is her companion. He kept us <u>company</u> as we listened to the radio.

2 Suddenly, we heard the announcer make an <u>announcement</u>.

3 "Answer a question <u>correctly</u> and you'll win a ticket to the circus. Let me make a correction. You'll win two tickets!"

4 Then he asked, "Which inventor made an <u>invention</u> that lets you talk to someone who is far away?"

5 Kate called in with the answer. "The <u>scientist</u> Alexander Graham Bell made scientific discoveries and invented the telephone."

Independent Practice

For numbers 1–4, use the underlined word in each sentence to help you answer each question.

1 Read the sentence below.

You can <u>enter</u> the circus tent from Beach Street, but we used the **entrance** on Bay Road.

What does the word "entrance" mean as it is used in the sentence?

A   a path

B   a crosswalk

C   a way to get into a place

D   a way to leave a place

2 Read the sentence below.

The seats in the tent were arranged in a <u>circle</u> around a **circular** stage.

What does the word "circular" mean as it is used in the sentence?

A   strong

B   round

C   long

D   raised

3 Read the sentence below.

My ticket had a <u>number</u> that matched one of the **numerous** seats.

What does the word "numerous" mean as it is used in the sentence?

A   lettered

B   ordered

C   few

D   many

4 Read the sentence below.

We watched dogs drive <u>bicycles</u> and a clown ride a **unicycle**.

What does the word "unicycle" mean as it is used in the sentence?

A   a vehicle with one wheel

B   a wagon pulled by dogs

C   a clown car

D   a small horse

Lesson 29
Using a Dictionary or Glossary

👥 **Introduction** Many words have more than one meaning, or **definition**. You can use a dictionary or a glossary to check the exact meaning of a word or a phrase.

- A **dictionary** lists words in alphabetical order. Each entry gives the pronunciation, the part of speech, and the meaning of the word.

> **plant** (plănt) *n.* 1. a seedling 2. a factory *v.* 3. to put seeds or seedlings into the ground to grow 4. to set firmly in place: *Lee plants four stakes in the soil to mark the corners of his garden.*

> When there is more than one meaning, each definition is numbered.

> A sample sentence can make a word's meaning clearer.

- A **glossary** is like a dictionary. It is an alphabetical list of vocabulary words in a book. Each entry explains the meaning of a word as it is used in that book.

> **pest** (pĕst) 1. a plant or an animal that causes a problem: *Flies can be pests at a picnic.* 2. an annoying person

To find the right meaning of a word, first read all the definitions. Then see which meaning makes sense in the sentence you are reading.

👥 **Guided Practice** **Read the passage. Use the dictionary and glossary entries above to find the meaning of each underlined word. Then write the number of the definition above the word.**

HINT Ask yourself how the underlined word is used. Is it a noun? Is it a verb? Then reread the sentence using the definition you chose. Does the definition make sense?

After you <u>plant</u> flowers in your garden, you care for them. You

<u>plant</u> poles in the ground to support any tall stems. You love your

garden, but so do beetles! Some beetles eat <u>plants</u>. Try putting

a birdhouse in your garden to attract birds. Many birds will eat

<u>pests</u>, such as beetles.

👤 Independent Practice

Use the dictionary entries to answer numbers 1–4.

> **gather** (găTH ur) *v.* **1.** to come together in a group **2.** to pick **3.** to conclude **4.** to collect information

> **spot** (spŏt) *n.* **1.** a stain or mark **2.** a place or location   *v.* **3.** to mark with dots **4.** to notice or see

1 Which definition matches how <u>gather</u> is used in this sentence?

In the morning, crows gather in the pumpkin patch.

A Definition 1

B Definition 2

C Definition 3

D Definition 4

3 Which definition matches how <u>spot</u> is used in this sentence?

The crow finds a juicy grub in one spot and swallows it.

A Definition 1

B Definition 2

C Definition 3

D Definition 4

> **probe** (prōb) *n.* **1.** a thin tool used by doctors and dentists **2.** a search   *v.* **3.** to search or explore **4.** to get information about a person or thing

4 Which definition matches how <u>spot</u> is used in this sentence?

The other crows spot many beetles chewing the pumpkin plants and quickly eat the beetles.

A Definition 1

B Definition 2

C Definition 3

D Definition 4

2 Which definition matches how <u>probe</u> is used in this sentence?

One crow uses its beak to probe the soil.

A Definition 1

B Definition 2

C Definition 3

D Definition 4

Literal and Nonliteral Meanings

👥 Introduction Words and phrases often have more than one meaning.

- Sometimes words and phrases mean exactly what they say. For example, the words *took steps* can mean "walked" or "stepped."

  > The hungry lion took steps toward the baby elephant.

- Sometimes words and phrases have a meaning that is different from their usual meaning. The words *took steps* can also mean "took action" or "acted."

  > The mother elephant quickly took steps to protect her baby.

When you read, keep in mind that words or phrases might have more than one meaning. Use what you know and nearby words to figure out what the writer really means.

🐾 Guided Practice Read each sentence. Circle the meaning of the underlined word or phrase.

HINT To figure out what the underlined part means, think about the words that come before and after it.

1 A tired elephant calf <u>drops off</u> after playing all morning.

      goes to sleep   **lets go**   **falls down**

2 A lion creeps through tall grass and <u>goes after</u> the calf.

      bothers   **follows**   **tries to get**

3 The mother elephant <u>trumpets</u> for help.

      asks   **makes a loud sound**   **plays the trumpet**

4 The calf wakes up but <u>freezes</u> when it sees the lion.

      turns to ice   **gets cold**   **is so scared it can't move**

Independent Practice

For numbers 1–5, read each sentence. Then choose the correct meaning of each underlined word or phrase.

1 Many adult elephants <u>turn up</u> to protect the calf.

    A hold their trunks up

    B look toward the sky

    C look toward the calf

    D arrive suddenly

2 These smart <u>giants</u> use their tusks to protect the calf.

    A grown-up elephants

    B important animals

    C large monsters

    D huge people

3 The elephants <u>cut the lion off</u> each time he tries to dash between them.

    A remove a part of the lion

    B keep the lion from other lions

    C block the lion's way

    D stop the lion from roaring

4 The lion <u>takes off</u> when he realizes he can't catch the calf.

    A flies

    B leaves

    C jumps up

    D becomes angry

5 The lion doesn't want to <u>go another round</u> with the elephants.

    A give up

    B walk in a loop

    C run in a circle

    D fight again

Lesson 31
Real-Life Connections

👥 Introduction
When reading, you can connect the words on the page to your own life or to the wider world. Connecting words with real-life events can make their meaning clearer.

- What do you think of when you read the word *friendly*? You might remember a time when a friendly classmate smiled at you.

  A friendly classmate smiled and said, "Hi."

- When you think about the word *friendly*, you might also remember what friendly people and animals in your town or city have done.

  A friendly lady in town gives neighbors vegetables from her garden.

  Friendly dogs wag their tails and want to be patted.

👥 Guided Practice
Circle the correct words to complete each sentence. Then work with a partner to think of more ways to complete each sentence.

HINT To help think of more ways to complete each sentence, ask your partner questions like these.
- When were you helpful?
- What do you do when you are curious about something?

1 A helpful person might _____ .

   do chores   **break a glass**   **trip and fall**

2 If a person is curious, she might _____ .

   go to sleep   **read a book**   **wrap a gift**

3 It would be selfish to _____ .

   take all the toys   **give presents**   **help others**

4 A student could interrupt a class by _____ .

   writing a story   **doing math**   **talking loudly**

Independent Practice

For numbers 1–5, choose the correct answer to each question.

1 How might a **patient** person act?

   A tell a friend to hurry up

   B run to be first in line

   C refuse to wait for someone

   D teach a baby something new

2 What might a **stubborn** person say?

   A "I like this new food after all."

   B "I won't eat that even if it's good for me."

   C "I agree with you about that."

   D "I'll stay home because you need my help."

3 What might a **generous** person do?

   A help a friend with homework

   B eat candy without sharing

   C disobey his parents

   D scare a friend's dog

4 How might someone cause **confusion**?

   A by solving a problem

   B by telling the truth

   C by giving poor directions

   D by speaking clearly

5 What is a **rude** thing to do?

   A invite a friend to a party

   B talk while others are talking

   C offer to wash the dishes

   D help a neighbor plant a garden

Shades of Meaning

Introduction Some words have similar definitions, but there are small differences in their meanings. These small differences are called **shades of meaning**.

- Think about the words *surprised* and *shocked*. They mean almost the same thing, but *shocked* has a stronger, or more forceful, meaning than *surprised* does.

> Max was surprised that so many people entered the poster contest.
>
> Max was shocked that so many people entered the poster contest.

- Look at the words below. They have similar definitions but different shades of meaning. They are arranged in order from the mildest meaning to the strongest.

> surprised ⟶ amazed ⟶ stunned ⟶ shocked

Guided Practice Complete each sentence by circling the word with the strongest meaning.

HINT Read each sentence using the four answer choices. Think about which word gives the sentence the most forceful feeling.

1 Max _____ that the judges would like his poster.

> **thought**   **believed**   **knew**   **guessed**

2 His artwork was _____ .

> **nice**   **great**   **good**   **fine**

3 Max felt _____ when mud splashed on it.

> **worried**   **upset**   **unhappy**   **angry**

4 He was _____ that the mud wiped off easily.

> **excited**   **glad**   **happy**   **pleased**

Independent Practice

For numbers 1–5, read each sentence. Then replace the underlined word by choosing the word with the strongest meaning.

1 Max was <u>worried</u> that his poster might not win a prize.

  A concerned

  B bothered

  C troubled

  D alarmed

2 He was <u>anxious</u> when his little brother walked toward the poster.

  A nervous

  B worried

  C panicky

  D uneasy

3 His little brother's hands were <u>dirty</u>!

  A filthy

  B muddy

  C soiled

  D stained

4 It would be <u>tough</u> to win a prize with a messy poster.

  A difficult

  B hard

  C rough

  D impossible

5 Max <u>supposed</u> his brother would not hurt his poster.

  A imagined

  B believed

  C felt

  D thought

Words for Time and Space

👥 Introduction
How can you help make your writing clear for readers? One way is to use words and phrases that explain when and where actions or events take place.

- Words and phrases that tell *when* show the time events happen or the order in which they happen. *First, second, next, often, at noon,* and *in the morning* are some words and phrases that tell when events happen.

When	Plan your garden in the winter.
	First, decide what to grow.

- Words and phrases that tell *where* show the position or direction of something. *Down, around, under, close to,* and *on the right* are some words and phrases that tell where.

Where	Vegetables grow best in sunny areas.
	Some flowers can grow under trees or climb up walls.

👥 Guided Practice

Complete each sentence. If the parentheses ( ) say *when*, add a word or phrase that tells *when*. If they say *where*, add a word or phrase that tells *where*.

HINT Think about what happens when you plant and care for a garden. What words and phrases that tell *when* or *where* will make the steps clear?

1 _____, get a shovel and loosen the soil. (when)

2 Plant your seeds, and be sure to water them _____
_____. (when)

3 The roots of the tiny seedlings will grow _____
_____ (where)

4 The stems and leaves will grow _____
_____. (where)

5 Don't forget to weed your garden _____
_____. (when)

Independent Practice

For numbers 1–5, complete each sentence by choosing the word or phrase that tells _when_ or _where_.

1 If you have packets of seeds, _____ read the directions.

   A slowly

   B first

   C carefully

   D you must

2 It's a good idea to plant _____.

   A vegetables

   B many seeds

   C in the morning

   D with a friend

3 You can grow corn, squash, and beans _____.

   A near one another

   B if you want

   C for food

   D for your family

4 Some seeds sprout _____.

   A in just a few days

   B with little water

   C but others do not

   D without much trouble

5 Once your vegetables grow, you can share them _____.

   A with neighbors

   B easily

   C too

   D at school

Glossary of Terms
Academic Talk Words and Phrases

academic vocabulary words that are commonly used in written texts but are not generally part of everyday speech

academic words see academic vocabulary

account a written or spoken report of an event or topic

act a main section, or part, of a play

alliteration repetition of initial consonant sounds in a piece of writing to create a special effect

allude to to mention something in an indirect way

analyze to closely and carefully examine a piece of text

beginning the start of something; the first part of a text, which introduces the characters and problem in a story or the topic and main idea in an informational text

bold print heavy, dark type; important words in a text are sometimes printed in bold print

caption a phrase or sentence set below a picture in a text that explains something about the picture

cast of characters a list of all the characters in a play, usually in order of appearance

cause something that brings about an effect or a result

cause and effect a relationship between things or events, in which one thing—the cause—brings about, or causes, something else—the effect

cause-and-effect text structure a text organization that tells about events and explains why they happen

central message a lesson about life the author of a story wants to share

challenge a problem or difficulty that needs to be solved

chapters sections, or parts, of stories or books

character person, animal, or made-up creature in a story or play

character traits special qualities of characters, such as shyness or honesty, that makes one character different from another

chronological text structure a text organization in which events are told in the order in which they happen

clues pieces of information that help you figure out something; hints

compare to describe how two or more things are similar

compare-contrast text structure a text organization that describes how two or more things are alike and different

comparison the process of showing how two or more things are alike and different

connected joined or linked together; when two or more things are connected, they are related in some way.

connection how the facts and ideas in a sentence or paragraph relate to each other, for example, some ideas have a cause-and-effect relationship, or connection; causal relations or sequence between two ideas

context clues words, phrases and sentences around an unknown word or phrase in a text that help to determine the word's meaning; context clues may be synonyms, antonyms, examples, or definitions.

contrast to describe how two or more things are different

contribute to add to something; to help bring about a result

describe to tell what something is like or to explain something

details facts, examples, and other pieces of information directly stated in a text

diagram a simple drawing that is used to explain something

dialogue the words the characters say in a story or play

digital source a text on a specific subject area or topic that is located on a computer website or provided in an electronic format

drama a story that is performed on a stage

effect something that happens as a result of something else

end the point at which something is completed; the last part of a text, in which the problem in a story is solved or the main idea in an informational text is summed up

events things that happen in stories and in the natural world

evidence facts, details, quotes, or other pieces of information used to support a claim, point, or an idea

Glossary of Terms

examples things that an author uses to represent an idea or a group of things

explain to describe or give details about something so it can be understood

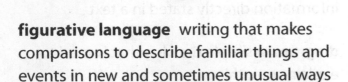

figurative language writing that makes comparisons to describe familiar things and events in new and sometimes unusual ways

first before all others in time, order, or importance

firsthand account something written about an event by a person who witnessed the event or who took part in it

first person describes the narrator of a story who is a character in the story and actually experiences what happens; a first-person narrator uses the pronouns *I, me*, and *we*

focus a center of interest or attention

genre a type of writing characterized by a particular style, form, or subject area; narrative poems, mysteries, realistic fiction, historical texts, and technical texts are examples of genres

glossary a list at the back of a book of important words from the text and their meanings

graph a chart that is used to show the relationship between two sets of numbers

headings words or a phrase at the beginning of a section of a text that tell what the section is about

historical describes something based on history

historical events important things that happened in the past

historical text an informational piece of writing that tells about people, events, and ideas from the past

hyperlinks features in digital texts that allow you to quickly access additional information

idea a thought, an opinion, or a belief that exists in the mind about what something is like or should be like

illustrations pictures that accompany a text and that often provide additional details about the text

images the pictures, or illustrations and photographs, in a text

important points the most important details, facts, examples, and other pieces of information in a text

index a list at the back of a book of all the topics in the book, in alphabetical order, and the page numbers where they can be found

infer to reach a reasonable conclusion about an idea or event not directly stated in a text based on text clues and background knowledge

inference the process of reaching a conclusion based on details in the text and your own background knowledge

influence to have an effect on something or someone

information facts and details about someone or something

integrate to put together or combine information on a topic from more than one source

Interaction the way people or things affect each other

interpret to explain the meaning or significance of certain information

K

key detail an important fact, example, or other piece of information in a text that helps explain a main idea

key facts important ideas in a text that can be proven true

key point an important idea about a topic

key words words in bold print that call attention to something important in a text

knowledgeably in a manner that shows a clear understanding of something or, to speak or write about a topic like an expert

last at the end; after all others; finally

lesson something to be learned—for example, from a story or an experience—that imparts new knowledge

literal describes the usual or most basic meaning of a word

lyric poem a type of poem that uses language in unusual ways to express thoughts and feelings about something

main idea something important that an author wants readers to understand about a topic

main purpose what an author of a text wants to tell, describe, or explain to the reader

main topic what a selection is mostly about

maps drawings that show the cities, roads, rivers, and other details of an area

meaning the thoughts or ideas meant to be conveyed, especially by language

Glossary of Terms

metaphor a kind of figurative language that compares two things that are not alike, without using the words *like* or *as*

meter the regular pattern of stressed and unstressed syllables in a verse, or line, of poetry

middle the central part of something; the part of a text after the beginning and before the end, in which the plot of a story or the main idea of an informational text is developed

mood a feeling a story creates in the reader; setting, word choice, and tone all contribute to mood

motivations the reasons why characters act, think, and feel as they do

mythology a collection of ancient stories belonging to a particular people that tell about their origin, history, gods, goddesses, and heroes

narrator the person who tells a story

nonliteral describes an unusual or unexpected meaning of a word

opposition strong disagreement or conflict; struggle

order the arrangement or sequence of things or events in time

paragraph a group of sentences about a particular idea or topic

personification a kind of figurative language that gives human qualities to animals or objects

persuade to cause someone to do something or to think a certain way about something, by giving them good reasons for it

phrase a short group of words that has meaning

play a story that is performed on stage by actors

plot the sequence of events in a story

points ideas that authors present to convince readers that something is true

point of view
Literary Text the perspective from which a piece of text is written
Informational Text the author's viewpoint that allows the reader to know how the author thinks and feels about a topic

primary source a description of an event from someone who experienced it, such as diaries, speeches, letters, or interviews

print source a text on a specific subject area or topic that is in print form, such as a book or magazine article

problem a challenge that the main character or characters face

problem-solution text structure a text organization that describes problems and solutions

procedures steps to follow to do something

prompt a writing assignment

prose any form of writing that is not poetry

qualitative measured by the quality of something rather than by quantity

quantitative describes information in the form of numbers or other data or, describes information in the form of quantities, or amounts, of things

quote a short passage, sentence, or phrase of exact wording from a text

R

reason an explanation for why an idea might be right or true

recount to retell events and details of a story in the order in which they happened using your own words

reflects thinks deeply or speaks seriously about something

regular beat the main rhythm in a piece of music; the main rhythm is created by having an equal amount of time between each occurrence of a beat

relationship the way in which two or more people, events, or things are connected

repetition the use of repeated words or ideas in a piece of writing for emphasis, or to show that something is important

respond to make a reply; to answer; to say or do something in reaction to something else

rhyme the repetition of the same or similar stressed sounds in words

rhythm the regular pattern of sounds in a poem or beats in a piece of music

scene a part of a play in which all the action takes place in the same setting

scientific text a piece of text that explains how or why something happens

script the written text of a drama, which is used by all people putting the drama on stage

search tools Internet utilities that allow users to quickly find information on the Web

Glossary of Terms

secondary source a description of an event based on research that includes key facts such as textbooks, biographies, and newspaper articles

secondhand account something written about an event by a person who did not experience it but rather heard or read about the event

sections smaller parts into which something is divided

setting when and where a story or play takes place

sequence the order in which events in a story or the steps in a procedure occur

sequence of events everything that happens in a story, in the order in which it happens

sidebars short, often boxed, articles included in longer texts that provide additional information related to the main text

significant large enough to be noticed or to have an effect

simile a kind of figurative language that uses the words *like* or *as* to compare two dissimilar things

solution the answer to a problem; or the way the main characters resolve the conflict at the center of a story

solved figured out; worked out a correct solution, or answer, to a problem

source a text on a specific subject area or topic; a source may be in printed or digital form

speaker the character whose "voice" you hear in a poem

stage directions instructions in a script that tell where a scene takes place, what the actors should do, and what should appear or happen on stage

stanza several verses, or lines, of a poem that are grouped together to describe an image, idea, or event

steps in a process a set of actions to do, or directions to make or do something

structural elements special features of texts; they vary from one form of written text to another

structure the particular way a writer organizes a text, such as acts for a drama or stanzas for a poem, that helps the reader understand the writer's meaning

subheading the title of a section, or part, of text; it tells what the section is about

subject a topic; something that is being talked or written about

Glossary of Terms

subject area a specific topic or field of study; science, mathematics, history, outer space, the ancient world, and the environment are examples of subject areas

summarize to briefly retell in your own words the most important ideas, events, and details in a text

summary a short but complete version of a text

support to help explain, or provide evidence for, a main idea in a text

T

table of contents a list at the front of a book of the sections or chapters of the book in the order in which they appear

technical text a piece of writing that tells how to make or do something

text evidence a detail, fact, or other information in a piece of writing that the author uses to support a point, or an idea

text features special parts of a text that help you locate information, such as specific facts and details, within the text; tables of contents, captions, subheadings, and glossaries are examples of text features

text structure the way an author organizes the ideas and details in a piece of writing; text structures include comparison, cause-effect, chronology, and problem-solution

theme an important message or lesson that an author wants to share either implicitly or explicitly about people or life

third person describes the narrator of a story who is not a character in the story but looks in at events from outside; a third-person narrator uses pronouns, such as *he* and *she*.

time line a chart that shows the dates of important events during a certain time period

tone the general feeling or attitude conveyed by a text

topic the general subject of a text

traditional literature stories, such as fables, fairy tales, and folktales, that were originally passed along by word of mouth and written down much later.

traits special qualities, such as courage, pride, or honesty, that people and characters in stories have

versions descriptions or accounts of the same thing, such as a story or an event, which contain some different details

visual elements pictures that appear with a text

visuals pictures that appear with a text, such as photographs, diagrams, and time lines; visuals are also referred to as *visual elements*.

Illustration Credits

pp. 9, 12, 24, 38, 40, 42, 54, 60-61, 71, 77, 80, 100-101, 106, 114-115, 122, 134, 135, 138, 139, 145, 146, 168, 174, 182-183, 199, 200, 214, 222-223, 228, 236, 237, 264-265, 275, 296, 351, 352, 354, 356, 360-362, 383, 384, 385, 386: QBS Learning

p. 10: Jenny Nutting Kelchin

pp. 33, 286, 343: Mary Jo Heil

pp. 52, 92, 120, 256, 366: Six Red Marbles

pp. 77, 87: Fian Arroyo

pp. 77, 110: Sarah Goodreau

p. 108: LoopAll/Shutterstock

p. 124: mir_vam/Shutterstock

pp. 77, 128-130: Ian Dale/Deborah Wolfe Ltd.

pp. 199, 250-251: Carlos Aón

p. 244: Tanya Maiboroda

p. 246: gitan100/Shutterstock

p. 282: Jenny Nutting Kelchen

pp. 351, 376-378: Mauro Mazzara

Photography Credits

pp. 9, 18-19: Power and Syred/Science Source

pp. 9, 28: KRCrowley/Alamy

pp. 9, 32-33 (background): kak2s/Shutterstock

pp. 9, 47 (bottom): Neftali/Shutterstock

p. 14: Byelikova Oksana/Shutterstock

p. 20: European Space Agency

p. 26: wavebreakmedia/Shutterstock

p. 32: Yaromir/Shutterstock

pp. 32-33 (bottom border): Irmairma/Shutterstock

p. 46 (coin): Vladimir Wrangel/Shutterstock

p. 47 (top): Nagel Photography/Shutterstock

p. 48: Everett Historical/Shutterstock

pp. 46-47 (background): Lorcel/Shutterstock

p. 56: Volodymyr Goinyk/Shutterstock

pp. 60-61: deepspacedave/Shutterstock

p. 66: Jim.Henderson/Wikimedia Commons

p. 67: Kirk Geisler/Shutterstock

p. 70: Courtesy NOAA

p. 78: Monkey Business Images/Shutterstock

p. 82: Erik Lam/Shutterstock

p. 94: TerraceStudio/Shutterstock

pp. 77, 96: Sinisa Botas/Shutterstock

pp. 122, 126: Studio Barcelona/Shutterstock

pp. 145, 148: ZUMA Press, Inc./Alamy

pp. 145, 162: AndreAnita/Shutterstock

pp. 145, 168-169: INTERFOTO/Alamy

pp. 145, 155 156: Marmaduke St. John/Alamy

pp. 145, 178: Jeff Schultes/Shutterstock

pp. 150, 153: Protasov AN/Shutterstock

p. 154: ABK/BSIP/Corbis

p. 160: Kumar Sriskandan/Alamy

p. 164: Anke van Wyk/Shutterstock

p. 169: Alfie Photography/Shutterstock

p. 170 (right): Fotos593/Shutterstock

p. 170 (left): Dr. Hernan Vargas/The Peregrine Fund

p. 176: Jason and Bonnie Grower/Shutterstock

p. 182 (photo border): Picsfive/Shutterstock

p. 182 (left): Napoleon Sarony

p. 183: Library of Congress Prints and Photographs Division Washington, D.C.

pp. 188, 189: Jennifer Mattox/Highlights for Children, Inc.

p. 192 (top): Kristina Postnikova/Shutterstock

p. 192 (bottom): pan demin/Shutterstock

p. 193: Paul Looyen/Shutterstock

pp. 199, 202: Paul S. Wolf/Shutterstock

pp. 199, 209 (bottom): Keneva Photography/Shutterstock

p. 204: LilKar/Shutterstock

p. 208: GooDween123/Shutterstock

p. 209 (top): Tony Campbell/Shutterstock

p. 216: Javier Brosch/Shutterstock

p. 218: Juice Team/Shutterstock

p. 230 (top): clearviewstock/Shutterstock

p. 230 (center left): YorkBerlin/Shutterstock

p. 230 (center right): TsuneoMP/Shutterstock

p. 232: Andrea Danti/Shutterstock

p. 242: Andrey Armyagov/Shutterstock

p. 258: Tetiana Savitska/Alamy

p. 260: VIZE/Shutterstock

p. 270: Leonid Ikan/Shutterstock

pp. 281, 284: Junko Kimura/Getty Images

pp. 281, 291 (bottom), 298: NASA

pp. 281, 300 (left): Prasanna Swaminathan/Shutterstock

pp. 281, 305: Ildi Papp/Shutterstock

pp. 281, 319: INTERFOTO/Alamy

pp. 281, 336: prudkov/Shutterstock

p. 290 (left): Christina Kennedy/Alamy

p. 290 (right): alexmak72427/Shutterstock

p. 291 (top): Richard Choy/Getty Images

p. 291 (center): Stocksnapper/Shutterstock

p. 300: BI/Barcroft Media/Getty Images

p. 304: Underwood & Underwood/Corbis

pp. 304-305 (background): Evlakhov Valeriy/Shutterstock

p. 310 (top): picturepartners/Shutterstock

p. 310 (bottom): Nikolasm/Shutterstock

p. 312: Elena Blokhina/Shutterstock

p. 314: Jess Kraft/Shutterstock

p. 318 (nest): Kazakov Maksim/Shutterstock

p. 318 (insect): Melinda Fawver/Shutterstock

p. 324: Chris Willson/Alamy

p. 326: Bettmann/Corbis

p. 328: Oleksiy Mark/Shutterstock

p. 335: Goodluz/Shutterstock

pp. 340, 341: swa182/Shutterstock

p. 370: Malchev/Shutterstock